The **SOLOMON** EXAM PREP *Guide*

SERIES 63

NASAA UNIFORM SECURITIES AGENT STATE LAW EXAMINATION

4TH EDITION

SOLOMON EXAM PREP®

A DIVISION OF FIRSTBOOKS.COM®

For more innovative exam preparation products:

www.solomonexamprep.com

THE SOLOMON EXAM PREP GUIDE: SERIES 63 – NASAA UNIFORM SECURITIES AGENT STATE LAW EXAMINATION 4TH EDITION

ISBN 13: 978-1-61007-093-5   ISBN-10:1-61007-093-3

Publisher: Solomon Exam Prep® | www.solomonexamprep.com

3 5 7 9 10 8 6 4 2

Printed in the U.S.A.

Table of Contents

APPENDIXES

Introduction

I remember sitting exactly where you are—staring at the first page of a study guide for the Series 63 exam. Perhaps like you, I found the exam to be a far more nerve-wracking experience than any exam I ever took during college, because passing this test would mean either a huge step toward a career in an amazing industry or a major roadblock in my career path of choice.

How did I do? I passed with a 100%.

Does that mean it was easy? *Not in the slightest.*

Rather, and this is the good news for you, it means that the exam is predictable. Even though it crams a lot of complex material into just 65 questions, the material can be mastered by anyone who is willing to commit the time. That's because the NASAA, the North American Securities Administrators Association, which designs the exam, has outlined everything you need to know, as well as given samples of the question formats. The NASAA tries to make the exam more difficult by writing questions that can seem tricky and nuanced. But if you've learned the material, you will have an excellent chance of success. Most of you who will be taking this exam will be working for broker-dealers, so most of the rules and regulations on the exam apply to broker-dealers and their representatives. But the NASAA also wants you to know about firms that give advice on securities as well. This means you will be tested on rules and regulations related to investment advisers and their representatives.

The text is organized into the following five chapters based on the content of the exam, plus a sixth chapter that we added to familiarize you with federal securities acts, about which the exam assumes you will be knowledgeable.

- Chapter One: Regulation of Investment Advisers and Investment Adviser Representatives—6 questions (10%)
- Chapter Two: Regulation of Broker-Dealers and Agents—18 questions (30%)
- Chapter Three: Securities, Issuers and Administrative Provisions—9 questions (15%)
- Chapter Four: Communications with Clients and Prospects—12 questions (20%)
- Chapter Five: Ethical Practices and Obligations—15 questions (25%)
- Chapter Six: Federal Securities Acts—0 questions (0%)

The key to passing the Series 63 comes down to three things, all of which this text is designed around. First you need to memorize a good amount of information to the point that it automatically pops into your brain when you see the subject mentioned in a specific question. If you can memorize the concepts, terms, and rules in this book, you should have no problem scoring a passing grade.

The second crucial element to passing the NASAA Uniform State Law Examination, the official name for the Series 63 exam, is to take as many different practice exams as possible, so that you become comfortable with the question formats and the ways the material can be tested. Notice that I say *different*. I say that because if you take the same practice exams over and over again, you'll memorize the answers to those questions instead of applying the knowledge you've learned. And while this text contains great practice exams, if you haven't already you should visit SolomonExamPrep.Com and purchase the online exam simulator. After reading this book, at least once carefully, you should take and PASS several practice exams in the Solomon Online Exam Simulator.

Lastly, to sufficiently dominate the exam, you need to keep in mind its purpose for existence—*to protect consumers*. The rules have been designed to protect the public from unscrupulous and poorly trained securities representatives. That means a lot of questions are going to focus on identifying both ethical and unethical behaviors. If you keep this, the exam's core purpose, in mind, it will often help you decide between two answers that both seem right on the surface.

A Word About Memorization …

While I have no doubt that you're excited to learn about the state regulation of securities agents, there's no way that all the stuff will stick with a simple reading of the book. Reading the book twice (or even three times) is much better.

But the best way to pass this and every other securities exam is to go buy 500–1,000 index cards (3x5 inch) at your local office supply store. Use one card for every unfamiliar term or concept that is covered in the book.

On one side of the card put the term or concept; on the other write a definition or explanation that is short enough to begin sticking in your brain after viewing it a few dozen times. Further, and this is important, by *handwriting* the cards yourself, your brain will interact with the information in a different and deeper way than by reading it. This helps the information to be stored with more permanence. Using an app or an electronic flashcard system doesn't have the same long-term memorization effect, studies show. The physical work of handwriting your own flashcards beats typing notes on an electronic device.

The best way to use these note cards once you've made them is to study them by a process of elimination. This means that you should spend 15–20 minutes every morning and evening going through the stack, attempting to define each term or explain each rule or concept listed on the front side of the card. If, upon flipping the card over, you were on target, you can then set that card to the side. The effect of this is to increasingly focus your studying time on only the concepts that are giving you trouble, by studying only the cards that are giving you trouble. As a bonus, it'll also sharpen your ability to answer when put on the spot.

A Word About Practice Exams ...

I'm an impatient guy. My first inclination when I study for anything is to go straight to a practice exam and see how much I already know. Likewise, when I get about halfway through a study guide, I get anxious to know if all this time studying has really made a difference, and again I want to flip to a practice exam to check out my progress.

This of course leads to wasted opportunities to take a practice exam for the first time, which will be one of the best measures of whether you really know the material and are ready for the actual exam. By taking the practice exams before you've studied all the material, you'll accomplish two things. First, you'll stress yourself out, since your score won't be nearly as high as when you've worked through the entire book. Second, you may bias the results of the practice exam by having seen the questions once before, perhaps later giving yourself a false sense of assurance that you know the material.

To help keep you focused on the task at hand and not the finish line, as well as to help you measure your progress as you go, Solomon Exam Prep includes short practice quizzes at the end of each chapter that address just the material covered in that chapter. Also, you can take additional quizzes on these chapters in the Solomon Exam Prep exam simulator. These questions are unique from what you'll find on the practice exams at the end of the book and will provide you with additional opportunities to hone your skills. Once you finish reading the text at least once, start taking practice exams in the Solomon Exam Prep online exam simulator. Ideally, you will want to take and pass at least a half-dozen of the Solomon online exam simulator practice exams. Take most of them un-timed and read every rationale, even for the questions you answer correctly.

A Last Word Before You Start ...

Normally, I'd end an introduction by wishing you good luck. But luck is something that only unprepared people need. Study hard, memorize as much as you can, and take as many practice exams as possible, and I can guarantee that luck will have nothing to do with the passing score you receive!

—*Ken Clark*, CFP

Series 63 Frequently Asked Questions

How do I register to take the Series 63?
To take the Series 63, a FINRA member firm must file a Form U4 application on your behalf through FINRA's Central Registration Depository (CRD), or you can file a Form U10 individually. You will have to get fingerprinted and answer a lengthy set of questions about your background. Individuals filing Form U10 will also need to meet the requirements of the regulatory authority they are registering with.

What does passing the Series 63 qualify me to do?
Passing the NASAA Series 63 exam qualifies you to sell securities within a state. You may need to pass the Series 6, 7, 62, 79 or 82 as well to be fully registered.

What score do I need to pass the exam?
A score of 72% is required for passing.

> ⚑ **Note:** Scores are rounded down to the lowest whole number, so a 71.9% would be a final score of 71%—not a passing score for the Series 63 exam.

How many questions are on the exam?
There are 60 scored and 5 unscored questions. The 5 unscored questions are randomly distributed, so test takers do not know which questions are not scored. The unscored questions are being tried out by the exam committee.

Are the questions put into any order?
No, the questions are randomly distributed.

If I get some questions correct, does the test adjust and give me progressively harder questions?
No, the questions are randomly distributed.

How long is the exam?
You'll have 75 minutes to complete the exam. You must go quickly to finish the exam in time. Keep an eye on the clock. You are allowed to take restroom breaks during the exam; however, the clock will continue counting down.

Do I need to be sponsored by a FINRA member firm?
No, sponsorship is not necessary.

Where can I take the exam?
Pearson and Prometric offer the Series 63 at test centers around the world.

Pearson Professional Centers
866-396-6273
www.pearsonvue.com/finra

Prometric Testing Centers
800-578-6273
www.prometric.com/finra

FINRA also offers an easy website to search for a testing center near you:
http://apps.finra.org/testcenter/1/locations.aspx

When can I take the test?
Daily, excluding holidays.

> ⚑ **Note:** Not all testing centers are open on Sundays. Check your preferred testing center for availability.

How much does the exam cost?
The cost of the exam is $125 at this writing.

CHAPTER ONE

Regulation of Investment Advisers and Investment Adviser Representatives

(6 questions on the exam)

1.1. INVESTMENT ADVISERS

Since this is the first of many chapters that sequentially follow the outline for the Series 63 exam prepared by the North American Securities Administrators Association (NASAA), it's worth taking a moment to explain the origins of this exam and the regulations you'll be studying. Understanding its origins and its authors' intentions should give you some major clues as to why you're studying what you're studying. In the process, you will sharpen your test-taking intuition, helping you to narrow the choices down to the correct answer for each question, while spending less time doing it.

One important note about terminology: when I refer to an investment adviser, that often is referring to an entire firm, and not just an individual professional, though it can represent that, too. Hence an investment adviser may be referred to as "they" or "it" throughout the book.

The Series 63 is, at its core, a test of the laws contained within the Uniform Securities Act (USA). The framework for this law was originally put into place in 1930, shortly after the greatest stock market crash in U.S. history, which helped kick off the Great Depression. Much of the motivation behind the law was that individual investors lost an enormous amount of wealth that had been invested in a largely unregulated stock market, by a largely unregulated industry of investment professionals.

Essentially, before this and a few other pieces of landmark legislation were put in place, the investing world was the financial equivalent of the old Wild West. When the Uniform Securities Act and other legislation were enacted, it was the equivalent of a new, gun-slinging sheriff coming to town.

The Uniform Securities Act is not federal legislation; the Securities Act of 1933, the Securities Exchange Act of 1934, and the Investment Company Act of 1940 fill that role. Rather, it is *model* legislation that was designed for states to use (and modify) for the regulation of securities at the individual state level. By creating it once and inviting states to use it, regulators helped to ensure some uniformity of laws from state to state, as well as the quick creation and implementation of laws, since the states did not have to start from scratch. Note: while there are more recent versions, the Series 63 tests the 1956 Uniform Securities Act.

More than anything else, the regulations contained in the Uniform Securities Act are in place to protect investors by ensuring three things. The first is that investment professionals and firms must meet standardized requirements prior to opening up shop. The second is to ensure that certain securities sold to consumers are properly registered before they hit the shelves for sale. Lastly, the regulations clearly outline key ethical standards and practices, so that no professional, firm, or securities issuer can claim they didn't know better.

Make sense? Good, let's dive into it!

1.1.1. INVESTMENT ADVISER—DEFINITION

The first category of people and companies regulated under the Uniform Securities Act are **investment advisers**. In its most basic definition, an investment adviser is someone who provides investment advice in exchange for compensation of some kind. As you'll quickly come to see however, the law makes it a little more complex than that simple definition, adding numerous exceptions that you'll be tested on.

The Investment Advisers Act of 1940 states:

> "Investment adviser" means any person who, for compensation, engages in the business of advising others, either directly or through publications or writings, as to the value of securities or as to the advisability of investing in, purchasing, or selling securities, or who, for compensation and as a part of a regular business, issues or promulgates analyses or reports concerning securities.

The term person, as defined by the Investment Advisers Act of 1940, means a natural person or entity (a company). This distinction is important because, generally speaking, investment advisers are typically not living, breathing individuals. Instead, an investment adviser is usually a business or firm that provides financial advisory services to clients. As we will see later, the individuals who actually work with clients and provide that advice are investment adviser representatives.

"Investment adviser" also includes financial planners and other persons who, as an integral component of other financially related services, provide the foregoing investment advisory services to others for compensation and as part of a business, or who hold themselves out as providing the foregoing investment advisory services to others for compensation.

As you may have noticed, the definition itself includes some people who provide investment advice alongside other services (such as being a financial planner) and those who write newsletters that contain investment recommendations and securities analysis.

On the exam, you'll likely be asked a question about whether or not someone would be considered an investment adviser. When this occurs, you'll be best served by memorizing the three pronged list issued under SEC Release IA-1092, as well as the list of exclusions from the definition of investment adviser. And finally, you'll need to know who *is not* required to register as an investment adviser because they are exempt from registration.

Under the SEC's three-pronged test, an investment adviser is a company or person that does all of the following:

- Offers advice or analyses concerning securities
- Is in the business of offering such advice (even it is not the primary service offered)
- Receives compensation for offering these services

SEC Release IA-1092 also commented directly that the definition of investment adviser includes consultants who advise on pension plans, as well as those who select and evaluate the pension plan's investment managers. Interestingly, the release also included sports and entertainment managers that advise clients on their investments in the definition of investment advisers.

Here's the full list of people/entities excluded from the definition of investment adviser under the Uniform Securities Act, along with a brief explanation below each one. This means these people do not have to register as investment advisers and are not subject to the regulations that were written for investment advisers.

(1) an investment adviser representative;

Explanation: An investment adviser representative is someone who works for an actual investment adviser, which requires a unique type of registration. Thus, they're not actually considered investment advisers.

(2) a bank, savings institution, or trust company;

Explanation: Since banks, savings institutions, and trust companies fall under separate regulations and oversight, they're not typically required to register as investment advisers on a state level.

(3) a lawyer, accountant, engineer, or teacher whose performance of [investment advice] is solely incidental to the practice of [the person's] profession;

Explanation: Anyone who gives investment advice as a smaller, non-integral part of another profession is not considered an investment adviser. If at any point, however, providing investment advice becomes the primary purpose of the relationship they have with someone, they immediately become defined as an investment adviser. You can remember these exclusions by the acronym LATE (Lawyer, Accountant, Teacher, Engineer).

(4) a broker-dealer or its agent whose performance of [investment advice] is solely incidental to the conduct of its business as a broker-dealer and who receives no special compensation for [the investment advice];

Explanation: While the definition of a broker-dealer will be explained more in

Chapter Two, it's sufficient now to say that the primary role of a stockbroker is to help clients buy and sell securities (stocks, bonds, etc.) and he or she is paid a commission for doing so. As long as the provision of investment advice is given as part of that process and any money paid is directly related to the transaction itself, an individual or firm is not considered an investment adviser.

(5) a publisher of any bona fide newspaper, news column, newsletter, news magazine, or business or financial publication or service whether communicated in hard copy form, or by electronic means, or otherwise, that does not consist of the rendering of advice on the basis of the specific investment situation of each client;

Explanation: Any publication (including virtual publications such as a website or blog) that is not primarily making investment recommendations and providing investment advice, even though it may include some such advice, is exempt from the definition of an investment adviser. However, if the sole focus of the publication becomes investment advice and security analysis based on clients' specific situations, then the publisher must register as an investment adviser.

(6) any person that is a federally covered investment adviser;

Explanation: If a professional is required to register as an adviser by a federal regulatory organization, then they are exempt from the definition of an investment adviser on a state level.

(7) such other persons not within the intent of [the definition of an investment adviser] as the [administrator] may by rule or order designate.

Explanation: The Uniform Securities Act may exempt other people and organizations from the definition of an investment adviser. Hence, the law itself basically reserves the right to be amended or expanded, both in this section and others.

Y EXERCISE

CHOOSE INVESTMENT ADVISER OR NOT AN INVESTMENT ADVISER

1. _____ Jim, who works for Your Interest, a firm that receives compensation for giving investment advice.

2. _____ Silvia, who teaches a class at a community college which includes several classes involving general strategies for financial investment.

3. _____ Valued Services, a broker-dealer firm that pays its employees a commission for securities traded as well as occasional compensation for giving advice on which investments are best suited for clients' portfolios.

4. ____ **Investments Publishing, the publisher of a subscription-based interactive website with a component that allows investors to enter personal information and receive advice that matches their needs.**

5. ____ **Beth, an agent for Security Group who gives investment advice but is only compensated for effecting transactions.**

ANSWERS

1. **Not an investment adviser.** Jim works for an investment adviser and thus is an investment adviser representative.

2. **Not an investment adviser.** Sylvia is a teacher and the investment advice that is part of her classes is incidental to the practice of her profession.

3. **Investment adviser.** Valued Services pays its employees to give investment advice and thus is considered to be an investment adviser as well as a broker-dealer.

4. **Investment adviser.** Investments Publishing provides a website that gives investment advice based on clients' specific situations and thus it is an investment adviser.

5. **Not an investment adviser.** Beth, though she gives investment advice, is not compensated for that advice. Thus she is not considered to be an investment adviser.

1.1.2. REGISTRATION OF INVESTMENT ADVISERS

With the exception of Wyoming, which does not require the registration of investment advisers, if a person or company meets the requirements of an investment adviser for their state, then registration with that state is required. The purpose of this is to both allow a state to track and examine investment advisers operating in their state, as well as to give consumers a way of accessing basic information about the advisers and the nature of their practice. Failure to register is a big deal and can result in substantial fines.

Of course, as with everything, there are exceptions to the rules about who must register, even though someone might otherwise meet their state's definition of an investment adviser.

The two exceptions to the registration requirement for people and firms that meet the definition of an investment adviser are:

```
[The investment adviser] has no place of business in this state and (A)
[the adviser's] only clients in this state are investment companies as
defined in the Investment Company Act of 1940, other investment advisers,
federal covered advisers, broker-dealers, banks, trust companies, sav-
ings and loan associations, insurance companies, employee benefit plans
with assets of not less than one million dollars ($1,000,000), and gov-
ernmental agencies or instrumentalities, whether acting for themselves
```

or as trustees with investment control, or other institutional investors as are designated by rule or order of the (administrator), or

Explanation: Investment advisers do not have to register in a state if they do not have an office in the state and their only clients in the state are institutional investors.

[The investment adviser has no place of business in this state and] (B) during the preceding twelve-month period has had no more than five clients, other than those specified in subparagraphs (A), whether or not [the adviser] or any of the persons to whom the communications are directed is then present in this state.

Explanation: This exception, often called the *de minimis* rule (Latin for "about minimal things"), is one of the most commonly used rules to avoid state registration and is something you should burn into your brain for the exam. It says that if an adviser has had no more than five non-institutional clients in a state during the previous 12 months, they are not required to register with that state.

Note: As we will see below, many advisers are required to register at the federal level rather than the state level; these advisers do not meet the definition of investment adviser under the Uniform Securities Act, so they are not required to register at the state level.

1.1.2.1. Federal vs. State Registration

While investment advisers are always subject to both the laws of their state and federal securities laws, the jurisdiction (state vs. federal) with which they must register ultimately depends on the size and nature of their advisory practice. In short, the bigger an adviser's practice and the broader its geographical reach, the more likely it is to require federal registration. Advisers who register at the federal level are called **federal covered advisers**. The law that separated the registration process into federal and state registration is called the **National Securities Markets Improvement Act (NSMIA)** of 1996.

The most common factor for determining where someone needs to register is how much client money an adviser has under management. In most cases, if an adviser has less than $100 million in client assets under their care, it must register on a state level. If it has $110 million or more in assets under management, then federal registration is required (the SEC). If it has at least $100 million but less than $110 million in assets under management, the adviser can choose to register on the federal level or on the state level.

Additional factors that may result in required federal registration include:

- Serving as an adviser to registered investment companies (such as mutual funds)

- Acting as a pension consultant, working with employee pension plans of $200 million or more in total value

- Being an affiliate of an SEC-registered adviser who shares the same home office as the adviser

- Being a mid-sized adviser ($25 million–$100 million assets under management) that is an adviser to a business development company

- Being a mid-sized adviser that is not required to register in the state in which they maintain their principal office (see the laws of the individual state) or which is not subject to examination as an adviser by that state (advisers in New York and Wyoming)

- Being an adviser that is not regulated in the state in which they maintain their principal office (advisers in Wyoming)

- Having a principal office outside of the U.S.

A federally registered adviser must switch to state registration if assets under management drop below $90 million.

In addition:

- Investment advisers that are required to register in 15 or more states are allowed to register federally instead if they wish.

- Investment advisers who provide advice exclusively through an interactive website (and have up to 14 clients through other means) and investment advisers who expect to be eligible for SEC registration within 120 days may also register federally if they meet certain additional requirements.

- The SEC may, through rule or order, permit other investment advisers to register federally.

Federally registered advisers are still required to file a notice with each state in which they have more than five non-institutional clients or a place of business and pay any required fees for investment advisers working in that state.

> **Note:** Investment advisers register at either the state level or the federal level. They are never required to register at both the state and federal level. But they may have to provide a notice filing to a state if they have a place of business in the state or have more than 5 non-institutional clients in the state. A notice filing usually involves sending a copy of the adviser's ADV to the state, paying a filing fee and registering any IARs who provide advice and have a place of business in the state.

> **Note:** The state cannot require additional registration information from an investment adviser than what was used to file with the SEC.

1.1.2.1.1. Federal Exclusions from the Definition of Investment Adviser

The following are exceptions to the *definition* of an **investment adviser**, meaning they don't fit into the definition of investment adviser under the Investment Advisers Act (and the Dodd-Frank Act). Note that many of these exceptions overlap with the ones listed under the Uniform Securities Act. As such, they do not register federally, and states cannot require these entities to register as investment advisers:

- A bank or bank holding company that is not an investment company and does not act as an investment adviser to an investment company
  - ▸ However, a separately identified department may act as an investment adviser without causing the entire bank to be counted as an investment adviser, and in this case, only the separate department would need to register.

- A lawyer, accountant, teacher, or engineer whose performance of advisory services is solely incidental to the practice of his or her profession

- A broker or dealer whose performance of advisory services is solely incidental to its business conduct and for which the broker or dealer receives no compensation

- The publisher of a newspaper or other publication of general and regular circulation

- A person who only gives advice on U.S. government securities and certain other exempted securities

- A nationally recognized statistical rating organization that does not give recommendations to buy, sell, or hold securities and does not manage assets that include securities for others

- A family office

- Other persons as designated by the SEC

1.1.2.1.2. Exemptions from Registration under the Advisers Act

The Advisers Act provides several exemptions from federal registration. Note that the section above discussed exceptions to the definition of investment adviser. Those firms did not need to register because they didn't meet the definition of investment adviser. This section focuses on investment advisors that are exempted from registration requirements. These exemptions are voluntary, and if a firm decides to take advantage of one of them, it may still be subject to state registration. Some of these exemptions were updated and modified under the Dodd-Frank Act of 2010. The firms that are exempted from federal registration requirements include:

- Advisers to insurance companies
- Advisers to charities
- Foreign private advisers with no place of business within the United States
- Advisers that only advise private funds with less than $150 million in assets under management in the United States
- Advisers to venture capital funds (not private equity funds)
- Advisers to licensed small business investment companies

1.1.2.2. **The Investment Adviser Registration Process**

To register at the state level as an investment adviser, persons must file the appropriate paperwork with the state through the federally run Investment Adviser Registration Depository system, or IARD for short. To register, an investment adviser must use this system to submit a Form ADV. Some states may require the filing of additional forms such as advisory contracts and financial statements as well.

The applicant must also give permission for an appropriate background check to be performed and sign a **consent to service of process**, which allows a state administrator to receive legal papers (summons, notice of lawsuits, etc.) on behalf of the adviser. Once the consent to service of process has been filed, it does not need to be renewed.

Part 1 of Form ADV (which is short for Adviser) is general information about the investment adviser such as:

- Information about the ownership and nature of their practice including the names of the principals involved
- The location of the main office
- The types of services offered
- Whether the adviser keeps custody of customer assets
- The location of books and records
- Any relevant regulatory/disciplinary history

Part 2 of Form ADV includes information relevant to the customer such as:

- Fees or fee structure for the services provided
- Types of clients and investments
- Methods of analyzing investments (e.g., technical versus fundamental)
- The educational and business background of the advisers

For state registration, firms submit Form ADV, Parts 1 and 2, to the administrator. Federal covered advisers, however, submit only Parts 1 and 2A to the SEC, and save Part 2B in their records. Part 2A is the brochure; Part 2B is the brochure supplement. The firm will also fill out Form U4s for all employees that will work as investment adviser representatives.

In addition to filing the appropriate forms, applicants for investment adviser registration must pass any exams required by their state, such as the Series 65 exam. However, some states may waive this requirement for advisers who hold certain designations, such as the CFP (Certified Financial Planner), CIC (Chartered Investment Counselor), ChFC (Chartered Financial Consultant), PFS (Personal Financial Specialist), or CFA (Chartered Financial Analyst).

An application for registration becomes effective at noon on the *30th day* after the application is initially filed, unless the state requires additional information or denies the application. If a state's administrator wishes to initiate a hearing based on an applicant's admission of a final judicial or administrative order made against them prior to registration, they have 90 days to do so following registration or they may no longer use that information to challenge an adviser's registration.

If a firm is registering with the SEC at the federal level, the SEC has *45 days* to approve or deny the application.

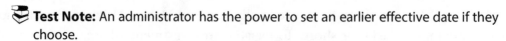 **Test Note:** An administrator has the power to set an earlier effective date if they choose.

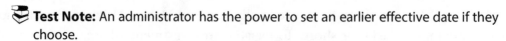 **Test Note:** While an applicant is waiting for their registration as a securities professional to become effective they may not perform any functions that would normally require registration (e.g., advising clients). They would be able to perform clerical tasks.

An adviser's registration remains in effect *until midnight of December 31* of the year for which the registration is filed. If a renewal was not filed, the registration is considered revoked. This means that an adviser who initially registers on November 15 must renew their registration less than two months later.

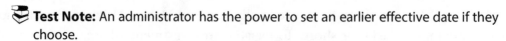 **Test Note:** When an adviser files an application for a successor firm for the unexpired portion of the year (from the time of filing to December 31), they do not need to pay a filing fee.

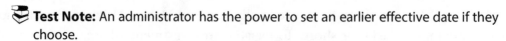 **Test Note:** If a securities professional becomes registered in the middle of the year, the filing fee is typically paid in full at the time of registration.

1.1.2.3. **Net Capital Requirements**

States commonly require investment advisers to meet net capital requirements both prior to registration and at all times while their registration remains active. This means that their personal net worth (assets minus debts) must not fall below a certain amount.

In calculating this net worth, the adviser must exclude all assets that cannot readily be converted into cash. This includes personal residences, automobiles, and any intangible assets such as patents or trademarks.

The amount of net capital they are required to have depends on the nature of their practice. Advisers that have actual custody of their client assets are required to maintain the most net capital.

The current NASAA recommended net capital requirements are:

- $35,000 for advisers with custody over client assets, except those advisers that only have custody for purposes of deducting their fees or managing a pooled investment

- $10,000 for advisers that do not have custody over client assets, but have discretionary authority over the transactions in their clients' accounts

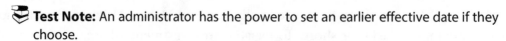 **Test Note:** Discretionary authority is when an adviser or agent has been granted permission to make trades in an account without receiving prior approval from the customer for each trade. A third-party trading agreement is different from a discretionary authority, since a third-party agreement grants someone else besides the adviser or agent permission to initiate trades in the account.

Any adviser who requires prepayment of client fees more than six months in advance, and for more than $500 per customer, must also maintain a positive net worth (hypothetically just $0.01) at all times.

Anyone not meeting the net capital requirements is required to notify their state's administrator and file the following documentation by the close of business on the next business day:

- A trial balance of all ledger accounts
- A statement of all client funds or securities that are not segregated
- The total of all clients' debit balances
- The total number of client accounts

In the event a company fails to meet its net capital requirements, the state securities administrator may permit the company a period of time to bring its net capital requirements into compliance, may issue sanctions against the company, and may make a proper showing to a court of law and request that the judge appoint a receiver in the firm's bankruptcy. The administrator may even order a company to cease operations or hand over operations to a third party. The administrator may also require the firm to purchase a surety bond for the amount of the deficiency. Because surety bonds are only sold in $5,000 increments, the firm will have to round up to the nearest $5,000.

According to the USA and the Investment Advisers Act of 1940, a state administrator cannot impose additional net capital or bonding requirements beyond what is required of the state where they have their principal place of business. This is true even if they are doing business in other states that have higher net capital requirements. In addition, a state securities administrator cannot require an investment adviser to maintain net capital requirements higher than what is listed in the Investment Advisers Act of 1940.

1.1.2.4. **Post-Registration Requirements**

In addition to the ongoing requirement to file the appropriate renewal forms on an annual basis, state-registered investment advisers must also meet ongoing requirements known as **post-registration requirements**. These requirements include:

- **Financial reports.** Advisers may be required to file reports regarding their own personal and their firm's financial condition. If the information filed on these forms becomes inaccurate at any point, updated reports must be filed as soon as possible.

- **Recordkeeping.** Advisers are required to meet the recordkeeping requirements put in place by each state in which they operate.

  ▸ According to both the USA and the Investment Advisers Act of 1940, advisers must keep virtually every form of client record and marketing literature on file for *five years*. This five-year period begins at the end of the fiscal year in which the record was created. Also, these records must be easily accessible for two of the five years.

▸ If an adviser goes out of business, records must be kept at least an additional *three years* past the date of the firm's closure.

▸ A state cannot require an investment adviser to maintain any books and records in addition to those required under the laws of the state in which the adviser's principal office is located, as long as the firm is registered and is complying with the requirements of that state.

▸ The administrator is allowed to view the books and records of an investment adviser within their own state and across states to aid an investigation.

- **Audits.** All registered investment advisers (RIAs) are subject to audits, also called examinations, by the states they're licensed in *at any time and for any reason that the administrator thinks is in the public interest.* As part of the audit, their state administrator may examine any records they deem useful. The administrator may examine books and records of investment advisers within their state or outside their state, and they may cooperate with other administrators when appropriate. Additionally, some states may require the adviser to pay a reasonable fee to conduct the audit. Section 222 of the Investment Advisers Act of 1940 prevents a state administrator from conducting an audit of a Federal Covered Adviser unless the adviser's principal office is in the state.

- **Access persons.** Access persons include employees, directors, officers, and fiduciaries with access to inside information about securities gained from their work with or for an investment adviser. The investments of access persons must be monitored on an ongoing basis, and the easiest way to do this is to have them send copies of their brokerage statements and trade confirmations to your firm.

- **Bond or insurance required for advisers with custody or authority.** If an adviser has custody of client funds or discretionary authority over a client's account, the state may require the adviser to post a surety bond. An adviser may make an appropriate deposit of cash or securities in lieu of posting a bond. If an adviser has a net capital that exceeds the amount required by the administrator, a surety bond cannot be required.

- **The brochure rule.** Investment advisers subject to state registration may be required by their state to provide certain basic information and disclosures about their business to prospective and existing clients prior to entering or renewing an advisory contract. This brochure must be written in plain English that avoids jargon. The disclosures include:
  ▸ Types of services provided
  ▸ Fee structures
  ▸ Conflicts of interest and additional fees that could be gained through any conflicts of interest
  ▸ Material disciplinary actions against the firm, its management, or advisory personnel
  ▸ Educational and business background of its management, or advisory personnel

This is often referred to as the brochure rule, since much of the information typically required would be found in many advisers' marketing brochures. The disclosure statement or brochure should be delivered to clients at least 48 hours before an advisory contract is signed, or the advisory client will have five business days to terminate the contract without penalty fees being charged by the adviser. However, the brochure must be delivered *before* the contract is signed. Additionally, the adviser must deliver or offer to deliver the brochure upon request.

> **Note:** Because different states may have different bonding, net capital, and recordkeeping requirements, the exam may require you to know that a state administrator cannot require an investment adviser to maintain bonding, net capital, or recordkeeping requirements different from those required by the state in which it maintains its principal office and place of business.

> **Note:** An administrator of another state can demand to examine the books of any adviser operating in their state or another state.

> **Note:** In addition, a state administrator cannot require an investment adviser to maintain bonding, net capital, or recordkeeping requirements that are greater than what is required at the federal level. This federal amount may be referred to on the test as the amount set by the Securities Exchange Act of 1934 or the SEC.

1.1.3. TERMINATION OF AN INVESTMENT ADVISER REGISTRATION

As previously mentioned, registration as an investment adviser is by no means permanent. At a bare minimum, state approval to operate can terminate on December 31 of any year simply because an adviser forgets to submit their renewal paperwork. But an adviser's registration can terminate or be restricted for a variety of other reasons including:

- **Denial.** Naturally, if a state's administrator has reason to believe an applicant would not serve the best interests of the public (such as if they are unqualified), an application can be denied outright.

- **Revocation.** If an adviser has acted in a way that has substantially harmed the public, the administrator may permanently revoke the adviser's registration in that state.

- **Suspension.** For less serious infractions, such as a failure to file proper paperwork, the administrator may temporarily suspend an adviser's registration.

- **Withdrawal.** An adviser may choose to terminate their registration at any time; using a Form ADV-W officially notifies a state's administrator of their intent to cease operations. The withdrawal request becomes effective 30 days after it is submitted. Once registration has been withdrawn, the applicant remains under the administrator's jurisdiction for a year.

- **Restriction/limitation.** An adviser's registration may be restricted to only operate in certain settings and capacities, for a variety of reasons as deemed in the best interest of the public.

🏋 EXERCISE

ANSWER TRUE OR FALSE

1. _____ An investment adviser with no place of business, 20 institutional clients, and 3 non-institutional clients in State A has to register there.

2. _____ An investment adviser with no place of business and six non-institutional clients in State A has to register there.

3. _____ An investment adviser with $200 million assets under management and six non-institutional clients in State A has to register there.

4. _____ An investment adviser with $75 million in assets under management that is registered in 16 states is allowed to register at the federal level.

5. _____ To register at the state level, an investment adviser needs to file both a Form ADV and and Form U4s for all employees that need to register as investment adviser representatives.

6. _____ An investment adviser must always have a net worth of at least $35,000.

7. _____ Investment advisers must keep most records on file for at least 5 years.

8. _____ A state administrator cannot require an investment adviser to maintain net capital amounts greater than that required at the federal level.

9. _____ Investment advisers cannot be audited more than once a year.

10. _____ An adviser's withdrawal of registration becomes effective as soon as it is filed with the state administrator.

ANSWERS

1. **False.** An investment adviser with no place of business in a state does not have to register there if its clients in that state are institutional clients plus no more than 5 non-institutional clients.

2. **True.** Having any more than five non-institutional clients in a state will require an investment adviser to register there.

3. **False.** An investment adviser with over $110 million in AUM must register at the federal level. Having more than five non-institutional clients in a state would require a notice filing, which is not the same as state registration.

4. **True.** Investment advisers with $25-$100 million in AUM that are registered in 15 or more states are allowed to register federally.

5. **True.** To register at the state level, an investment adviser needs to fill out a form ADV. A Form

U4 is used to register representatives of an investment adviser, also known as investment adviser representatives. The firm will need to fill out a Form U4 for each employee that will work as a representative.

6. **False.** The NASAA recommends that an investment adviser with custody over client assets has $35,000 or more in net capital, but this suggested requirement does not apply to all investment advisers.

7. **True.** As a post-registration requirement, investment advisers must keep most records on file for at least 5 years.

8. **True.** State administrators cannot require an investment adviser to maintain net capital amounts in excess of federal requirements.

9. **False.** Investment advisers are subject to audits at any time and for any reason that an administrator thinks such an audit to be in the public interest.

10. **False.** An adviser's registration withdrawal becomes effective 30 days after it is submitted.

1.1.3.1. **Reasons for Disciplining an Adviser**

According to the Uniform Securities Act, there are 12 (yes, you need to know them all) categories for which an adviser might be disciplined by a state securities administrator, if the order is in the public interest. It is not uncommon for disciplinary action against an adviser to contain charges in multiple categories.

Since the exact wording of the code is quite extensive at this point, each of the 12 areas has been simplified below. Be sure to review the entire code at least once.

- **Filing incomplete applications.** The bottom line is that any adviser filing an application that is missing material (important) information can have action brought against them.

- **Willfully violating securities regulations.** If a person breaks any of the rules within the Uniform Securities Act or a predecessor act, such as the Securities Exchange Act of 1934, the Securities Act of 1933, or the Investment Company Act of 1940, he or she can be held accountable and disciplined.

- **Within the last 10 years, having prior felony convictions or securities-related misdemeanors.** While a previous felony does not necessarily mean an adviser's registration application won't be approved, it's definitely a huge hurdle. If the felony occurred within the previous 10 years, it absolutely must be disclosed to the state administrator and an explanation must be provided. All securities-related misdemeanors that occurred within the last 10 years must also be disclosed.

- **Court-ordered limitations.** If a court confirms the administrator's charges by limiting or prohibiting an adviser's right to operate, this could (and probably would) result in an action against the adviser's registration as well.

- **Prior disciplinary orders.** If an adviser is subject to an order by the administrator denying, suspending, or revoking their registration, the administrator may use this as a basis to deny an application for a new registration.

- **Within the last 10 years, other securities act violations.** If within the past 10 years any industry regulatory body, such as the SEC, determined that a person willfully violated the Securities Act of 1933, the Securities Exchange Act of 1934, the Investment Advisers Act of 1940, the Investment Company Act of 1940, or the Commodity Exchange Act, they may be subject to discipline against their registration.

- **Unethical behavior.** Any unethical or dishonest behavior, in any financial arena or industry, may be grounds for disciplinary action.

- **Insolvency.** If an adviser becomes financially insolvent, either because the person's debts exceed the person's assets or because the person cannot meet their financial obligations when they're due, their registration may be restricted or revoked.

- **Foreign violations.** An adviser who is found by a foreign court or regulatory body to be in violation of foreign laws may be subject to domestic action against their registration. In addition, if within the past five years an adviser's registration has been denied, revoked, or suspended by a foreign regulator or the adviser was kicked out of a foreign exchange or self-regulatory organization, the administrator may act against the adviser's registration.

- **Unqualified adviser.** Any adviser who is deemed unqualified by their state's administrator may have their license disciplined. However, if an adviser is qualified by training and/or knowledge, they are considered qualified, regardless of how much experience they have.

- **Failure to supervise.** Advisers are responsible for all those that work on their behalf. If they fail to reasonably supervise an investment adviser representative or another individual, their registration can be adversely affected.

- **Failure to file.** If the registration or renewal fees required by a state are not paid, a registration may be denied, though the denial order must be vacated once the filing fees are paid.

> **Test Note:** An administrator cannot deny the license of an investment adviser (or an investment adviser representative, a broker-dealer or a broker-dealer agent) based on lack of experience if the applicant is qualified by training or knowledge or both.

1.2. PRACTICAL APPLICATION

Amy Adams is new to the securities industry and has just passed the required licensing exams. She's been hired by Wealth Management, Inc., a firm with hundreds of clients and more than $500 million under management. Since Amy will be providing advice as part of the business of a larger firm, she does not typically have to register as an investment adviser herself. Rather, she has to register with their state as an investment adviser representative. In other words, she's a representative of someone else who is registered as an investment adviser.

However, Amy Adams's firm *does* have to register as an investment adviser. As part of this process, the firm must first determine whether or not it has to register as an investment adviser with each state it operates in, or just once with the federal government (Securities and Exchange Commission). Because her firm is one of the largest in the region, there's no doubt that the firm would exceed the $110 million asset limit for state registration, in addition to having over five non-institutional clients in more than 15 states.

Because Amy's firm acts as custodian for their clients' assets (instead of using another firm to hold the assets they manage), they would be required to meet the largest net capital requirement of $35,000. If they did not maintain custody, but did have discretionary authority, then the net capital limit would drop to $10,000.

Due to the large number of investment professionals employed by Amy's firm, the firm employs several compliance professionals to ensure that their annual registration as an investment adviser is not revoked by someone accidentally not filing paperwork in a timely manner or by the careless and unethical activities of its investment professionals.

1.3. INVESTMENT ADVISOR REPRESENTATIVES

While some investment advisers are one-man or -woman shops, others may employ dozens, hundreds, or even thousands of investment professionals. These employees often work with individual clients and give individualized advice, seemingly working as investment advisers themselves. Yet, due to their employee status working for another investment adviser, they're not considered investment advisers themselves. They are in fact considered investment adviser *representatives*.

While that might seem like splitting hairs, this unique classification essentially ensures that qualified professionals can provide investment advice to the public without having to start their own firms, meet net capital requirements, etc. At the same time, it also guarantees that those professionals who do work for an existing investment adviser are individually accountable for their actions and have something to lose (their right to provide investment advice) should they decide to not walk the narrow ethical path.

1.3.1. INVESTMENT ADVISER REPRESENTATIVE—DEFINITION

Here's the official definition of an **investment adviser representative**, or **IAR**, from the Uniform Securities Act:

any partner, officer, director of (or a person occupying a similar status or performing similar functions) or other individual employed by or associated with an investment adviser that is registered or required to be registered under this act, or who has a place of business located in this state and is employed by or associated with a federal covered adviser; and who does any of the following: (1) makes any recommendations or otherwise renders advice regarding securities, (2) manages accounts or portfolios of clients, (3) determines which recommendation or advice regarding securities should be given, (4) solicits, offers or negotiates for the sale of or sells investment advisory services, or (5) supervises employees who perform any of the foregoing.

As you can tell from the official definition, there's nothing second-rate about being an investment adviser representative. More often than not, IARs are the professionals finding a firm's clients, giving them the bulk of their investment advice, and helping clients manage their portfolios. In fact, the description of an IAR looks very similar to that of the actual investment adviser they work for. At the core, they give advice as their primary business and receive compensation for doing so. The only real difference, aside from meeting different regulatory requirements, is that an investment adviser representative is essentially just an investment adviser who has chosen to work for another investment adviser under their existing registration.

1.3.1.1. Investment Adviser Representative Registration

First and foremost, to register as an investment adviser representative, someone would naturally have to have found an actual investment adviser who wants to hire him or her. Being an IAR, by definition, requires someone to be affiliated in some way with an actual registered investment adviser.

When an employment arrangement is agreed upon, the appropriate paperwork must be filed with the state through the federally run Investment Adviser Registration Depository system, or IARD, just as it is for the actual investment adviser. The primary difference is that the paperwork, while often completed by the investment adviser representative, is submitted by the investment adviser who will be employing him or her. This helps prevent investment advisers from suddenly finding themselves with a bunch of IARs that they didn't actually hire.

On behalf of the IAR, the investment adviser must submit a **Form U4**, which is a generic application for registration. The Form U4 requires information about an applicant which includes ten years of employment history and five years of residential history, any previous criminal convictions, guilty pleas, or pleas of no contest. Bankruptcy proceedings or compromise with creditors which involved either the applicant or a firm he or she controlled must also be disclosed on the Form U4.

The applicant must also give permission for an appropriate background check to be performed and sign a **consent to service of process**, which allows a state administrator to receive legal papers (summons, notice of lawsuits, etc.) on behalf of the IAR. Once the consent to service of process has been filed, it does not need to be renewed.

In addition to filing the appropriate forms, applicants for investment adviser representative registration must pass any exams required by their state, such as the Series 65 or Series 66 exam. However, some states may waive this requirement for IARs who hold certain designations, such as the CFP (Certified Financial Planner). Also, Wyoming and New York do not require investment adviser representatives to register.

An application for registration as an investment adviser representative becomes effective at noon on the *30th day* after the application is initially filed, unless the state requires additional information or denies the application. If a state's administrator wishes to initiate a hearing based on an applicant's admission of a final judicial or administrative order made against them prior to registration, they have 90 days to do so following registration or they may no longer use that information to challenge an investment adviser representative's registration.

A representative's registration remains in effect *until midnight of December 31* of the year for which the registration is filed. If a renewal is not filed, the registration is considered revoked. This means that an IAR who initially registers on December 28 must still renew his or her registration just a few days later, on January 1. In other words, licenses cannot be prorated.

1.3.1.2. Registration Exceptions

IARs do not have to register in a state if they do not have an office in the state and they have five or fewer non-institutional clients in the state (the *de minimis* exemption).

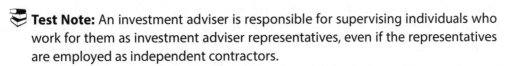 **Test Note:** An investment adviser is responsible for supervising individuals who work for them as investment adviser representatives, even if the representatives are employed as independent contractors.

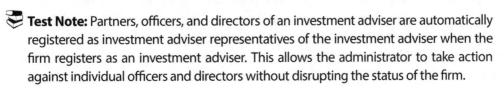 **Test Note:** Partners, officers, and directors of an investment adviser are automatically registered as investment adviser representatives of the investment adviser when the firm registers as an investment adviser. This allows the administrator to take action against individual officers and directors without disrupting the status of the firm.

IARs who work for federally covered investment advisers may need to register in the state where their office is located. It is also important to note that IARs never register at the federal level.

1.3.1.3. Net Capital Requirements

Unlike the investment adviser they work for, investment adviser representatives do not have to prove that they can meet certain capital requirements to register. In other words, even if they have a negative net worth (owe more than they're worth), an investment adviser can still register them as their representative.

1.3.1.4. **Post-Registration Requirements**

There are very few post-registration requirements for investment adviser representatives, aside from the IAR not breaking the law and the IAR's firm renewing his or her registration in a timely manner. The most likely post-registration requirement would be many states' requirement to engage in some type of continuing education during each renewal period.

1.3.2. **TERMINATION OF AN IAR**

Because investment adviser representatives work for an investment adviser as an employee or associate, they tend to come and go more frequently than actual investment advisers. That's not hard to imagine, since professionals are constantly being hired and fired from firms, as well as changing jobs or switching firms for their own reasons.

In all these cases, additional filings are required with the states in which the investment adviser is registered. The responsibility for these filings is supposed to fall on the investment adviser (employer), not the investment adviser representative (employee). This makes sense, since disgruntled or distracted former employees may not care about properly filing paperwork in an industry they may never work in again. However, if the employer is a federal covered adviser, then the IAR is responsible for notifying the administrator.

When does a Notice of Termination need to be filed? The Uniform Securities Act says promptly. That's code for *do it right away*.

1.3.2.1. **Disciplinary Action against an IAR**

As with investment advisers, lifetime registration as an investment adviser representative is by no means guaranteed after someone is initially approved. State approval as an IAR terminates on December 31 of each year. If not properly renewed, an IAR's registration is revoked. For a full list of reasons registration can be terminated, please see "Termination of an Investment Adviser Registration" on page 23. However, for IARs, there is one exception: in the case of withdrawal, an adviser may terminate an IAR's registration at any time by filing Form U5. The withdrawal request becomes effective 30 days after it is submitted. The adviser is then required to supply the IAR with a copy of the Form U5 within 30 days of the date that the employee left the firm. Once registration has been withdrawn, the applicant remains under the administrator's jurisdiction for a year.

According to the Uniform Securities Act, most of the same 12 categories for which an investment adviser can be disciplined also apply to an investment adviser's representative (except for failure to supervise), assuming the order is in the public interest. As before, it is not uncommon for disciplinary action against an IAR to contain charges in multiple categories.

Please see "Reasons for Disciplining an Adviser" on page 25 for the full list of situations that could result in disciplinary action.

EXERCISE

ANSWER TRUE OR FALSE

1. ____Partners, officers, and directors of an investment adviser are required to register as IARs only if they regularly give investment advice.

2. ____ IARs who work for federally-covered investment advisers register at the federal level.

3. ____IARs are not subject to net capital requirements.

4. ____IARs are subject to most of the same post-registration requirements as the firms for which they work.

5. ____IARs in some cases are responsible for notifying a state administrator in the case of their termination.

ANSWERS

1. **False.** Partners, officers, and directors of an IA are automatically registered as IARs when the firm registers.

2. **False.** IARs only register at the state level. They cannot register federally.

3. **True.** Unlike the IAs for which they work, IARs never have to meet net capital requirements.

4. **False.** While IAs have many post-registration requirements, IARs are typically only required to engage in some sort of continuing education during each renewal period.

5. **True.** IARs who work for a federal covered adviser are responsible for notifying the administrator in the case of their termination.

☐ What legislation is the Series 63 heavily based upon?

☐ Who uses the Uniform Securities Act?

☐ What is the basic definition of an investment adviser?

☐ What are the seven exceptions to the definition of investment adviser?

☐ What are the two primary reasons for requiring investment adviser registration?

☐ What are the two exceptions from state registration for investment advisers?

☐ Advisers that have no place of business within a state are not required to register if their only clients in that state are which kind?

☐ What is the *de minimis* rule?

☐ What amount of assets under management requires federal registration?

☐ An adviser may federally register if it would be required to register in how many states?

☐ When do registrations typically become effective?

☐ When do registrations typically expire?

☐ What are the most common post-registration requirements?

☐ How long must investment adviser records be kept?

☐ What recordkeeping responsibility does an adviser have if it goes out of business?

☐ What is the brochure rule?

☐ What types of action can be taken against someone's license or application?

☐ What are the twelve main reasons an adviser may be disciplined?

☐ What is the definition of an investment adviser representative?

☐ What is the standard for exemption from registration for an IAR?

☐ Who typically handles the registration of an IAR?

☐ When does an IAR application typically become effective?

☐ When does an IAR's registration expire?

☐ What are the net capital requirements for an IAR?

☐ What is the most common post-registration requirement for an IAR?

☐ When must a state be notified of a terminated IAR?

Chapter 1 Practice Questions

1. **All of the following are factors that are considered when determining if someone is an investment adviser except:**

   A. Receiving compensation
   B. Assets under management
   C. Providing advice
   D. Job description

2. **Which of the following would most likely be considered an investment adviser?**

   A. A lawyer overseeing the management of a client's trust
   B. A college professor who teaches a class on investing
   C. A personal finance author who focuses on planning for retirement
   D. A publisher of a subscription-based online newsletter that includes an interactive component where investors can put in information and receive advice specific to their needs

3. **Which of the following are exceptions to the definition of an investment adviser subject to state registration?**

   I. An investment adviser representative
   II. An investment adviser with $150 million in client assets under management
   III. The publisher of a general interest business magazine
   IV. A bank or savings institution

   A. II only
   B. II and III
   C. I, II, and III
   D. I, II, III, and IV

4. **All of the following would allow someone with no office in the state, but who otherwise is clearly defined as an investment adviser, to avoid state registration except:**

   A. The *de minimis* rule
   B. The adviser's only clients were institutional clients.
   C. Their assets under management did not exceed $100 million.
   D. The adviser had no more than five non-institutional clients.

5. **The net capital requirement for an adviser who has discretion, but not custody, over a client account is:**

   A. $0
   B. $500
   C. $10,000
   D. $35,000

6. **According to the Uniform Securities Act, an investment adviser may be disciplined because of:**

    I.   A felony from fifteen years ago
    II. A non-material error on their registration application
    III. Insolvency
    IV. A non-securities-related misdemeanor from five years ago

    A. I only
    B. III only
    C. II and III
    D. I, II, III and IV

7. **All of the following are situations that would require an investment adviser to meet a net capital requirement except:**

    A. Not qualifying for federal registration
    B. Requiring clients to pay fees 6 months in advance
    C. Custody of client assets
    D. Discretion over client assets

8. **The requirement for investment advisers to provide certain information to prospective clients is known as:**

    A. The *de minimis* rule
    B. The brochure rule
    C. U4
    D. Form ADV-W

9. **Common post-registration requirements include:**

    I.   Consent to service
    II. Audit compliance
    III. Financial reporting
    IV. Posting a bond

    A. I and II
    B. I, II, and IV
    C. II, III, and IV
    D. I, II, III, and IV

10. **All of the following are methods by which an adviser's registration may be terminated or restricted except:**

    A. Lapse
    B. Withdrawal
    C. Suspension
    D. Revocation

11. **All of the following would likely be considered an investment adviser representative except a(n):**

    A. Customer service rep who is paid bonuses based on how clients rate his service
    B. Stockbroker who receives an agreed-upon dollar fee for giving advice to each client
    C. Wealth manager who receives a fee equal to a percentage of the assets she manages
    D. Investment professional whose firm pays him a salary regardless of how many clients he advises

12. **Which of the following is the key distinguishing feature between an investment adviser and an IAR?**

    A. The adviser works for the IAR.
    B. The IAR works for the adviser.
    C. The IAR must meet a net capital requirement.
    D. Only the investment adviser, not the IAR, can make recommendations to clients.

13. **Which of the following would not need to register as an investment adviser representative?**

    I. Someone who performs only clerical duties
    II. Someone who serves no more than five non-institutional clients per year in a state besides their home state
    III. An IAR who receives less than $500 in annual fees
    IV. Someone who is working as an agent for a broker-dealer and only gives incidental advice

    A. I and III only
    B. I, II, III, and IV
    C. I, II, and III
    D. I, II, and IV

14. **An investment adviser representative will typically be required to meet all of the following registration and post-registration requirements except:**

    A. Exam or evidence of qualification
    B. Have a sponsoring firm
    C. Background check
    D. Net capital requirements

15. **An investment adviser representative's registration must typically be renewed by:**

    A. December 31 of each year
    B. One year from the original registration
    C. Two years from the original registration
    D. 30 days after his or her firm renews their primary registration

16. **Which of the following parties is/are responsible for filing an investment adviser representative's termination of registration when he or she leaves a state-registered firm?**

    I.   The IAR
    II. The investment adviser
    III. Their state
    IV. The SEC

    A. I only
    B. II only
    C. I and II
    D. III and IV

17. **All of the following are reasons an IAR may have action taken against his or her registration except:**

    A. Failing to register with the SEC when working with international clients
    B. Omitting material information from their registration
    C. A felony drunk driving conviction seven years prior to his or her initial registration
    D. Failing to respond to his or her state administrator's request for information

18. **Jackson works for an investment adviser. He calls prospective clients and solicits advisory business for the firm. He is paid for every new appointment he schedules, but he doesn't actually meet with any of the prospects himself. Which of the following is true?**

    A. Jackson must register as an investment adviser representative for his firm.
    B. Jackson does not need to register as an investment adviser representative because he doesn't give advice to clients.
    C. Jackson must register as an agent for his firm.
    D. Jackson does not need to register as an investment adviser representative as long as he doesn't split fees with other representatives.

19. **Which of the following are common reasons a state may take action against an IAR?**

    I.   Failure to meet bonding requirements
    II. Failure to meet conditions placed on their registration
    III. Failure to supervise
    IV. Working for multiple investment advisers at the same time

    A. II only
    B. II and III only
    C. II, III, and IV
    D. I, II, III, and IV

20. All of the following are exempt from registration as an IAR with a state except:

A. A federally covered adviser, with 12 clients and no physical office in the state

B. Someone employed by a federally covered adviser with four clients and one office in the state

C. A stockbroker with $14 million in client assets under management, who is paid only when transactions occur

D. The publisher of a newsletter that only gives investment advice on small company stocks

Chapter 1 Practice Question Answers

1. **Answer B.** While assets under management are a measure used to determine whether or not someone is required to register with the SEC or simply with their state, it doesn't determine if someone is an adviser or not. Whether or not someone actually provides advice and whether or not they receive compensation directly related to that advice are definitely measures of whether someone is an adviser. Someone's job description does affect whether or not they're considered an investment adviser; if giving advice simply occurs as something incidental to another job (such as being a lawyer or teacher), then the person would not be required to register as an investment adviser.

2. **Answer: D.** While the publishers of general newspapers, newsletters, and magazines are not required to register as investment advisers, publishers of newsletters that focus specifically on security analysis and recommendations based on clients' individual situations must register as investment advisers. The lawyer, professor, and personal finance author do not need to register since any investment advice they give is secondary to their primary role.

3. **Answer: D.** All choices are considered exceptions to who must register at the state level as an investment adviser. Investment adviser representatives register as such, not as investment advisers. Investment advisers with more than $110 million are required to register on a federal level. The publisher of a general interest magazine is not considered an investment adviser. Banks and savings institutions are not required to register as investment advisers.

4. **Answer: C.** If an adviser's assets are under $100 million, they are mostly likely required to register on a state level. The *de minimis* rule allows advisers with no more than five clients in a state to avoid registration. Advisers working with only institutional clients are not required to register as investment advisers.

5. **Answer: C.** Advisers who have discretion (the right to execute transactions without a client's specific consent) are required to demonstrate net capital (assets minus liabilities) of $10,000. This requirement is raised to $35,000 if the investment adviser has custody of their clients' assets, even if they don't have discretion. Advisers who collect more than $500 worth of prepaid fees per client six or more months in advance are required to demonstrate a positive net capital balance at all times.

6. **Answer: B.** Insolvency (not being able to meet one's financial obligations) is a reason that a state securities administrator may act against an adviser's registration. A felony must have occurred in the last 10 years to be a reason an adviser's registration is acted against. Securities-related misdemeanors within the last 10 years may also serve as a cause for action, but misdemeanors unrelated to the securities industry may not. Non-material errors (typos, missing signature, etc.) do need to be fixed, but are not by themselves a reason an adviser's registration may be acted upon.

7. **Answer: A.** Whether an adviser is state or federally registered has no bearing on whether or not an adviser has to meet net capital requirements. Requiring clients to pay fees six or more months in advance, having custody over clients' assets, or having discretion over clients' accounts all require an adviser to meet net capital requirements.

8. **Answer: B.** The brochure rule requires advisers to supply prospective clients with basic

information about their practice. Many advisers simply provide a copy of their Form ADV, Part II, to meet this requirement. The *de minimis* rule states that if an adviser has no more than five non-institutional clients in a state, they do not need to register with that state as an adviser. The Form U4 is used as a standardized application for registration by investment advisers and broker-dealers. The Form ADV-W is used by investment advisers to voluntarily withdraw their registration.

9. **Answer: C.** After an adviser's initial registration, they may be required to undergo audits at any time, submit financial reports, and post a bond or provide an appropriate deposit of cash or securities. Providing consent to service is part of the initial registration process.

10. **Answer: A.** An adviser's registration may be restricted or terminated by denial, revocation, suspension, or withdrawal. A withdrawal occurs when an adviser willingly submits a Form ADV-W and terminates their registration. A temporary suspension of registration may be issued by a state administrator as a penalty for violating state laws.

11. **Answer: A.** Someone working for an investment adviser who performs only clerical (think secretary) or ministerial (think customer service) duties does not need to register as an investment adviser representative. The moment they begin providing advice to the customers of that investment adviser for compensation, however, they would very likely be considered an IAR. All the other professionals mentioned in the question, even though their fees are calculated differently from one another, still receive a fee for providing investment advice. The stockbroker would be exempt from registration only if his sole compensation was transaction-related commissions.

12. **Answer: B.** The key distinguishing factor between an investment adviser and an investment adviser representative is that the IAR works for the investment adviser. Hence, they're called the firm's representative. IARs very often do provide investment advice based on their own unique preferences, research, and beliefs, but they do so under the investment adviser's supervision. There are no net capital requirements for IARs like there are for the firm that employs them.

13. **Answer: D.** Someone who performs clerical duties would not meet the definition of an IAR and therefore would not need to register as such. Someone who works as an agent for a broker-dealer (think stockbroker) does not need to register if her advice is given incidentally, as part of helping the customer conduct a transaction. If she were to receive compensation for providing investment advice that was not specifically tied to completing transactions, then she would likely have to register. Lastly, an IAR is exempt from having to register in a state where she has no office and fewer than five non-institutional clients in the past 12 months.

14. **Answer: D.** Investment adviser representatives do not have to meet the net capital requirements their employing firms do. However, they do have to pass an exam or have a designation (such as Certified Financial Planner), be employed by an advisory firm, and pass a background check.

15. **Answer: A.** The registration for an investment adviser representative, just like for his or her employing investment adviser, must be renewed by December 31 of each year. It does not matter how long the current registration has been valid. The reference to 30 days applies to when an investment adviser representative's registration becomes valid after an application has been submitted, if the state securities administrator does nothing to block it.

16. **Answer: B.** When an investment adviser representative's employment with a state-registered adviser ends, that firm must notify the state promptly of the adviser's termination. If an IAR's employment with a federal covered adviser is terminated, then the IAR must notify the state.

17. **Answer: A.** Although working with international clients may require certain notifications and types of documentation, investment adviser representatives are not required to register with the SEC prior to working with them. Omission of material information on an application, felonies that occurred up to 10 years prior to registration, and failure to respond to a state administrator's request for information (audits) can all be grounds for action against an IAR's registration.

18. **Answer: A.** An employee who solicits advisory business for an investment advisory firm is included in the definition of an IAR and must register as such.

19. **Answer: A.** Failure to meet conditions set by a state (such as continuing education) could result in disciplinary action against an investment adviser representative. IARs are not subject to bonding requirements. An IAR's registration may not be acted against for a failure to supervise under the Uniform Securities Act. There are no rules in the Uniform Securities Act that prevent an IAR from working for multiple investment advisers.

20. **Answer: B.** The fact that the IAR and his firm have an office in that state means that the IAR is required to register, regardless of the number of clients he serves. Stockbrokers who are paid commissions based on transactions are not required to register, as long as the advice they give is not separately compensated. The publisher of a newsletter falls under an exception from the definition of an investment adviser.

CHAPTER TWO
Regulation of Broker-Dealers and Agents

(18 questions on the exam)

2.1. BROKER-DEALERS

So far, everything discussed in this study guide has pertained to investment advisers and their representatives. These are people and firms who, for a fee, provide investment advice. It's very important to note though, that they receive their fee for providing advice, regardless of whether or not the advice actually leads to the purchase or sale of securities (investments). In other words, sometimes they get paid for simply telling people to stay put and not move their money from one investment to another.

By contrast, broker-dealers and their agents get paid when their customers complete a transaction (buying or selling). If no buying or selling takes place in an account, no fees or commissions are generated. Any investment advice a broker-dealer or their agent gives, even though some seem to give a lot, is considered incidental to the transaction itself, unless a separate agreement is in place to provide investment advice.

While that may seem like a pretty cloudy line between being an investment adviser and a broker-dealer, it's one that regulators take very seriously. To operate in either capacity, you have to be appropriately registered. Interestingly enough, regulators have no problem with the same person or firm acting in both capacities, even for the same client, as long as it is done in an ethical manner. But again, the professional or firm must be properly registered in each capacity. Always keep in mind that those giving investment advice for a fee must be registered as investment advisers or investment adviser representatives; those effecting transactions must be registered as broker-dealers (or, as we will see later, as agents).

2.1.1. BROKER-DEALER—DEFINITION

While the term investment adviser from Chapter One is fairly self-explanatory, the term **broker-dealer** is often much more confusing for test takers. Take a look at the definition from the Uniform Securities Act and see if the picture comes any more into focus.

"Broker-dealer" means any person engaged in the business of effecting transactions in securities for the account of others or for [the person's] own account.

Before we go any further, let's stop and address the definition of 'person' as it applies to broker-dealers. The USA defines a person as "an individual, a corporation, a partnership, an association, a joint-stock company, a trust where the interests of the beneficiaries are evidenced by a security, an unincorporated organization, a government, or a political subdivision of a government." As is the case with investment advisers, this is an important distinction to make. In reality, broker-dealers are rarely persons in the living, breathing sense of the word. Instead, they are almost always the firm or business that employs actual living, breathing people to effect securities transactions. Those people, as we will soon learn, are called agents.

So what about the rest of the definition of broker-dealer? One thing that you might notice about it is that it does not specify exactly what a broker dealer is.

The easiest way to understand these two terms is to start with the heart of the definition above. Brokers and dealers help people *effect transactions in securities* (buy or sell stocks, bonds, etc.). That means they are involved in the mechanics of money and securities changing hands on behalf of their customers.

While the words broker and dealer are often combined, each actually represents a different entity. The difference between operating as a broker or a dealer comes in the second part of that definition, where it says they do it "for the account of others or for [their] own account." In short, **brokers** act as the go-between for two parties interested in making a transaction, whereas **dealers** are simply buying from or selling to the consumer out of the inventory of securities that they already own.

An easy way to visualize this is by thinking about the sale of real estate. A real estate broker helps a buyer find a seller, or a seller find a buyer. They're a financial matchmaker, if you will. Someone who decides to skip the middleman, list their home "For Sale by Owner," essentially handles the deal themselves. Their home is their inventory that they're selling directly to the public. In the most basic sense, brokers make money by charging a commission on the transactions they help effect; dealers make money by charging a client a markup on securities sold out of their own accounts or by purchasing securities for their accounts at a markdown.

In addition to effecting trades between investors, broker-dealers also help to bring securities to the market for the first time, for instance in an IPO (initial public offering). In these instances, broker-dealers act as investment bankers and underwriters for an offering. They assist a private company in selling its securities to the public in order to raise capital. The broker-dealer will also profit from the sale of shares by receiving an agreed-upon percentage of each sale.

When investors trade securities, it is called the secondary market, while when issuers sell securities to the public for the first time it is called the primary market. Broker-dealers assist their customers in both the primary and secondary markets. In each case, a broker-dealer receives money for assisting someone to buy and/or sell securities. But does that mean that any entity that helps two people complete a transaction, or buys and sells for its own account, is a broker-dealer? As always, there's a list of exceptions that will very likely be tested on the Series 63.

Exceptions to the definition of a broker-dealer at the state level:

(1) an agent

🗣 **Explanation:** Just as an employee of an investment adviser is called an investment adviser representative, the proper terminology for an employee of a broker-dealer is agent. Since there is a separate type of registration for agents of broker-dealers, they don't have to register as broker-dealers.

(2) an issuer

🗣 **Explanation:** Issuers (creators) of securities, as well as the securities they issue, are subject to separate registration requirements from broker-dealers when they conduct these activities.

(3) a bank, savings institution, or trust company

🗣 **Explanation:** Under the Uniform Securities Act of 1956, banks, savings institutions, and trust companies are exempt from registration as broker-dealers.

🏋 EXERCISE

CHOOSE BROKER-DEALER OR NOT A BROKER-DEALER

1. _____ James is an employee of Securities-R-Us, a broker-dealer firm. He helps clients effect transactions.

2. _____ The city of Raleigh, North Carolina, issues municipal securities, which it sells to the general public.

3. _____ ABC is a firm that specializes in selling securities from its own account to retail clients.

4. _____ ABC Mutual Funds is a firm that specializes in sponsoring mutual funds and selling the fund shares to investors.

2.1.2. REGISTRATION OF BROKER-DEALERS

Persons or firms who do not have a physical office in a state do not have to register in the state if their only clients are:

Answers: 1. Not a broker-dealer; 2. Not a broker-dealer; 3. Broker-dealer; 4. Broker-dealer

(i) the issuers of the securities involved in the transactions

Explanation: In other words, if the only transactions someone does in the state are with the people who created the securities being bought or sold, registration is not required. So, if IBM were to issue a new type of bond and a person or firm were to buy those bonds directly from IBM, the person or firm would not be required to register in the state in which IBM is selling them the bonds.

(ii) other broker-dealers

Explanation: Similar to not being required to register when dealing with a security's issuer, someone dealing only with another broker-dealer is not required to register in that state. In essence, the law does not require a person or firm to jump through the hoops of registration if they're dealing only with individuals or firms who are industry professionals and don't need nearly as much regulatory protection.

(iii) [institutional investors]

Explanation: As when dealing with the actual issuers of securities and other broker-dealers, individuals and firms dealing only with *institutional* investors don't need to register. These institutional investors, who handle very large amounts of money, are viewed as having enough sophistication to watch their own backs without as much help from regulators.

Since it'll come up again and again, you should memorize the fact that an institutional investor is someone or something that fits into one of the following categories:

- A bank, savings institution, or trust company
- An insurance company
- An investment company (mutual fund)
- A broker-dealer
- A pension or profit-sharing trust
- Another financial institution or institutional buyer

Test Note: A person or firm who has an office in a state must register in that state. A person or firm who does not have an office in a state does not have to register in a state if they have only institutional clients. A person or firm who does not have an office in a state does have to register in a state if they have even one noninstitutional client.

Test Note: Different rules use different standards for who counts as an institutional client. For example, broker-dealers may avoid registration based on the above list of institutional buyers. Investment advisers, on the other hand, have a registration exemption based on limiting their business to institutional investors (plus up to five non-institutional investors). FINRA has its own definition of who counts as an institutional investor for purposes of communications. While there is much overlap between these three categories ("institutional buyers" and "institutional investors" in the Uniform Securities Act, and "institutional investors" in FINRA's rules), they are not identical.

A person is also not considered to meet the definition of a broker-dealer in a given state if:

the person is licensed under the securities act of a state in which the person maintains a place of business and the person offers and sells in this state to a person who is an existing customer of the person and whose residence is not in this state.

> 🗣 **Explanation:** In other words, a broker-dealer that has an office only in State A and sells in State A to an existing client who resides in State B is not required to register in State B.

> 📖 **Test Note:** Subsidiaries of bank holding companies that effect securities transactions with the public must register as broker-dealers. Commercial banks are exempt.

To summarize, if a broker-dealer has an office in State A, it must register in State A. If it has an office in State A and sells securities in State B, it must register in State B unless it meets one of the above conditions. If it only has an office in State A and sells securities from that office to an existing client from State B, it does not have to register in State B.

2.1.2.1. **Exceptions for Canadian Broker-Dealers**

While a broker-dealer from Canada may not come and set up shop in any state without jumping through the required regulatory and registration hoops, there are some exceptions that permit them to operate within a state using a limited registration.

These exceptions are built around the basic premise that the Canadian firm *does not* have offices in that state, in which case they can transact securities with a client located in that state if:

- The client is from Canada, and is temporarily in that state, and had a relationship with the Canadian broker-dealer prior to entering the state.

- The client is engaging in transactions for a self-directed, tax-advantaged retirement plan held in Canada, for which they are the holder or contributor.

- The client is an institutional investor.

Agents (stockbrokers) working for one of the broker-dealers in the previous three situations may also use a limited registration.

To obtain this limited registration, the Canadian broker-dealer would have to:

- File an application in the form required by the jurisdiction in which it has its principal office

- File a consent to service of process

- Provide evidence of good standing in the jurisdiction where the broker-dealer is registered

- File proof of membership in a Canadian self-regulatory organization (SRO) or Canadian stock exchange

- Make records available to the administrator for business done in that state

- Inform the administrator of any criminal action taken against the broker-dealer

- Disclose to clients in the state that the Canadian broker-dealer is not subject to the state's full regulatory requirements

- Pay a filing fee

2.1.2.2. Exceptions for Certain Foreign Broker-Dealers

The Securities Exchange Act of 1934 also provides conditional exemptions from registration for foreign broker-dealers that engage in certain specified activities involving U.S. investors. Foreign broker-dealers are defined by the SEC as any non-U.S. resident 'person' that is not an office or branch of or a natural person associated with a registered broker-dealer and whose securities activities would otherwise qualify the 'person' as a broker or a dealer. Basically, if they are outside the U.S., not affiliated with registered broker-dealers, and engaged in the business of effecting securities transactions, foreign broker-dealers may be eligible for this exemption.

However, these foreign broker-dealers are limited to participating in a handful of specific activities to avoid registration requirements. These activities include:

- Effecting unsolicited securities transactions, meaning transactions that are initiated by the customer

- Providing research reports to American institutional investors

- Soliciting and effecting transactions with or for most American institutional investors through a registered broker-dealer

- Soliciting and effecting transactions directly with or for registered broker-dealers, banks serving as broker-dealers, certain international organizations, foreign persons temporarily present in the U.S., American citizens resident outside the U.S., and agencies or branches of U.S. persons permanently located outside of the U.S.

SUMMARY

ENTITIES THAT DO NOT NEED TO REGISTER WITH THE STATE AS BROKER-DEALERS

Is Not a Broker-Dealer	Broker-Dealer Exempt from State Registration
Agent	BD without office in state whose only clients are: • Issuers of securities • Other broker-dealers • Institutional investors
Issuer of securities	BD with office in state who sells to existing client from a different state while at that office
Bank, savings institution, or trust company	Canadian broker-dealer that: • Sells to existing client temporarily in a state • Has a client in the state engaged in Canadian self-directed tax-advantaged retirement plan • Sells only to institutional investors (in each case, however, broker-dealer needs to obtain a limited registration)
	Foreign broker-dealer involved in limited activities

 EXERCISE

ANSWER YES OR NO

1. _____ A firm has an office in State A and three non-institutional clients in State B. Does the firm need to be registered in State B?

2. _____ A firm has an office in State C, but its only client is a corporation located in state D. The corporation issued the securities being bought and sold. Does the firm need to be registered in State D?

3. _____ A firm has an office in State E and has three clients in State F. Those clients are a mutual fund, a savings institution, and a retail investor. Does the firm need to be registered in State F?

4. _____ On January 15, North Star Investment, a Canadian broker-dealer, reaches an agreement to effect trades for Jim Maple, who is vacationing in Florida at the time. Two days later, a North Star agent makes a transaction for Jim, who is still in Florida. Does North Star need to be registered in Florida?

5. _____ Lira Financial, an Italian-based brokerage firm with no office in the United States, regularly trades securities with International Intentions, a broker-dealer located in North Carolina. Does Lira need to be registered in North Carolina?

ANSWERS

1. **Yes.** For broker-dealers, having even one non-institutional client in a state requires registration in that state.

2. **No.** If the only client that a broker-dealer has in a state is an issuer of the securities involved in a transaction, the broker-dealer does not need to register in that state (as long as it does not have an office in the state).

3. **Yes.** The firm would not need to register if the only clients it had in State F were the mutual fund and savings institution, but having even one retail (i.e., non-institutional) investor means it must register in that state.

4. **Yes.** For a Canadian broker-dealer to be exempt from regular state registration, it must have a pre-existing relationship with a vacationing Canadian client.

5. **No.** Since International Intentions is a broker-dealer, the foreign-based Lira Financial does not have to register in North Carolina.

2.1.2.3. The Registration Process

Broker-dealers must almost always register at a federal level, in addition to meeting state registration requirements. The only time that registration is permitted *only* at the state level is if all transactions and all aspects of the transactions are conducted or expected to be conducted within state boundaries. Since the vast majority of broker-dealers will at some point use third-party services located out of their state, virtually no broker-dealers choose to go this route.

To register federally, a broker-dealer must complete a two-step process. First, the BD must register with the SEC using the Central Depository Registration system to file a **Form BD**. This form requires important background information about the broker-dealer, including key personnel, contact information, and disclosures of any previous regulatory violations. The second step is to register with FINRA, which is done by filing Form NMA (New Member Application form). Additionally, the broker-dealer must join the Securities Investor Protection Corporation (SIPC). The SEC must then review the application and approve it within *45 days* or initiate proceedings to determine whether or not the registration should be denied.

A broker-dealer's application for registration at the state level becomes effective at noon on the *30th day* after the application is initially filed, unless the state requires additional information or denies the application. If a state's administrator wishes to initiate a hearing based on an applicant's admission of a final judicial or administrative order made against them prior to registration, they have 90 days to do so following registration or they may no longer use that information to challenge a broker-dealer's registration.

A broker-dealer's registration remains in effect *until midnight of December 31* of the year for which the registration is filed. If a renewal was not filed, the registration is considered revoked. This means that a broker-dealer who initially registers on November 15 must renew its registration less than two months later.

When a broker-dealer files an application for a successor firm for the unexpired portion of the year (from the time of filing to December 31), they do not need to pay a filing fee.

2.1.2.4. **Net Capital Requirements**

As with investment advisers, broker-dealers are required by states to meet net capital requirements both prior to registration and at all times while their registration remains active. Unlike the simpler investment adviser's requirements, however, the broker-dealer capital requirements use complex formulas that go beyond the scope of the Series 63 exam. It's sufficient to know that broker-dealers are subject to substantial net capital requirements.

You will also need to know that the state cannot require broker-dealers to meet net capital requirements that exceed SEC net capital requirements.

> **Test Note:** The administrator may require registered broker-dealers, agents, and investment advisers who have custody of or discretionary authority over client funds or securities to post bonds in amounts that the administrator prescribes. These amounts are subject to the limitations and conditions of the Securities Exchange Act of 1934 for broker-dealers and the Investment Advisers Act of 1940 for investment advisers. Any appropriate deposit of cash or securities shall be accepted in lieu of any bond so required. No bond may be required of any registrant whose net capital, or, in the case of an investment adviser whose minimum financial requirements exceed the amounts required by the Administrator.

2.1.2.5. **Post-Registration Requirements**

In addition to the ongoing requirement to file the appropriate renewal forms on an annual basis, broker-dealers must meet ongoing requirements known as **post-registration requirements**. These requirements include:

- **Financial reports.** Broker-dealers are required to file regular reports regarding their firm's financial condition. If the information filed on these forms or on a firm's Form BD becomes inaccurate at any point, updated reports must be filed as soon as possible.

- **Recordkeeping.** Broker-dealers must keep most forms of client records and marketing literature on file for three years, the first two years in an easily accessible place, even if the broker-dealer goes out of business. Some records must be kept for six years.

- **Audits.** All broker-dealers are subject to audits by the states they're licensed in as well as by federal regulators *at any time*. As part of the audit, their state administrator may examine any records they deem useful. Additionally, some states may require the broker-dealer to pay a reasonable fee to conduct the audit.

- **Bond or insurance required for broker-dealers with custody or authority.** States may require the broker-dealer to post a bond or provide an appropriate deposit of cash or securities.

Test Note: The National Securities Markets Improvement Act (NSMIA) prohibits the states from making any capital, bonding, custody, reporting or record keeping requirements that are different from or greater than the SEC requirements. This law requires the state requirements on these topics to be consistent with the SEC requirements.

2.1.3. BROKER-DEALER SUPERVISION OF AGENTS

Supervision of agents is one of the key responsibilities of a broker-dealer. In Section 15(b)(4) of the Exchange Act, the SEC notes that it may take punitive action against any broker-dealer that has willfully violated, enabled the violation, or failed to supervise a violator of applicable securities law and regulations under its employ. This means that if a broker-dealer does not adequately supervise one of its employees (a.k.a. an agent: more on them later), the Feds can get involved. The Act goes on to say, however, that no supervisor will have failed in his duties if a supervisory system and procedures have been established and dutifully applied to prevent and detect such violations.

For an acceptable supervisory system, each member firm is required to have a written description of supervisory responsibilities and a set of written supervisory procedures that will govern the activities of its registered employees. The firm must make sure that there are supervisory controls and periodic inspections to check that procedures are being complied with.

FINRA has similar rules on the books, and it has outlined in some detail a procedural framework by which a supervisor's responsibilities will be known and procedures set in place for their execution. Each member firm is required to establish in writing a clear delineation of supervisory responsibilities and a set of written supervisory procedures (WSPs) to govern the activities of its registered employees. Compliance with these procedures is accomplished through supervisory controls, periodic inspections, and reviews. Each firm must also maintain an **Office of Supervisory Jurisdiction (OSJ)**, which is an office where supervisory activities take place. These activities include:

- Final approval of new customer accounts
- Review and endorsement of customer orders
- Final approval of retail communications used by agents
- Supervision of activities of persons at one or more of the member firm's branch offices (a **branch office** is any location where one or more associated employees is involved in soliciting or effecting the purchase or sale of any security)

Additionally, each branch office is required to designate one representative or principal to have supervisory authority and responsibility for the activities of that office and any non-branch offices in its jurisdiction. Each associate of the firm must participate in an annual compliance meeting, whose purpose is to assure that all employees remain current on changes in compliance requirements. Written procedures should describe how this mandatory meeting will take shape and who must attend. The firm must also establish, in writing, procedures for the review and approval of all agent-initiated transactions.

Failure to meet any of these requirements may result in administrative action as described in the USA.

 EXERCISE

ANSWER YES OR NO—HAS THE AGENT BEEN PROPERLY SUPERVISED?

1. _____ An agent of a broker-dealer commits securities fraud; however, the broker-dealer has an appropriate supervisory system in place.

2. _____ An agent of a broker-dealer has a spotless record on all transactions she has effected, but she has not attended a compliance meeting in the past 18 months.

3. _____ A firm has a set of procedures, each of which follows FINRA and SEC guidelines, yet those procedures have not been put in writing.

ANSWERS

1. **Yes.** So long as an appropriate supervisory system and procedures have been put in place, the actions of this agent do not constitute a failure to supervise. Note, however, the agent is subject to administrative penalties.

2. **No.** Agents of broker-dealers are required to attend an annual compliance meeting. So, despite her otherwise spotless conduct, this agent's nonattendance at an annual meeting represents a failure on behalf of her firm to comply with FINRA regulations.

3. **No.** Supervisory procedures must be in writing to comply with FINRA requirements.

2.1.4. TERMINATION OF A BROKER-DEALER'S REGISTRATION

Recall that registration as a broker-dealer is by no means permanent. At bare minimum, state and federal approval to operate can terminate on December 31 of any year simply because a broker-dealer forgets to submit its renewal paperwork. For a full list of reasons registration can be terminated, please see "Termination of an Investment Adviser Registration" on page 23. However, for broker-dealers, there is one exception: a broker-dealer may choose to terminate its registration at any time by filing a Form BDW. The withdrawal request becomes effective 30 days after it is submitted. Once the registration has been withdrawn, the applicant remains under the administrator's jurisdiction for a year.

2.1.4.1. **Reasons for Disciplining a Broker-Dealer**

According to the Uniform Securities Act, broker-dealers may be disciplined for the same reasons as investment advisers and investment adviser representatives, if the order is in the public interest. Please see "Reasons for Disciplining an Adviser" on page 25 for the full list of situations that could result in disciplinary action.

2.2. PRACTICAL APPLICATION

Like virtually all investment professionals, Amy Adams will never register as a broker-dealer. In reality, the number of broker-dealers in the country is somewhere in the thousands and the vast majority of these are firms, not individual professionals. However, these broker-dealers may literally employ hundreds of thousands of investment professionals as agents.

The firm that Amy Adams works for is one such firm. In addition to acting as an investment advisor to some of its customers for an agreed-upon fee as discussed in Chapter One, it also acts as a broker-dealer for the same and other customers. In this role, Wealth Management Inc. buys securities from and sells securities to its clients, both for its own account and in the open market. For these services, her firm often receives a commission for helping to enact the transaction.

Because of its substantial size and breadth of activities, Amy Adams's firm has to register both with federal regulators as a broker-dealer, as well as with each state it operates in. These individual states subject the firm to complex net capital requirements and substantial bonding.

In working for this firm, Amy Adams is required to register as an agent of the firm, who acts on its behalf with its clients. This registration is done separately from the broker-dealer's registration.

2.3. AGENTS OF BROKER-DEALERS AND AGENTS OF ISSUERS

If you took the SAT in high school or any number of graduate school exams, one thing is certain—you're familiar with the analogy question. These were the questions that would ask you something like "shoes are to feet as glove is to ____." ("Hand" is the answer, in case you were stumped). Well, to permanently solidify in your mind what an agent is, an analogy may do the trick. So, here goes:

Investment adviser representative is to investment adviser
as *agent* is to *broker-dealer or issuer*.

In other words, an agent has a nearly identical relationship to a broker-dealer or issuer of securities that an investment adviser representative (IAR) has to the investment advisory firm that employs him. Remember that the broker-dealer or investment adviser is generally a firm; the agent or investment adviser representative is the person that represents the firm. For the agent this means that he is essentially the person on the ground who deals with customers, acting on behalf of the broker-dealer or issuer.

In the most classic sense of the word, this is what most people think of when they think of a stock or bond broker, who places buy and sell orders on behalf of his clients. However, as the investment industry has evolved, agents have also evolved from the classic image of a stockbroker to roles ranging from comprehensive wealth managers (who provide sophisticated investment advice), to salaried employees that are essentially clerks and cashiers at discount brokerages. In all cases, though, these individuals are the bridge between investors and the broker-dealer the agent has chosen to work with, which is a role that states deem worthy of registration and regulation.

2.3.1. AGENT—DEFINITION

For the sake of being thorough, you should know how the Uniform Securities Act defines an agent, word-for-word. While it's highly unlikely that you'll be quizzed on the exact definition, an understanding of it will underlie numerous questions on the exam.

An **agent** is:

```
any individual other than a broker-dealer who represents a broker-dealer or
issuer in effecting or attempting to effect purchases or sales of securities.
```

One interesting point to note in the Uniform Securities Act's definition of an agent is that people are considered agents even if they *attempt* to effect transactions. In other words, anyone who is viewed as marketing securities or transaction services to the public must be registered, even if their *attempts* do not result in forming a business relationship at that time. This means that future agents and employees of broker-dealers may not begin marketing their services until their registration as an agent is complete.

The definition of an agent under the Uniform Securities Act is subject to a long list of exceptions, as with investment advisers and broker-dealers.

2.3.1.1. Agents Representing Broker-Dealers

Agents representing broker-dealers *do not* have to register with the state if:

- They have no place of business in the state and their only clients are institutional investors.

- They are registered in State A and have an existing client who is on vacation in State B (up to 30 days); the customer must be a client who has had an account with the broker-dealer for 30 days prior to the transaction.

- They have an existing client who is moving to another state (must register within 10 days of learning of the move).

- They work for a Canadian broker-dealer that qualifies for the Canadian broker-dealer exemption as previously described, and they only conduct the types of transactions permitted under that exemption.

- They work for a broker-dealer selling investments that are not securities, such as annuities, insurance, or commodities. Please note that non-securities are not the same as exempt securities and as a result will subject the agent to different registration requirements.

- They work for a broker-dealer that is exempt from registration (for instance, a foreign broker-dealer that qualifies for the exemption described above).

Note that under the Uniform Securities Act of 1956, there is no *de minimis* for broker-dealers or agents of broker-dealers. If a broker-dealer or agent has even one non-institutional client in a state, they will have to register in that state.

Not every member of the staff of a broker-dealer is required to register as an agent. Here is a summary of the rules regarding clerical staff. Clerical staff who work for a broker-dealer:

- Are exempt from registration, as long as they don't solicit or accept orders

- Can give out stock or bond quotes over the phone without registering

- Can give out account information over the phone without registering

- Can fax documents for customer signatures without registering

- *Cannot* give investment advice to clients without registering

- *Cannot* accept solicited or unsolicited orders without registering

 **EXERCISE**

PLEASE CHOOSE A, B, OR BOTH

1. _____ John works for a brokerage firm. John has an office in State A and has a retail client named Mary. In his first two weeks as her agent, John effected three securities transactions for Mary before she travelled to State B on a one-week vacation. Then, John made a fourth transaction for Mary while she was in State B. In which state or states should John be registered?

2. _____ Steve, who has an office in State A, has a client named Brenda. He has worked with Brenda for five years, but unfortunately Brenda recently moved to State B. Steve wants to effect a transaction for Brenda today, two weeks after she made her move. In which state or states should Steve be registered?

3. _____ Quinne is an agent with an office in State A where she sells only exempt Treasury securities. She also has 10 institutional investors in State B. In which state or states should Quinne be registered?

ANSWERS

1. **Both.** Since John has an office in State A, he must register there. Also, though Mary has been vacationing in State B for less than 30 days, she was not a client of John's for the requisite minimum of 30 days before travelling there, and thus he needs to register in that state in order to make transactions for her.

2. **Both.** Since Steve has an office in State B, he must register there. Also, since Brenda has lived in State B for more than 10 days, Steve must register there in order to continue to effect transactions for her.

3. **A.** Since Quinne has an office in State A and sells exempt securities, which are different from non-securities investments, she must register there. However, since her only clients in state B are institutional investors, she does not need to register in that state.

2.3.1.2. Agents Representing Issuers

Agents representing issuers *do not* have to register with the state if:

- They only engage in transactions in certain exempt securities.

- **Explanation:** If an agent works for an issuer of certain exempt securities (e.g., United States government), and she effects transactions only in these securities (e.g., sells government bonds), the agent will not have to register. These exempt securities include:

  - Federal and municipal securities

  - Securities issued by foreign governments with which the U.S. has diplomatic relations

  - Securities issued by commercial banks, savings institutions, or trust companies

  - Investment grade commercial paper (notes) that has a maturity of 9 or fewer months, is issued in denominations of at least $50,000, and receives a rating in one of the three highest rating categories from a nationally recognized statistical rating organization

  - Investment contracts issued in connection with an employee benefit plan if the administrator is notified in writing 30 days before the inception of the plan

- They engage in transactions only for existing employees, partners or directors of the issuer and their pay is not tied to how much they actually help sell.

- They engage in exempt transactions.

Explanation: Common exempt transactions include:

- Isolated non-issuer transactions

- Transactions between issuers and underwriters

- Private placements

- Transactions in federal covered securities for qualified purchasers. (A qualified purchaser is an individual or family-owned company with $5 million to invest, or any other company with $25 million to invest.)

*See Chapter Three for a full list.

Remember, though, that just because an agent represents an issuer of securities does not mean he is necessarily exempt from state registration. If the securities issued are not exempt or if a transaction itself is not exempt, an agent representing an issuer must register. And, of course, as you should remember from above, all of these registration exemptions only apply to agents of issuers and not to agents of broker-dealers.

The definition of an agent also states that:

A partner, officer, or director of a broker-dealer or issuer, or a person occupying a similar status or performing similar functions, is an agent only if [that person] otherwise comes within this definition.

Explanation: If a partner, officer, or director of a firm does not effect securities transactions on behalf of the firm, then he or she is not an agent. If he or she does engage in agent activities, then he or she is an agent.

Test Note: Partners, officers, and directors of a broker-dealer are automatically registered as agents of the broker-dealer when the firm registers as a broker-dealer, if they are actively engaged in the business and perform the functions of an agent. This allows the administrator to take action against individual officers and directors without disrupting the status of the firm.

Test Note: Silent partners who are not actively engaged in the business would not be registered as agents. Similarly, officers of a firm who are not engaged in soliciting or effecting transactions would not register as an agent. For example, the Vice President of Human Resources or the CFO would not need to register as an agent.

Test Note: A person is only considered an agent if they are subject to the control of a broker-dealer or issuer. A person who effects securities transactions for others but who is not subject to the control of a firm would be considered a broker-dealer.

Agents of Broker-Dealers Are Exempt from State Registration If They:	Agents of Securities Issuers Are Exempt from State Registration If They:
Have no place of business in a state and have: • Only institutional clients • An existing client on vacation in the state (up to 30 days) • An existing client who recently moved to the state (must register within 10 days of learning of the move)	Engage only in transactions involving exempt securities
Work for a Canadian broker-dealer that qualifies for the Canadian broker-dealer exception	Engage only in exempt transactions
Work for a broker-dealer that only sells non-securities investments	Engage only in transactions for existing employees, partners, or directors of the issuer and are not compensated based on the amount of securities sold.
Work for a broker-dealer that is otherwise exempt from registration	

2.3.1.3. **Limits on Employment or Association**

While the USA is more nebulous on the limits of employment and association with investment adviser representatives, it draws some clear lines in the sand for agents of broker-dealers. Specifically, there are two clear limits placed on employment or affiliation with a broker-dealer or issuer:

- Broker-dealers and issuers in a state may only employ properly registered agents in that state. There is no rule allowing people who meet the definition of an agent to operate in a state if they have fewer than a certain number of non-institutional clients.

- An agent's registration is only valid so long as she is employed by a registered broker-dealer or issuer. In other words, the registration of an agent who quits or loses her job ceases to be effective.

2.3.1.4. **The Registration Process**

To register as an agent, a sponsoring broker-dealer or issuer must use the Central Depository Registration system to file a Form U4 and the individual must pass whatever exams are required for the types of securities he will be selling. Additionally, potential agents must pass a background check that looks for previous criminal as well as regulatory violations. The applicant must file a consent to service of process, which allows a state administrator to receive legal papers (summons, notice of lawsuits, etc.) on behalf of the agent. As part of a broker-dealer's state registration, the broker-dealer must also file a consent to service of process. Once the consent to service of process has been filed, it does not need to be renewed.

The Form U4 requires history about the agent, including ten years of employment history and five years of residential history. Additionally, applicants must list any previous criminal convictions, guilty pleas, or pleas of no contest on the U4. The applicant must disclose whether he or a firm he has controlled has been subject to bankruptcy or a compromise with creditors in the past ten years.

An application for registration becomes effective at noon on the *30th day* after the application is initially filed, unless the state requires additional information or denies the application. If a state's administrator wishes to initiate a hearing based on an applicant's admission of a final judicial or administrative order made against him prior to registration, the administrator has 90 days to do so following registration or it may no longer use that information to challenge an agent's registration.

An agent's registration remains in effect *until midnight of December 31* of the year for which the registration is filed. If a renewal was not filed, the registration is considered revoked. This means that by December 31, the broker-dealer must renew even the registration of an agent who was initially registered on November 15.

2.3.1.5. **Net Capital Requirements**

Unlike investment advisers and broker-dealers, agents are not required to meet net capital requirements.

2.3.1.6. **Post-Registration Requirements**

Agents are not subject to as many post-registration requirements as the broker-dealers they represent, but they are expected to help their broker-dealers meet all recordkeeping requirements and comply with all audits as needed. Agents are responsible for meeting any conditions for ongoing registration set by their state, however, and providing any documentation needed as evidence of meeting such conditions.

2.3.2. **TERMINATION OF AN AGENT'S REGISTRATION**

We have seen that an agent's registration is not permanent. At bare minimum, it can terminate on December 31 of any year simply because the broker-dealer forgets to submit their renewal paperwork. Additionally, as with broker-dealers, investment advisers, and investment adviser representatives, it can also terminate or be restricted at any time for a variety of other reasons. For a full list of reasons registration can be terminated, please see "Termination of an Investment Adviser Registration" on page 23. However, for agents, there is one exception: in the case of withdrawal, a broker-dealer may terminate an agent's registration at any time by filing Form U5. The withdrawal request becomes effective 30 days after it is submitted. The broker-dealer is then required to supply the agent with a copy of the Form U5 within 30 days of the date that the employee left the firm. Once registration has been withdrawn, the applicant remains under the administrator's jurisdiction for a year.

Whenever an agent begins or ceases engaging in the activities that make him an agent, both the agent and the broker-dealer or issuer he works for must promptly notify the administrator. The broker-dealer will inform the administrator by filing Form U5.

When an agent switches from one broker-dealer to another, the old employer, the new employer, and the agent are all responsible for promptly notifying the state administrator of this change. In such an event, the previous employer must fill out a Form U5 to terminate the agent's employment and the new employer must complete a Form U4 to begin the agent's employment.

2.3.2.1. Reasons for Disciplining an Agent

According to the Uniform Securities Act, agents may be disciplined for the same reasons as broker-dealers, investment advisers, and investment adviser representatives, assuming the order is in the public interest. Please see "Reasons for Disciplining an Adviser" on page 25 for the full list of situations that could result in disciplinary action.

 **EXERCISE**

ANSWER TRUE OR FALSE

1. **True or false. Partners, officers, and directors of a broker-dealer must always register as agents of a broker-dealer.**

2. **True or false. Clerical staff members are always exempt from agent registration requirements.**

3. **True or false. Agents are not required to meet net capital requirements.**

FILL IN THE BLANK

4. **_____ is the form which must be filed by a sponsoring broker-dealer or issuer before an agent can be registered.**

5. **_____ is the form that is filed by a broker-dealer in order to terminate an agent's registration.**

ANSWERS

1. **False.** Unlike in the case of registration of investment adviser representatives, partners, officers, and directors of broker-dealers are not required to register as agents in all cases. It is only when they begin performing the tasks of an agent (i.e., helping to effect securities transactions) that they are required to register.

2. **False.** Clerical staff members are only exempt from registration as agents if they do not give investment advice to or accept orders from clients.

3. **True.** Unlike broker-dealers, agents are not required to meet net capital requirements.

4. **Form U4.** A Form U4 must be filed by a sponsoring broker-dealer or an issuer for an agent's registration to become effective.

5. **Form U5.** A form U5 must be filed by a broker-dealer in order to terminate an agent's registration.

2.4. **PRACTICAL APPLICATION**

When Amy Adams was originally hired by the first firm she worked for, she was hired as a stockbroker. Though her firm's advertisements mentioned wealth management and helping clients see the big picture, Amy's legal job description was "agent of a broker-dealer." She initially gave advice as part of helping clients buy and sell different securities, but she was only compensated when they actually completed a transaction.

In short, her job was to go out, find prospective clients, and sell them investments offered through her firm. To be qualified to do this, Amy had to pass a number of licensing exams and give her permission for a background check to be conducted. It was not until after Amy decided to leave the firm that she fully realized that agents cannot remain registered separate from the broker-dealers that employ them.

☐ What is the basic definition of a broker?

☐ What is the basic definition of a dealer?

☐ What does "effect transactions" mean?

☐ Who is excepted from the definition of a broker-dealer?

☐ What is an agent of a broker-dealer?

☐ What is the basic definition of an issuer?

☐ What are the six general categories of institutional investors?

☐ How does a customer's state of residence affect the need to register as a broker-dealer?

☐ What are the rules regarding customers for a broker-dealer to avoid state registration?

☐ When may Canadian broker-dealers use a limited registration?

☐ A broker-dealer may only register at the state level if what requirement is met?

☐ When do registrations typically become effective?

☐ When do registrations typically expire?

☐ What are the most common post-registration requirements for broker-dealers?

☐ How long must broker-dealer records be kept?

☐ What recordkeeping responsibility does a broker-dealer have if it goes out of business?

☐ What must a broker-dealer do in order to fulfill its supervisory obligations?

☐ What types of action can be taken against a broker-dealer's license or application?

☐ What are the twelve main reasons broker-dealers may be disciplined?

☐ What is the basic definition of an agent?

☐ What is the relationship between a broker-dealer and an agent?

☐ Who is generally excepted from the definition of an agent? What are the two limits on employment or association of agents?

☐ Who is responsible for the registration of agents?

☐ What standard form is required to register an agent?

☐ What are the net capital requirements for an agent?

☐ What is the most common post-registration requirement for agents?

☐ What are the primary actions that can be taken against an agent's registration?

☐ What are the main categories of violations for which an agent can be disciplined?

SUGGESTED NOTECARDS

Chapter 2 Practice Questions

1. **Which of the following best describes the activities of a broker?**

    A. Buying securities for its own account
    B. Selling securities from its own account
    C. Day trading securities for its own account
    D. None of these choices

2. **All of the following are exceptions to the definition of a broker-dealer except:**

    A. A broker-dealer's agent
    B. An issuer
    C. An investment adviser
    D. A bank

3. **When a firm acts as a dealer in a securities transaction with one of its clients, the parties exchanging funds and securities include:**

    I.   The firm
    II. The firm's client
    III. Another firm's client
    IV. A securities issuer

    A. I and II
    B. II and III
    C. I, II, and III
    D. I, II, III, and IV

4. **A broker-dealer registered in one state does not need to register in another state if it has:**

    A. Less than $50,000,000 in assets
    B. Over $100,000,000 in assets
    C. No non-institutional clients in that state
    D. Five or fewer non-institutional clients in that state

5. **All of the following are generally requirements for registration of a broker-dealer except:**

    A. Completing a Form ADV
    B. Meeting net capital requirements
    C. Meeting bonding requirements
    D. Acceptance of registration by a state's securities administrator

6. **A broker-dealer who works only with the following investors and does not have an office in the state would not be required to be registered with the state:**

   I.   Other broker-dealers
   II. An individual with $1 million in assets
   III. A pension trust
   IV. Investment companies (mutual funds)

   A. I only
   B. I and III
   C. I, II, and III
   D. I, III, and IV

7. **The state securities administrator may set the net capital requirements for broker-dealers operating in their state:**

   A. Without limits
   B. No higher than 150% of the national requirements
   C. No higher than 125% of the national requirements
   D. The same as the national requirements

8. **In addition to registering with federal regulators, a broker-dealer must register with:**

   A. All states in which they have a client
   B. Any state whose securities they sell
   C. The SIPC
   D. The FDIC

9. **A Canadian broker-dealer may operate in a state with limited registration if:**

   I.   It is registered in Canada.
   II. The client of the broker-dealer is a Canadian temporarily visiting the state, with whom a previous relationship exists.
   III. The client of the broker-dealer is a permanent resident of the state, but opened the account while in Canada.
   IV. The broker-dealer only deals in foreign securities.

   A. I only
   B. I and II
   C. II and III
   D. II and IV

10. **All of the following are true of broker-dealer audits except:**

    A. They can happen at any time.
    B. Auditors cannot view confidential client records.
    C. Broker-dealers may be required to cover the cost of an audit.
    D. Both state administrators and federal regulators can initiate an audit of a broker dealer.

11. **One major difference between an agent and an investment adviser representative is that:**

    A. An agent cannot give investment advice.
    B. Investment adviser representatives do not need to be affiliated with an actual firm to provide advice.
    C. Agents receive compensation for effecting transactions.
    D. Agents are not subject to post-registration requirements.

12. **All of the following individuals would be considered an agent except someone who:**

    A. Sells non-exempt securities to the public on behalf of an issuer for a commission
    B. Sells exempt securities to the public on behalf of a broker-dealer for a commission
    C. Takes orders from customers without providing any investment advice
    D. Is an institutional investor buying and selling for/from his own account

13. **Which of the following are generally registration requirements for agents?**

    I. Passing required exams
    II. Passing a background check
    III. Working for an investment advisory firm
    IV. Meeting net capital requirements

    A. I and II
    B. II and III
    C. I, II, and III
    D. I, II, III, and IV

14. **Agents do not likely need to register if:**

    A. They have five or fewer clients in a state.
    B. They are also registered as an investment adviser representative.
    C. They receive a salary from an issuer for helping the issuer re-purchase their own securities and the issuer provides notice to the administrator of any such offer and the administrator doesn't object.
    D. They sell only securities of the federal government or mutual funds that invest only in government bonds.

15. **Which of the following best describes the limitations that an individual serving in a clerical or ministerial role at a broker-dealer must meet to be exempt from registration as an agent?**

    A. They do not have contact with customers.
    B. They do not discuss a customer's account with that customer.
    C. They do not help effect transactions.
    D. They can give investment advice only if receiving a salary.

16. The registration of agents is limited by the following standards:

   I.   They must be employed by a broker-dealer or issuer.
   II. They must have a college degree from an accredited institution.
   III. They must be an individual.
   IV. They are not permitted to give investment advice.

   A. I only
   B. I and III
   C. II and III
   D. I, III, and IV

17. Sarah works for XYZ Corporation, a publicly traded corporation. XYZ is offering its employees a chance to purchase shares of the corporation directly from the company. Sarah has been assigned to manage the sale of the shares. Which of the following is true under the Uniform Securities Act?

   A. Sarah would need to be registered as an agent of the issuer in all circumstances.
   B. Sarah would not need to be registered as an agent of the issuer if she doesn't receive compensation that is tied to the sale.
   C. Sarah cannot help with the sale unless she is registered as an agent of a broker-dealer.
   D. None of the choices is true.

18. Generally, the agents of a broker-dealer that is exempt from registration are:

   A. Not required to register either
   B. Still required to register
   C. Are only required to register if they have more than five customers in a state
   D. Are only required to register if they have more than $100,000,000 in assets

19. An agent's registration may be limited or revoked for:

   I.   Defrauding investors
   II. Failing to file paperwork by the required deadlines
   III. The insolvency of their sponsoring broker-dealer
   IV. Securities violations that occur in other countries

   A. I only
   B. I and II
   C. I, II, and III
   D. I, II, III, and IV

20. **All of the following are disciplinary actions that a state may take against individual agents except:**

    A. Revoking their registration
    B. Withdrawing their registration
    C. Suspending their registration
    D. Denying the renewal of their registration

Chapter 2 Practice Question Answers

1. **Answer: D.** When a broker-dealer acts in its broker capacity, it acts as the go-between for its customer and someone else interested in buying or selling a security. This stands in contrast to when a firm acts in its dealer capacity and buys, sells, or trades for its own account.

2. **Answer: C.** Being an investment adviser by itself does not disqualify someone from also being a broker-dealer. In fact, many broker-dealers also act as investment advisers. When this is the case, dual registration is required. A broker-dealer's agent, an issuer, and banking institutions, among other exceptions, are excluded from the definition of a broker-dealer.

3. **Answer: A.** When a firm acts as a dealer, the only two parties exchanging securities or cash are the firm and its customer. Acting as a dealer means that the firm is buying or selling for its own account, instead of acting as a go-between for their client and another investor.

4. **Answer: C.** Broker-dealers with zero clients (not counting exempt clients like other broker-dealers, investment companies, etc.) are not required to register if the broker-dealer does not have an office in that state. The five-client rule applies to investment adviser registration, as does the level of assets under management.

5. **Answer: A.** Broker-dealers are not necessarily required to fill out a Form ADV, only a Form BD. Broker-dealers are subject to net capital and bonding requirements, as well as their state security administrator's licensure requirements.

6. **Answer: D.** Broker-dealers that work only with certain clients are exempt from registration requirements. Among the list of clients which do not require registration are other broker-dealers, pension and profit-sharing trusts, and investment companies (mutual funds). An individual with $1 million would not generally be considered an institutional investor.

7. **Answer: D.** The net capital requirements set by the state may not be different from those required by national law. The same is true for margin, custody, recordkeeping, bonding, and reporting requirements.

8. **Answer: C.** Federally regulated broker-dealers (which represent the vast majority) are required to register with the Securities Investor Protection Corporation (SIPC). They do not necessarily have to register in every state they have a client, due to exceptions covering the numerous types of clients they have. Broker-dealers do not have to register in every state whose securities they sell, nor do they have to register with the FDIC, which regulates banks.

9. **Answer: B.** A Canadian broker-dealer must be registered in its home province or territory in order to use a limited registration, in addition to being a member in good standing of a self-regulatory organization or stock exchange. A limited registration can be used for Canadian broker-dealers working with foreign clients temporarily in a state, but not clients who started their relationship with the firm while out of the state, but who are now permanent residents of the state. Broker-dealers dealing only in foreign securities do need to register.

10. **Answer: B.** In order to hold broker-dealers accountable and protect the public, auditors have access to all records and documentation they deem necessary. There are no such things as confidential records that an auditor cannot view. Audits can happen at any time, may be required to be paid for by the broker-dealer, and can be initiated by both state and federal regulators.

11. **Answer: C.** To receive compensation for helping to effect transactions, individuals must be registered as agents unless they qualify for one of the exceptions listed in the Uniform Securities Act. Agents can give investment advice as long as it is incidental to helping someone buy or sell a security. Investment adviser representatives (IARs) cannot operate separately from the investment advisory firms they work for. Lastly, agents are required to meet post-registration requirements or conditions set by each state in which they are registered.

12. **Answer: D.** Investors, when buying or selling for their own accounts, do not need to register as agents since they are not working on behalf of a broker-dealer or issuer. Individuals selling exempt and non-exempt securities on behalf of a broker-dealer must register as agents regardless of how they are paid. Individuals selling non-exempt securities on behalf of an issuer must typically register as well. If the individual had been selling certain exempt securities on behalf on an issuer, he would have been exempt from registration. Even if an individual working for a broker-dealer takes securities orders from customers without providing any advice, he or she is still required to register as an agent.

13. **Answer: A.** While agents are required to pass any required exams and a background check, they do not have to meet net capital requirements like a broker-dealer or investment advisory firm. Agents must work for either a broker-dealer or an issuer, not an investment advisory firm.

14. **Answer: C.** When individuals work on behalf of an issuer to help that issuer re-purchase its own securities, they are not required to register as agents if either 1) they are not paid to do so or 2) the issuer notifies the administrator in advance and the administrator does not object. However, if they were to begin selling the issuer's securities at any point, they may be subject to registration requirements depending on how they are paid. The *de minimis* rule, which allows investment advisers to avoid registration in a state, does not apply to agents. While selling securities issued by the federal government may exempt some from agent registration, selling any type of mutual fund, regardless of its underlying investments, would require registration.

15. **Answer: C.** Customer service and administrative personnel are permitted to have contact with customers, including discussing basic details of their account, as long as they do not help effect a transaction. When they do become part of helping to effect a transaction, regardless of how they are paid, they are required to register.

16. **Answer: B.** Agents must be employed by a broker-dealer or an issuer and must be individuals. There is no requirement for an agent to have a college degree. Agents are permitted to give investment advice as long as it is incidental to (happens in the course of) helping someone effect a securities transaction.

17. **Answer: B.** An employee of an issuer is exempt from registering as an agent of the issuer if he or she is helping with the sale of the company's own securities to company employees and his/her compensation is not directly or indirectly tied to the sale. If the employee does receive compensation for the sale, the employee would have to register as an agent of the issuer.

18. **Answer: A.** Generally, if a broker-dealer is exempt from registration, then so are its agents.

19. **Answer: D.** An agent's registration may be suspended or revoked for all the reasons listed.

20. **Answer: B.** A state's security administrator may revoke, suspend, or deny the renewal of an agent's registration. An agent's registration can only be withdrawn by the agent, a broker-dealer, or an issuer.

CHAPTER THREE

Securities, Issuers, and Administrative Provisions

(9 questions on the exam)

3.1. REGULATION OF SECURITIES AND ISSUERS

Thus far in this study guide, we've talked mostly about how the Uniform Securities Act regulates the people and firms involved with helping people buy and sell securities and decide which securities to buy. While this is typically where the exam focuses much of its attention (since you'll probably be engaged in those activities before you do anything else), questions about the issuers of securities and the securities themselves are also fair game.

That doesn't mean you're going to be asked questions about which stock is better for a customer, or how to decide which bond pays a higher after-tax yield. Rather, it means you may be asked about how securities are initially cleared for sale to the public and what rules their issuers must abide by.

It's important to remember, as the material covered begins to shift a little, the intent of the Uniform Securities Act remains the same. It's there to protect the investing public, who may not have a working knowledge of complex investments or the time to research them, from being taken advantage of by professionals and companies who should know better. In other words, when you're taking the exam, keep telling yourself that you're looking for answers that would protect and favor the little guy.

3.1.1. ISSUER AND SECURITIES—DEFINITIONS

Once again, the Uniform Securities Act attempts to make it very clear who would be considered an issuer of securities. An **issuer** is:

```
a person who issues or proposes to issue a security
```

A big old thanks here to the authors of the Uniform Securities Act for using the word we're trying to define, in the definition itself. That doesn't actually tell us what someone does that makes them an issuer.

In layman's terms, an issuer is someone who creates, or publicly declares that they will be creating, a security that can be purchased by investors. Even though the USA's definition says "person," the definition is not limited to natural, living, and breathing persons. A person also must be 18 or over and legally competent. Thus, a 14-year-old, a dead person, or an individual who has been declared incompetent would not be considered a person under the USA. The USA may also include entities that are considered legal persons, including companies, governments and their agencies, and even non-profit associations.

Pretty simple, huh? *Not really*.

What makes this a little more complex is that the word security is thrown in. In a decision called "The Howey Decision," the U.S. Supreme Court came up with four characteristics that define a security. A security involves (1) an investment of money that (2) involves a common enterprise (3) in which the investors expect to make a profit, and (4) the profits will be derived from the efforts of someone other than the investor. This definition will help you to determine whether a particular example on the exam is an investment contract or not.

The Uniform Securities Act only addresses financial instruments that are considered securities. The Uniform Securities Act specifically states that a security (which will inevitably be issued by an issuer), can be a:

- Stock (preferred or common shares, treasury stock)
- Bond (corporate or government, including debentures)
- Any evidence of indebtedness
- Certificate of interest
- Participation in any profit sharing agreement
- Collateral trust certificate
- Preorganization certificate or subscription
- Transferable share
- Mutual fund (regardless of what it invests in)
- Option (puts, calls, futures, etc.)
- Oil and gas partnership
- Certificate of participation in an oil, gas or mining
- Certificate of deposit for a security (ADRs and GDRs)
- Voting trust certificate
- Warrant or right for a security
- Investment contract
- Real Estate Investment Trust (REIT)

Seems pretty broad, huh? In fact, a security can be defined as pretty much anything that can be easily purchased or sold that represents ownership in something else or a debt of others. Further, to be considered a security, none of the above items even need to be sold on one of the well-known stock or bond exchanges. Even ownership in a small, local company can be deemed a security. It's no wonder that some well-meaning folks who begin selling ownership in their family business to their neighbors in a small town can run afoul of securities laws!

For the record, there are a couple of things that are not directly regulated by the Uniform Securities Act, since they are not considered securities. You may see an exception type question on the exam asking you about these.

Currently, the non-securities not regulated by the USA are:

- Fixed annuity and other insurance contracts (including endowment policies) that don't have a variable feature allowing the owner to pick their investments out of a menu of choices, similar to a 401k. In other words, if you see the word variable associated with an insurance contract, it is subject to regulation. The most common types of exempt insurance contracts are endowment policies, term life insurance, whole life insurance, and universal life insurance.
- Commodities such as gold, pork bellies, and frozen orange juice
- Futures contracts on commodities
- Precious metals
- Currency such as rare coins
- Real estate used as a personal residence
- Collectibles such as antiques, art, and fine wine
- Retirement plans (e.g. IRAs and Keogh plans)

Test Note: Financial instruments that have the word certificate in them are often securities (e.g. certificates of deposit for a security, voting trust certificates, collateral trust certificates, preorganization certificates, certificates of interest in oil or a gas mining title). Certificates of Deposit (CDs) that are offered by a bank, however, are not considered securities.

Test Note: If an individual owns a single oil well, which he operates, the oil well would not be considered a security. Consider another situation, however, in which the investor purchases an interest in the oil well where he invests a certain amount of money for partial ownership of the oil well, but he doesn't expect to manage the oil well himself. This interest in the oil well would be considered a security because the investor has invested money in a common enterprise in which he expects to make a profit through the efforts of others.

Test Note: Note that while a futures contract is not a security, an option on a futures contract (also called futures contract option) is considered a security. Whenever you see the word "option," it is considered a security.

SUMMARY

COMMON TYPES OF SECURITIES AND NON-SECURITIES

Security	Not a Security
• Stock	• Fixed annuity
• Bond	• Non-variable insurance contract
• Mutual fund	• Commodity
• Option	• Futures contract on commodities
• Oil and gas partnership	• Precious metals
• ADR	• Currency
• GDR	• Real estate used as a personal residence
• Voting trust certificate	• Collectibles
• Real estate investment trust	• Retirement plans
• Warrant or right for a security	
• Investment contract	

Key Words for Securities	Key Words for Non-Securities
Certificate	Fixed
Interest in	Non-variable
Option	
Variable	

⟍ EXERCISE

CHOOSE IF A SECURITY OR NOT A SECURITY

1. _____ A valuable antique musical instrument

2. _____ A variable annuity

3. _____ A term life insurance policy

4. _____ A bond issued by a local school district

5. _____ Interest in a collection of antique musical instruments

6. _____ An option on commodities

7. _____ A personal residence

ANSWERS

1. **Not a security.** Collectibles, such as antiques, are not considered to be securities.

2. **Security.** Annuities without variable features are not considered to be securities. In contrast, variable annuities are securities.

3. **Not a security.** Because it is a fixed and non-variable type of insurance contract, a term life insurance policy is not an annuity.

4. **Security.** All bonds are considered to be securities.

5. **Security.** An interest in something, meaning a situation in which an investment in a common enterprise in which an investor expects to make a profit through the efforts of others, is a security.

6. **Security.** Options on commodities or anything else are considered to be securities.

7. **Not a security.** Real estate used as a personal residence is not considered to be a security.

3.1.2. **REGISTRATION OF SECURITIES**

Just like investment advisers, agents, and the other professionals discussed so far, securities must be registered with the state securities administrator and a registration fee must be paid. And as with these other parties, securities are potentially exempt from state registration if they are registered at the federal level or meet one of the exemptions outlined in the Uniform Securities Act (more on these in a bit).

The actual registration of a security doesn't have to be handled by the issuer. In fact, most times it is handled by an underwriter or broker-dealer who has been hired by the issuer. Regardless, however, registration of any security is valid for one year and can only be voluntarily withdrawn with the approval of the state securities administrator.

3.1.2.1. **The Registration Statement**

The **registration statement** is an important part of the process by which securities are registered with the SEC. Required information includes a description of the issuer's business and the security being offered, certified financial statements, and underwriter compensation. The registration statement must be signed by officers and directors. The USA says that when filing a registration statement with a state—whether filing by coordination or by qualification—the issuer must indicate the amount of securities to be offered in the state, other states in which the securities have been registered, and any adverse order, judgment, or decree entered in connection with the offering by the regulatory authorities in each state or by any court or the SEC.

3.1.2.2. **Incorporation by Reference**

Occasionally, the exam will ask you about a concept called **incorporation by reference**. This is a general legal concept that is also applied under the Uniform Securities Act. Essentially what it says is that a document filed about the same security or issuer within the previous five years can simply be *referenced* in a new filing, without having to include a copy of the previous filing.

3.1.2.3. **Types of Registration**

The registration process itself varies slightly depending on the nature of the security being registered, previous registrations in other jurisdictions, etc. The three registration methods are:

- Registration by qualification
- Registration by coordination
- Registration by filing

Federal covered securities may be sold in a state with a notice filing, which will be discussed later.

Regardless of the type of registration, all issuers of securities must

- Provide a signed consent to service of process to the state
- Pay filing fees to the state

3.1.2.3.1. **Registration by Qualification**

When an issuer registers a security by qualification, it means that the issuer is starting from scratch in proving that its security meets the basic regulatory requirements to protect the public. This means that it needs to provide a registration statement to its state securities administrator containing a boatload of information. This is the most laborious type of state registration and is generally used for intrastate securities or those securities that will be sold in only one state.

A registration by qualification requires:

- All the basics about the company (name, address, state of organization, etc.)

- The general nature of the business, including key assets

- A summary of the business environment in which the company operates

- All the relevant details about the security being issued (issue price, number of shares, face value of stock, maturity or redemption dates of debt, etc.)

- The total amount of money to be collected through the offering

- The total value of debt and stock already in existence for the issuer

- A company balance sheet that is no more than four months old

- The three previous years of annual income statements (profit and loss statements)

- A breakdown of each director, officer, or anyone owning more than 10% of the issuer's securities. The breakdown must include their addresses and five-year work history (for directors and officers only), their pay for the previous twelve months and estimated pay for the coming twelve months, and the amount of the issuer's securities held by each person as of 30 days before the filing.

- A description of any pending lawsuits against the company that would materially affect the value of the security being issued

- Copies of all prospectuses, advertisements, circulars, etc., related to the issue

- A sample of the actual security (stock or bond certificate)

- A copy of a legal opinion issued by an attorney about the legality of the issue

- Written consent for any reports issued by professionals (appraisers, engineers, etc.) used in valuing the company or its assets

- The intended uses of the proceeds, the amount of funds to be raised from other sources for these purposes, and the identities of those sources

- A description of any stock options, along with how many options will be held by officers/directors/10% owners

- Any other information the administrator requires

Once this information is filed with a state securities administrator, the registration becomes effective *when the administrator declares it to be effective*.

3.1.2.3.1.1. *Prospectus Delivery Requirements*

To further protect investors from shady new issues, the law requires a prospectus (detailed description of the issue) to be delivered by the completion of the transaction, which means the time that the security settles, to each investor who purchases a newly issued security.

A prospectus contains a large amount of the factual data about a security offering and helps give the investing public the information they need to make an educated choice about purchasing a security. Key information included on a prospectus includes:

- Name of security and issuer
- Type of security being issued
- Price of security
- Amount and denomination of security being issued
- Information about the issuer and the parties aiding the sale

3.1.2.3.2. **Registration by Coordination**

As the name implies, registration by coordination is used to coordinate both the state and federal filings of a securities issue. In other words, this form of registration is used primarily by companies that are registering their securities for the first time with the SEC at the same time that they are registering them with certain states. This most commonly occurs with larger issuers who would like their securities to be made available to investors in multiple states.

The most important step is filing the appropriate registration statement at the federal level *before* trying to register securities at the state level. All state level registrations under a registration by coordination happen after the federal registration and reuse much of that paperwork.

As part of the required registration statement, an issuer attempting a registration by coordination may be required to submit:

- Three copies of the latest prospectus
- A copy of the company's articles of incorporation and by-laws
- A copy of the agreement between the issuer and their underwriter
- A copy of any instrument governing the issuance of the security
- A copy of the security itself
- Anything else the state administrator requests

Any updates to the prospectus at the federal level must also be supplied to the state's securities administrator.

Once all the appropriate information is filed, the registration at the state level becomes effective *when the federal registration also becomes effective*, so long as the statement has been on file with the state for at least ten days and a range of offering prices and underwriting commissions has been on file for at least two business days.

The issuer must notify the state securities administrator when the federal registration becomes effective. At this time, the issuer must also notify the administrator of the offering price and the underwriting commissions. The administrator will, in turn, acknowledge this receipt.

3.1.2.3.2.1. *Special Subscription Form*

The administrator may require that securities registered by qualification or coordination be sold using a specific form called a subscription or sale contract form. The administrator may also require that a signed form of each contract be filed with the administrator and retained up to three years.

3.1.2.3.3. Registration by Filing

Registration by filing (also known as registration by notification) is an option for issuers that have registered a security federally. If the issuer meets certain conditions, they may register on the state level by providing the state with certain basic information and documentation. What you really need to know is that this type of filing is for established companies that have already registered a security with the SEC.

A security registered under the Securities Act of 1933 may only register by filing if the following conditions are met:

- The issuer is organized under U.S. laws, is organized under the laws of a state, or has an agent in the U.S. for service of process.

- The issuer has been in business in the U.S. for the past 36 months and has filed all their materials with the SEC for the last 36 months.

- The issuer has a security registered under the Securities Exchange Act of 1934 held by at least 500 shareholders.

- There have been 4 market makers in the security registered under the Securities Exchange Act for a period of at least 30 days during the 3 months preceding the offering of the security being registered.

- If the security being registered is an equity security, it must be offered at no less than $5 per share.

A security of a mutual fund or unit investment trust can be registered by filing if it meets a shorter list of conditions.

When a security is registered through filing, the following pieces of information must be provided to the state administrator:

- A statement demonstrating eligibility for registration by filing
- The name, address, and form of organization of the issuer
- A description of the security being registered
- A copy of the latest prospectus filed with the SEC

If this information has been on file with the state administrator for five business days and any filing fees have been paid, then the registration becomes effective simultaneously to when the federal registration becomes effective (assuming there is no stop order or related proceedings pending). The registrant must inform the state securities administrator when the federal registration becomes effective.

3.1.2.4. Federal Covered Securities and Their Sale at the State Level

Under NSMIA, a class of securities called **federal covered securities** only need to be registered at the federal level and do not have to be registered at the state level. This is meant to help avoid redundant filings for issuers and unneeded oversight for regulators.

The following *securities* are federal covered securities and must be registered at the federal level, which means they will not be registered at the state level. Federal covered securities include the following:

- Securities listed on the New York Stock Exchange, the NASDAQ Exchange, the American Stock Exchange, or another national exchange

- Debt securities or preferred stock of any of the companies that have stocks listed on the exchanges above

- Securities issued by an investment company that qualifies under the Investment Company Act of 1940

The following *transactions* would not be regulated by the state because they are covered by federal regulations:

- Transactions in most securities that are exempt from federal registration (U.S. government securities, municipal securities)

- Offers or sales to qualified purchasers under Regulation D of the Securities Act of 1933 (private placements)

- Most transactions that are exempt under federal law

Federal registration does not mean that a state regulator cannot get involved in how individuals and firms offer or sell these securities if someone is using fraudulent or deceptive schemes to market the securities. If this is the case, a state's administrator has a duty to intervene, though it will be expected to coordinate any action against the issuer with federal regulators.

3.1.2.4.1. Notice Filings

A notice filing is just a heads-up to a state's administrator that a federal covered security will be offered for sale in its jurisdiction. This heads up is required of issuers of federal covered securities. It is important to note that the issuers are not officially registering their securities at the state level. Instead, they are simply notifying the states that they will be selling the securities in their states. The state cannot impose additional filing requirements on these issuers that exceed the federal requirements. The issuers will still have to pay fees to the states that they will be selling in. Issuers usually don't mind notice filing too much because the requirements are few. They must simply:

- Submit all the documents that are used to register the security on a federal level to the state's securities administrator prior to sale

- Deliver to the state administrator copies of all amendments to the federal documents at the same time that the amendments are submitted to the federal government

- Provide a report describing the value of the federal covered securities that will be sold in the state

- Provide a consent to service of process

- Pay any filing fees required by the state

State securities registrations and notice filings expire one year after their effective date. They are renewable as long as copies of the appropriate paperwork are filed with the state on or before the one-year anniversary.

 Test Note: December 31 is only an important date for the registration of individuals and firms in the securities industry; December 31 is not an important date for the registration of securities because the registration of a security expires after one year from its effective registration date. For example, the registration for a security which goes into effect on November 25 will be effective until November 25 of the following year.

TYPES OF REGISTRATION AND FILING

Type of Registration	Description	What type of issuer does this apply to?
Registration by qualification	• Most laborious, asks for the most information	• Usually intrastate offerings • Can be used by any issuer
Registration by coordination	• File at the same time as SEC registration (actually immediately after) • Most common form of IPO	• Used for companies that have not issued securities before, but will be issuing them for the first time with the SEC • Issuers know that they want to sell the securities across states • **Example Issuers:** Over the counter and exchange listed IPOs
Registration by filing	• File with state because issuer is going to start selling securities in the state • The issuer must have already registered the securities with the SEC, but the securities are not federal covered securities	• Used for companies whose securities are already registered with the SEC, but want to start selling in a state • Not available to federal covered securities • **Example Issuers:** OTC securities that are registered with the SEC
Notice filing	• This is not a true registration, just a heads up to the state administrator that the issuer will be selling securities in the state • Easiest process • Allows the administrator to collect filing fees from the issuer • State registration requirements cannot exceed federal registration requirements	• Only required for federal covered securities as defined by NSMIA. • **Example Issuers:** Exchange listed securities

SUMMARY

✝ EXERCISE

MATCH THE MODE OF REGISTRATION OR FILING WITH THE SECURITIES ISSUE

A. Registration by qualification
B. Registration by coordination
C. Registration by filing
D. Notice filing

1. _____ Solar Corp has a security that is listed on the NYSE. Solar wishes to sell the security in several states.

2. _____ Enamel Brand has registered its stock with the SEC and makes regular reports to the SEC. The stock trades on the OTCBB. Enamel Brand wishes to sell its latest issue in State A.

3. _____ Tech Burst is a new company that is preparing its first IPO. It is only interested in making its securities available for sale in its home state.

4. _____ Playback Music Limited is a new company that is preparing its first IPO. It is interested in making its securities available for sale in several different states.

ANSWERS

1. **D.** Solar Corp is a federal covered security because it is listed on the NYSE. Notice filing is the mode by which a state administrator is made aware that a federal covered security will be available for sale in its state.

2. **C.** Registration by filing is open to issuers that have registered a security federally. It allows them to register at the state level by providing an administrator with certain basic information. This type of registration is usually used by issuers that have securities that are registered with the SEC but are not traded on a national exchange.

3. **A.** Registration by qualification is typically done by new companies that are only selling their securities issue in one state.

4. **B.** Registration by coordination is used to coordinate both the federal and state filings of a securities issue. It is used primarily by newer companies registering their securities for the first time with the SEC while also registering them in multiple states.

3.1.3. POST-REGISTRATION REQUIREMENTS

Once a security is issued, the issuer is subject to a minimal set of **post-registration requirements**. This is in large part due to the fact that a security, unlike an investment adviser or agent, cannot by itself make bad choices that harm investors.

Typically, an issuer of a security is subject to regular administrative reports that must be filed with the state securities administrator, as well as filing any amendments to the security's description or amount. The most often that these reports can be required is quarterly, though many issuers may not be required to file them at all. The administrator may also require that offers for a security comply with federal prospectus delivery requirements.

3.1.4. EXEMPTIONS TO ISSUER AND SECURITY REGISTRATION

When it comes to exemptions to registration requirements for securities and issuers, the Uniform Securities Act (and in turn, the Series 63 exam) continues to be as much about the exemptions from the rules as the rules themselves. In this case, even the exemptions have exemptions. In the case of registering securities, there are two levels of exemptions, Section 402(a) and 402(b) exemptions.

Section 402(b) exemptions are those exemptions that must be granted individually for each transaction, whereas **Section 402(a) exemptions** apply to every transaction of a security.

So let's start with the easy ones, or the Section 402(a) securities, that are *always exempt*.

3.1.4.1. Section 402(a) Exemptions

Under Section 402(a) of the Uniform Securities Act, the following types of securities are exempt from registration requirements, meaning they do not need to be registered with individual states:

- **U.S. government and municipal securities**—securities (usually bonds) issued or guaranteed by the United States government, a state government, a city or municipality, or any agencies related to these government entities

> **Note:** Municipal bonds may be subject to registration in the states in which they are issued.

- **Foreign government securities**—securities (usually bonds) issued or guaranteed by a foreign government or its political subdivisions, with which the United States maintains diplomatic relations, as long as the security is recognized as a valid obligation by the issuer or guarantor

- **Depository securities**—securities issued or guaranteed by a bank organized under U.S. law or by a bank, savings institution, or trust company organized and supervised under the laws of any state (usually a Certificate of Deposit or CD)

- **Loan association securities**—securities issued or guaranteed by a U.S. savings and loan association or a similar association that is authorized to do business in the state

- **Insurance company securities**—securities issued or guaranteed by an insurance company authorized to operate in the state (note: this exemption may not apply to variable annuities)

- **Credit union securities**—securities issued or guaranteed by a federal credit union or a state-supervised credit union or similar association

- **Public utility securities**—securities issued or guaranteed by a railroad, common carrier, public utility or holding company that is regulated by the United States, an individual state, Canada, or a Canadian province

- **Exchange-traded securities**—securities approved for trading on the NYSE, AMEX, Chicago, or other major exchanges

- **Nonprofit securities**—securities issued by a nonprofit religious, educational, benevolent, fraternal, charitable, social, athletic, or reformatory organization or a chamber of commerce or trade or professional association

- **Commercial paper**—investment grade commercial paper that has a maturity of nine or fewer months, is issued in denominations of at least $50,000, and receives a rating in one of the three highest rating categories from a nationally recognized statistical rating organization

- **Employee benefit plan investment contracts**—investment contracts issued in connection with an employee benefit plan if the administrator is notified in writing 30 days before the inception of the plan

Test Note: If you see the term "exempt securities" on the exam, this should signal to you that the securities do not need to be registered. On the other hand, the term "non-exempt" securities are securities that always need to be registered. Remember that exempt securities are subject to anti-fraud laws, however.

3.1.4.2. **Section 402(b) Exemptions**

Unlike Section 402(a), which provides blanket exemptions from registration to certain securities, Section 402(b) of the USA exempts certain securities from registration as long as they are limited to certain transactions. In other words, as long as securities that would otherwise require registration only change hands in one of the following circumstances, registration *is not* required.

In order to understand 402(b) exemptions it is important to understand the difference between issuer transactions and non-issuer transactions. When an issuer raises money by selling securities to investors, the sale is an issuer transaction. The proceeds of the sale go to the issuer. Securities bought in an initial public offering (IPO) and sales of mutual fund shares are both considered issuer transactions. An issuer repurchasing its own securities would also be an issuer transaction. An issuer transaction takes place in the primary market.

Test Note: If an exam question mentions an underwriter or the primary market, it is usually referring to an issuer transaction.

In contrast, a non-issuer transaction is when one party sells a security to another party, and neither party is the issuer. The proceeds of this kind of transaction do not go to the issuer, and these kinds of transactions take place in the secondary market.

Test Note: Generally sales of mutual fund shares are considered issuer transactions because when an investor buys shares of a mutual fund, the shares are issued new, and when the investor wants to sell these shares, they are then redeemed by the fund. If a mutual fund decides to sell some of the securities that are owned by the fund, however, this transaction is considered a non-issuer transaction.

Exempt transactions for which a security is not required to be registered are:

- **Isolated non-issuer transactions**—transactions between two private parties, even if effected through a broker-dealer, that do not occur frequently

- **Senior securities transactions**—non-issuer transactions by or through a registered broker-dealer in a security that is senior in rank to the issuer's common stock both in terms of payments and liquidation, and the issuer has not defaulted in the past three fiscal years and is engaged in business (not a shell company)

- **Transactions in certain federally registered securities**—non-issuer transactions in an outstanding security if the issuer has a security registered under either the Securities Exchange Act of 1934 or the Investment Company Act of 1940; if the security is registered under the Securities Exchange Act of 1934, the registration information must have been on file for at least 180 days

- **Unsolicited transactions**—non-issuer transactions effected by or through a registered broker-dealer of an unsolicited order or offer to purchase (the administrator may require that the broker-dealer keep on record a customer confirmation that the sale was unsolicited)

- **Underwriter transactions**—transactions between the issuer and an underwriter or among underwriters

- **Whole mortgage-backed bond transactions**—transactions in a bond or other evidence of indebtedness secured by a mortgage or other security agreement provided the security is offered and sold with the mortgage or other security agreement as a unit

- **Bankruptcy and fiduciary transactions**—transactions by fiduciaries such as an executor, administrator, sheriff, marshal, receiver, trustee in bankruptcy, guardian, or conservator

- **Transactions by a pledgee**—transactions executed by a bona fide pledgee without the purpose of evading the law (For example, when stock is put up as collateral, this is considered an exempt transaction, because the investor is not attempting to buy or sell the security, but is instead holding onto the security.)

- **Institutional investor transactions**—offers or sales to an institutional investor, such as an insurance company, pension fund, or college endowment, do not require registration, since these investors are considered much more sophisticated than the general investing public

- **Private placement transactions**—sales or offers to sell securities of an issuer (also called offerings), if
  ‣ The offer is directed to no more than ten purchasers (besides institutional investors) present in this state during any 12 consecutive months
  ‣ A commission or other remuneration is not paid or given, directly or indirectly, for soliciting a prospective buyer in this state
  ‣ The issuer reasonably believes that all the purchasers in this state, aside from institutional investors, are purchasing for investment

- **Preorganization certificate transactions**—offers or sales of a preorganization certificate or subscription if:
  ‣ No commission or other remuneration is paid or given directly or indirectly for soliciting any prospective subscriber
  ‣ The number of subscribers does not exceed ten
  ‣ No payment is made by any subscriber

- **Transactions with existing security holders**—transactions with existing security holders of the issuer, if either:
  ‣ A commission or other remuneration, other than a standby commission, is not paid or given
  ‣ The issuer first files a notice specifying the terms of the offer and the administrator does not disallow the exemption within the next five full business days

- **Offers of securities registered on the state and federal level**—offers to sell, but not an actual sale, of a security if a registration statement has been filed under both this act and the Securities Act of 1933 and no stop order or refusal order is in effect and no public proceedings or examinations looking toward such an order are pending under either act

- **Non-issuer distributions**—non-issuer transactions by or through a registered broker-dealer and a resale transaction by a sponsor of a unit investment trust in a security that has been in the hands of the public for at least 90 days, if the security and the issuer meet the following standards:
  ‣ The issuer is engaged in business (not a shell company)
  ‣ The security is sold at a price reasonably related to its current market price
  ‣ The security is not an unsold allotment to the broker-dealer as an underwriter
  ‣ Specified information about the issuer is in a nationally recognized securities manual or filed with the Securities and Exchange Commission

▸ The issuer is sufficiently well-established, based on pre-existing stock (exchange-listed), duration of operation (3 years), or total assets ($2,000,000 within 18 months before the transaction), or is a unit investment trust

- **Small offerings offered under the JOBS Act**—the JOBS Act, passed in 2012 to help stimulate the economy, included a provision allowing an exemption from registration of a small amount of securities if certain requirements are met for any 12-month period. The requirements are:
  ▸ The issuer sells a maximum of $1,000,000 in securities to all purchasers
  ▸ No single investor purchases more than the greater of $2,000 of the company's securities or 5% of the investor's net worth or annual income (10% if their annual income exceeds $100,000)
  ▸ The sales are conducted through a registered broker-dealer or a funding portal

Whenever anyone claims an exemption or an exception under the USA, the burden of proving the exemption or exception lies with the person claiming it. Thus if an agent transacts in an unregistered security, it is the agent's responsibility to show that the security or transaction is exempt. The administrator is never required to take the burden of proof for showing that a transaction or security is non-exempt—transactions and securities are assumed to be non-exempt unless it is shown otherwise.

 Test Note: A securities professional may not sell non-exempt unregistered securities. This is never allowed.

SECTION 402 EXEMPTIONS: SECURITIES AND SECURITIES TRANSACTIONS

Section 402(a) Exemptions	Section 402(b) Exemptions
Types of Securities	**Types of Transactions**
• U.S. government and municipal securities	• Isolated non-issuer transactions
• Foreign government securities	• Senior securities transactions
• Depository securities	• Transactions in certain federally registered securities
• Loan association securities	• Unsolicited transactions
• Insurance company securities	• Underwriter transactions
• Credit union securities	• Whole mortgage-backed bond transactions
• Public utility securities	• Bankruptcy and fiduciary transactions
• Exchange-traded securities	• Transactions by a pledgee
• Nonprofit securities (a.k.a. church bonds)	• Institutional investor transactions
• Commercial paper	• Private placement transactions
• Employee benefit plan investment contracts	• Preorganization certificate transactions
	• Transactions with existing security holders
	• Offers of securities registered on the state and federal level
	• Non-issuer distributions
	• Small offerings under the JOBS Act

EXERCISE

CHOOSE EXEMPT OR NON-EXEMPT

1. _____ Foreign government bonds

2. _____ Bank certificates of deposit (CDs)

3. _____ Shares of a fund that only has nonprofit securities within the fund

4. _____ An offer directed only to institutional investors

5. _____ An offering for which the issuer sells $1,100,000 in securities to all purchasers, the largest securities purchase by a single investor is $1,500, and for which sales are conducted through a funding portal.

ANSWERS

1. **Exempt.** Securities issued or guaranteed by a foreign government are generally exempt.

2. **Exempt.** Securities issued or guaranteed by a U.S. bank, such as bank CDs, are exempt.

3. **Not exempt.** Although nonprofit securities are exempt, shares of a fund which only invests in nonprofit securities are not.

4. **Exempt.** Offers or sales made solely to institutional investors are exempt.

5. **Not exempt.** Under the JOBS Act, securities are exempt from registration if their total issue is $1,000,000 or less, no single investor purchases more than $2,000 of those securities or an amount in excess of 5% of the investor's net worth, and the sales are conducted through a registered broker-dealer or a funding portal.

3.1.5. SALES, OFFERS, AND OTHER TRANSACTIONS

An important distinction that shows up in some form in at least one question on the exam is the difference between an offer to buy or sell securities, an actual transaction, and other exchanges of securities that don't constitute an offer or transaction.

A **sale** or **purchase** is an actual exchange of securities for some type of compensation, or a contract to do one of these things in the future. In addition to the typical cash-for-securities exchange, the following can all constitute purchases and sales:

- Trading securities for other securities
- Trading securities for other types of assets
- Trading securities for services
- Exercising options
- Making gifts of assessable securities

An **offer** is any attempt to invite another party to engage in a purchase or sale transaction, which includes advertisements for securities. *For the exam, remember that regulators are concerned with which state an offer originates in and which state it is directed to.* Each of those states, if they are different, will require an issuer to either register or meet an exemption. In addition, these also determine which state administrator has jurisdiction over the transaction.

Five important examples to remember that are considered offers are:

- A warrant or right to purchase a security at a set price in the future (warrants are often given as sweeteners on bond purchases)
- A security given as a bonus for purchasing other securities or other items of value
- Gift of assessable stock (see test note for an explanation of assessable stock)
- Sales calls
- Any mailed marketing material

There are some notable exceptions to the definition of an offer that you may be asked about on the exam. They include:

- Stock dividends that are paid to shareholders without them having to pay anything additional

- Stock splits where shareholders pay nothing additional

- Any communication or action related to a legitimate corporate action such as a reorganization, merger, consolidation, etc.

- Any pledge or loan

- Exchanges of securities made in connection with a judicially approved reorganization

- Gifts of non-assessable stock (these are the current type of stock)

Test Note: Almost all stock is non-assessable today and gifts of non-assessable stock are not considered an offer or a sale. Assessable stock, in contrast, is stock in which fees can be levied for future improvements or expansions. This kind of stock is extremely rare. Because fees can be assessed on this kind of stock, a gift of this kind of stock is not considered a gift, and it is considered to be both an offer and a sale of a security. What you need to remember for the exam is that a gift of assessable stock is considered to be both an offer and a sale of a security, whereas a gift of non-assessable stock is not considered to be either an offer or a sale of a security.

3.1.5.1. **Exceptions for Media from Other States**

Certain kinds of communications may not be considered an offer within a state. Specifically, advertisements in bona fide newspapers and other publications of regular circulation that are not published within a given state do not constitute offers within that state. Also, if two-thirds of a publication's circulation is outside the state in which it is published (such as for national magazines), then its advertisements do not count as offers even in the state in which the publication is published. Radio and television programs that originate outside of a given state do not constitute offers within that state. Note that radio ads, television ads, and state and local newspaper ads count as offers in their state of origin, so the administrator of that state will have jurisdiction over such offers.

3.1.6. STATE JURISDICTION OVER FRAUDULENT SECURITIES ACTIVITIES

Exempt securities are still subject to penalties for securities fraud at the state level. The state's administrator has a duty to intervene whenever he thinks that fraudulent behavior related to securities professionals or the registration of securities is taking place. In the case of federal covered securities, the administrator is expected to coordinate any action against the issuer or securities professionals with federal regulators.

Remember, however, that this jurisdiction only applies to securities and securities-related offenses. In the case of fraudulent behavior related to non-securities, such as those listed earlier, or to individuals working solely in selling and trading such items, the state administrator has no jurisdiction. For instance, an agent selling fraudulent term life policies would not be under the jurisdiction of the administrator, but the same agent selling bogus variable life policies would be.

3.1.7. TERMINATION OF A SECURITIES REGISTRATION

As previously mentioned, a securities registration is effective for one year from its effective date (or potentially longer, if a non-exempt offering lasts for more than a year). A securities registration may not be withdrawn within one year of its effective date. After that period, it may be withdrawn only at the discretion of the state securities administrator.

The state securities administrator may deny, suspend, or revoke a securities registration by issuing a stop order. A stop order may also be issued to stop the offer and sale of a federal covered security (other than an exchange-listed security) that fails to submit a notice filing or is in violation of other security registration requirements. These stop orders are not meant to be punitive, but are used by the securities administrator to protect the public from securities and issuers that have not met important requirements to be ready for public distribution.

3.1.7.1. Reasons for Issuing a Stop Order

In order for a state securities administrator to issue a stop order, the order must be in the public interest, and one of the following conditions must be true:

- The registration is materially incomplete, false, or misleading.

- Any of the following persons have willfully violated state securities law:
  ‣ The filer of the registration statement
  ‣ The issuer or any officer, director, or partner of the issuer
  ‣ Any underwriter

- Another state or federal regulator or court entered a stop order or injunction against the security within the past year.

- The issuer's business includes illegal activities.

- The offering is fraudulent.

- The offering involves unreasonable amounts of commissions and other compensation, or unreasonable amounts or kinds of options.

- A security applies for registration by notification but is not eligible.

- A security applies for registration by coordination, but it does not forward amendments to the federal prospectus to the state securities administrator.

- The applicant fails to pay the proper filing fee, but the administrator may only enter a denial order and must vacate the order once the fee has been paid.

The administrator may not institute a stop order proceeding against an effective registration statement on the basis of information the administrator knew when the registration statement became effective, unless the proceeding is instituted within 30 days of when the registration statement took effect.

The administrator may summarily suspend or postpone a registration statement that has been subject to a stop order proceeding, pending final determination. When the administrator does this, he or she must notify the registrant, the issuer, and the person on whose behalf the securities are offered. The administrator must also provide opportunity for a hearing and written findings of fact and conclusions of law. A hearing must be provided within 15 days of a written request for one.

Test Note: Note that "in the best interest of the public" is not enough for the administrator to issue a stop order on a security. They must also have one of the additional reasons above.

EXERCISE

ANSWER TRUE OR FALSE

1. _____ Exercising an option on a security is considered a sale.

2. _____ Sales calls are not considered to be offers.

3. _____ A radio communication broadcast from State A and heard in State B is considered to be an offer in both State A and State B.

4. _____ State administrators have some jurisdiction over federal covered securities.

5. _____An administrator can never institute a stop order against a registration statement on the basis of information that he or she knew at the time that registration went into effect.

ANSWERS

1. **True.** The exercise of options on securities is always considered to be a sale.

2. **False.** Sales calls are always considered to be offers.

3. **False.** A radio broadcast is only considered to be an offer in the state where the broadcast originated.

4. **True.** Securities listed on national exchanges, such as NYSE, are federal covered securities, and fraudulent activity involving these securities is under the jurisdiction of the state administrator if the fraudulent activity occurs within the state.

5. **False.** An administrator can issue a stop order proceeding against a registration statement on the basis of information that was known when the registration took effect for up to 30 days after the effective date.

3.2. PRACTICAL APPLICATION

Amy Adams learned early on in her career that networking was one of the most effective ways to find new clients. To help that process along, she joined the local chamber of commerce and began rubbing elbows with local business owners. One of the business owners she met was Sally, who owned a very popular chain of car washes.

One day at one of the Chamber of Commerce's meet and greets, Sally began asking Amy for some informal advice about selling a portion of her car washes to investors in order to raise additional funds to build even more car washes. Naturally, Amy was more than excited to have such a successful businessperson turn to her for advice.

Amy and Sally drew out some potential numbers on a cocktail napkin, coming to the conclusion that Sally would need approximately 50 investors to invest $50,000. Amy didn't think that would be a stretch, based on the fact that she had dozens of clients with at least that much cash in their accounts and due to the fact that Sally was a well-known and respected business person.

Amy went back to her office, excited to share the news about this potential relationship with her sales manager. To her surprise, she was greeted with a panicked look and some hurried questions about whether or not she had actually solicited anyone to invest yet. Not sure why her sales manager wasn't doing cartwheels over this new potential opportunity, Amy asked him to explain his lack of enthusiasm. Her manager went on to tell her that asking people, especially her firm's clients, to invest or buy shares in a business could very well cost Amy her securities license if proper procedures weren't followed. Specifically, it could constitute multiple violations of the Uniform Securities Act, for failing to register the securities properly as well as Amy selling away from her firm.

To avoid making matters any worse, Amy, with her sales manager on the line, called Sally and expressed excitement about the potential of working with her business. The manager went on to explain to her that such transactions need to be properly routed through their firm's investment banking department and someone would contact her immediately to explore those options.

In the end, the investment banking department at Amy's firm helped Sally's car wash find investors, raising more money than either Sally or Amy had dreamed. In the process, Amy received a nice referral fee from the investment banking department, while also picking up Sally's personal and retirement account business. Best of all, the securities were registered properly and offered in a way that conformed to the laws of their state.

3.3. REMEDIES AND ADMINISTRATIVE PROVISIONS

You've spent the last few chapters of this study guide learning what securities professionals, firms, and issuers are supposed to do to stay on the right side of securities administrators. This section is about what happens when they cross that line. As previously mentioned, the actual consequences of violations might vary slightly from state to state, since the Uniform Securities Act is meant to be a template that each state can build upon.

Regardless of how your state has crafted its laws, it's important to remember who sits at the top of the food chain. The administrator, who may go by a different official title in your state, is the head honcho. She is the one responsible for making sure that the laws a specific state has adopted are actually enforced. Her office is where the buck stops. Naturally, this position is vested with a number of unique powers.

3.3.1. AUTHORITY OF THE ADMINISTRATOR

While a state's securities administrator has a large amount of power, one of the role's highest responsibilities is to coordinate with other state and federal regulators. This expectation underlies all others, with state administrators expected to not act in a way that only benefits their state. With this in mind, a state securities administrator is charged with the following duties:

- Initiate investigations of potential securities violations involving residents of her state, as well as securities issued or transacted in her state

- Collect evidence needed to proceed with investigations

- Issue subpoenas requiring people to testify under oath before the administrator's staff

- Request courts and law enforcement to pursue appropriate action against violators (an administrator can't actually arrest people, send them to jail, issue search warrants, issue injunctions, etc.)

- Communicate and publish investigative and hearing results to the public

- Make, amend, or rescind orders and rules, in line with the laws set by their state (rules apply to all professionals and firms in a state; orders are specific to just one party)

- Administer oaths and affirmations

- Require the production of documents and records

- Issue and apply to enforce the subpoenas at the request of other state securities administrators

Important Note: The Uniform Securities Act also makes it very clear that a securities administrator and its personnel cannot use the information they gather as part of their job for their personal gain.

3.3.2. ADMINISTRATIVE ACTIONS

A state securities administrator has a bunch of tools at its disposal to ensure that securities professionals, firms, and issuers operating in their state do what they're supposed to. Generally, the first step in any action is for the administrator to require someone to either testify in person or supply needed information in written form. If a person or firm fails to do this, the administrator may do one or more of the following:

- Hold the person in contumacy

- Order the person to appear and testify before the administrator (even if it would require them to incriminate or provide evidence against themselves)

- Request that an appropriate court issue an injunction, including restricting or prohibiting the offer or sale of securities or the providing of investment advice

- Issue a cease and desist order (requires professionals to cease all securities related transactions immediately without a hearing)

- Bring an action before a court to enforce compliance with the Uniform Securities Act

- Issue an order revoking, denying, suspending, or canceling a registration or license

In the event that an administrative order is issued by a state's administrator, the order itself is effective immediately. However, an order that denies, suspends, or revokes a person's or security's registration can only be given with prior notice to all interested parties, opportunity for a hearing, and written findings of fact and conclusions of law. These are not required for summary suspensions or postponements (temporary action against a registration), nor are they required for cease and desist orders. If a hearing is not indicated as part of the initial contact received from the state, a professional or firm may request a hearing. If a person requests a hearing regarding a summary order (an order made before final determination has been reached), the state administrator must set a date within 15 days.

Test Note: Contumacy is when a person who is subject to an investigation ignores a subpoena or refuses to supply the required information. When faced with contumacy, the administrator can apply to a court in his state and ask for help. The court can issue an order requiring the person to appear before the administrator or to produce the required documents. If the person fails to obey the order, they can be held in contempt of court which can lead to time in jail.

Test Note: Be sure to know the difference between stop orders and the cease and desist orders mentioned above. Stop orders are aimed at securities registrations, whereas cease and desist orders are aimed at persons.

Test Note: Cancelling a license is a non-punitive termination of a license that occurs when a registered professional dies, becomes mentally incompetent, or disappears without a forwarding address.

3.3.3. OTHER PENALTIES AND LIABILITIES

In addition to revoking, denying, or suspending someone's registration, a state administrator can pursue civil liabilities, criminal penalties, and financial damages against a registered person or firm. The decision of which to pursue depends on a number of things, including the severity of the violation and the willingness of the professional or firm to work with the administrator.

The Uniform Securities Act states that persons who violate the Act through securities transactions or investment advice are subject to civil liabilities. But, if a violation or violations are serious enough, the administrator may request that state prosecutors pursue criminal charges. If a professional or firm is found guilty of criminal violations, it can be subjected to up to a $5,000 fine and three years in jail, *per violation!* In order to be subject to criminal penalties, however, the state needs to prove that the violations were *willful* (intentional) instead of accidental or out of negligence.

Generally, a criminal violation has a statute of limitations, or a period of time in which the charge must be brought for a court to consider it. For criminal violations the statute of limitations is five years (from the date of the violation).

Note that this section only addresses the penalties for criminal violations *under the Uniform Securities Act*. An action that is both a violation of the Uniform Securities Act and a violation of other state laws could result in the violator being prosecuted under all applicable laws and receiving other penalties in addition to those listed here.

3.3.3.1. Damages and Liabilities

In addition to whatever penalties the state administrator smacks on someone or asks prosecutors to pursue, the client or prospect that was injured by a violation can also sue to recover damages. In fact, lawsuits against brokers and advisers by their clients probably occur as often as actions initiated by the administrator.

In the event that a client does bring suit and a judge or jury finds in their favor, a professional or firm can be required to pay damages that are equal to one or more of the following, minus any income earned on the investments in question:

- Fees and commissions previously paid
- Amount paid for the security
- Amount paid for investment advice
- Amount lost due to investment advice
- Interest that would have been otherwise earned
- Court and legal costs

Generally, a civil lawsuit has a statute of limitations, or a period of time in which the suit must be brought, for a court to consider it. Currently, the statute of limitations for civil liabilities is either:

- Two years from the date the client discovers the violation

or

- Three years from the date of the violation itself, whichever occurs first

The cause of action for a lawsuit survives any potential plaintiff or defendant. This means that the estate of someone who was responsible for a civil liability may be sued even after the individual has died, and that the heirs of someone who had been subject to financial loss from a violation may sue as well.

3.3.3.2. **Rescission**

One unique provision available to securities issuers, investment advisers, and broker-dealers to help them avoid administrative action is known as **rescission**. Under rescission, a professional or issuer offers a client the right to undo advice they were given or a security that they purchased. As part of that process, their original investment is returned to them along with a reasonable rate of interest minus any income gained on the investment.

When a client is offered a letter of rescission, they have 30 days to accept. If they do not, then the offer is considered declined.

3.3.4. **OTHER PROVISIONS**

The Uniform Securities Act outlines a number of other administrative rules regarding the role of the administrator's office. The biggest of these are the rules surrounding a **final order,** when the administrator decides what final action to take on an initial order that was previously issued. Essentially, this is the finished product after an investigation (and possibly a hearing) has been conducted. The order may be:

- Vacated (charges or penalties dropped)
- Finalized (charges and penalties confirmed)
- Modified (charges and penalties changed)

From time to time, the state administrator may also issue what is known as an **interpretive opinion**. Under one of these, the administrator cuts off discussion at the pass and says that it *will not* pursue further actions against a person, firm, or issuer. Naturally, the administrator can only do this if it can establish that the person has not violated any law.

The state administrator may require that an applicant for initial registration as a broker-dealer, agent, investment adviser, or investment adviser representative publish an announcement of their application in one or more specified newspapers published in the state.

ADMINISTRATIVE JURISDICTION

What is an administrator allowed to do?	What is an administrator not allowed to do?
• Initiate investigations of potential securities violations involving residents of his state or issues transacted in state • Collect evidence for investigations • Issue and enforce subpoenas (including at the request of other state administrators) • Request courts and law enforcement to pursue action against securities violators • Make, amend, and rescind orders in line with state laws • Communicate and publish investigative and hearings results • Administer oaths and affirmations • Require the production of documents and records • Hold a person in contumacy • Order a person to testify • Request a court to issue an injunction • Issue a cease and desist order • Issue an order revoking, denying, suspending, or cancelling a registration or license	• Issue an injunction • Send a securities violator to prison • Levy fines • Hold trials • Amend state laws • Offer rescission

SUMMARY

ⵦ EXERCISE

ANSWER TRUE OR FALSE

1. _____ **If a person does not respond to an administrator's request for information, the administrator can rescind the person.**

2. _____ **An administrator can issue a cease and desist order without requesting a court injunction.**

3. _____ **An administrator has the authority to imprison professionals who violate securities regulations.**

4. _____ **The statute of limitations for civil violations is three years from the date of a violation itself or two years from the date an investor discovers that a violation took place.**

5. _____ **In the case of a final order that is vacated, all charges and penalties are dropped.**

ANSWERS

1. **False.** In such a case, the administrator can hold the person in contumacy. Only an issuer or securities professional can offer rescission.

2. **True.** Issuing a cease and desist order is an action that an administrator can take on his own.

3. **False.** Although an administrator can request courts and law enforcement to pursue appropriate action against violators, he cannot actually arrest or imprison anyone.

4. **True.** Criminal violations have a statute of limitations of five years; civil violations can be prosecuted within three years of the date that the violation occurred or within two years of the date that the investor discovered a violation took place.

5. **True.** A vacated final order means that all charges have been dropped.

3.4. PRACTICAL APPLICATION

From the day she was initially hired, Amy Adams had a healthy respect for Matt the Branch Manager. He was a dedicated manager who valued the integrity of his team as much as he did the growth of their business. When it came to the buck stopping with someone, Amy was sure that Matt was the top of the food chain in her world.

That was until she got a cease and desist order from her state's securities administrator. The order, which requested that she cease all securities-related activities immediately, made Amy's heart sink when she first read it. This meant she would not be able to work at the job she loved so much and that she would not be paid for her services. Apparently, someone in the administrator's office discovered that Amy's Social Security number had already been used to register another professional in her state. In fact, the professional that apparently had the same Social Security number had her registration revoked five years prior due to substantial ethical and legal violations.

Included in the letter was a copy of Amy's application for registration and a request that Amy provide any additional information that might clear up this matter, along with copies of various forms of identification and the paperwork she completed with her firm at the time she was hired. As Amy reviewed the information with Matt the Manager, she noticed that the Social Security number on her application was not in fact her Social Security number, but that one digit had been incorrectly entered.

At this discovery, Matt the Manager breathed a sigh of relief. He told Amy Adams to take the rest of the week off and that the firm's compliance department would supply the needed information to the administrator and ask for an interpretive opinion. He promised to have a couple of the firm's top advisers cover Amy's accounts while the mess got sorted out.

Less than a week later, Amy received her interpretive ruling from the administrator. The ruling stated that Amy had in fact done nothing wrong, that the incorrect Social Security number included was due to a clerical error, and that no further action was being pursued. Amy returned to work with a newfound realization that the buck truly stops with her state securities administrator, not her firm's management.

SUGGESTED NOTECARDS

- ☐ Define issuer.
- ☐ Define security.
- ☐ Give two examples of a non-security investment.
- ☐ What is a registration statement?
- ☐ What is found on a registration statement?
- ☐ What does incorporation by reference mean?
- ☐ What is a special subscription form?
- ☐ What are the three types of securities registration?
- ☐ Define registration by qualification.
- ☐ Define registration by coordination.
- ☐ Define registration by filing.
- ☐ Define notice filing.
- ☐ What are the requirements for a registration by qualification?
- ☐ What is a stop order?
- ☐ What must be submitted by an issuer performing a registration by coordination?
- ☐ How long must a registration statement be on file before it is valid?
- ☐ Define a Section 402(a) registration exemption.
- ☐ Define a Section 402(b) registration exemption.
- ☐ What securities are exempt under Section 402(a)?
- ☐ What transactions are exempt under Section 402(b)?
- ☐ What is the difference between an offer and a sale of a security?
- ☐ What actions are excluded from the definition of an offer?
- ☐ What securities are required to be registered on a federal level?
- ☐ What jurisdiction does a state have over federal securities?
- ☐ What is a stop order?
- ☐ What specific powers does an administrator have?
- ☐ What must happen for an administrator to pursue criminal charges?
- ☐ What measures can an administrator take to ensure that securities professionals and securities issues comply with regulatory standards?
- ☐ How long can an administrator take in granting a requested hearing?
- ☐ What are the maximum penalties for criminal violations?
- ☐ What damages and liabilities can a registrant be liable for?
- ☐ What is the statute of limitations in pursuing a lawsuit against a registrant?
- ☐ What is rescission?
- ☐ What are the time limits on rescission?
- ☐ What is a final order?
- ☐ What is an interpretive opinion?

Chapter 3 Practice Questions

1. **Which of the following would not be considered a non-exempt issuance of securities?**

   A. A bank offering CDs to its customers

   B. A bank attempting to raise money for expansion by selling shares of ownership that will trade on the NASDAQ

   C. A corporation raising money through the sale of bonds in their company

   D. A small business with less than $10,000,000 in sales that is offering ownership opportunities through radio advertisements on the local news radio station

2. **All of the following would be considered a security except:**

   A. Publicly traded stock

   B. Publicly traded bond

   C. A variable annuity

   D. A commodities future

3. **Which of the following are found on all registration statements?**

   I.   The type of security being issued

   II. The quantity of the security being issued

   III. The amount expected to be raised by issuing

   IV. The contact information of the issuer

   A. I and II only

   B. II and III

   C. I, II, and III

   D. I, II, III, and IV

4. **When a security has not been previously issued and does not qualify for federal registration, the issuer most likely will be required to register the security by:**

   A. Coordination

   B. Qualification

   C. Notice filing

   D. Examination

5. **All of the following are required when an issuer registers by qualification except:**

   A. Financial statements of the issuer

   B. Regulatory and legal history of the issuer

   C. A list of all officers owning more than 1%

   D. A sample of the actual security

6. **Which of the following securities are exempt from registration?**

   I. Companies that only invest in foreign investments
   II. Securities of an insurance company licensed to operate in the state
   III. U.S. government securities
   IV. Securities issued by a local municipality

   A. I and II
   B. I and III
   C. I, II, and III
   D. II, III, and IV

7. **All of the following transactions are exempt under Section 402(b) except:**

   A. Isolated non-issuer transactions
   B. Transactions by the executor of an estate
   C. The initial public offering of a bank's shares
   D. Transactions among underwriters

8. **Section 402(a) exemptions focus on:**

   A. Issuers
   B. Securities
   C. Transactions
   D. Investors

9. **Which of the following are taken into consideration when determining whether a state has jurisdiction over a securities offering:**

   I. Where the person offering was located
   II. Where the person receiving the offer was located
   III. Where a check for the purchase was mailed to
   IV. Where a check for the purchase was mailed from

   A. I only
   B. I and II
   C. I, II, and III
   D. I, II, III, and IV

10. **A state securities administrator would have jurisdiction over all of the following except:**

    A. Non-federally registered securities being offered in their state
    B. Non-federally registered securities being offered only to out-of-state residents by a broker-dealer in their state
    C. Federally registered securities that are part of a fraudulent scheme within their state
    D. Foreign securities purchased by a resident of their state while on vacation outside of their state

11. Which of the following is a power held by a state securities administrator?

    A. Sue a registrant for civil damages

    B. Arrest a registrant accused of criminal activity

    C. Modify the Uniform Securities Act

    D. Conduct investigations

12. All of the following are investigative activities conducted by the administrator except:

    A. Subpoena individuals

    B. Hold hearings

    C. Issue search warrants

    D. Review firm records

13. Which of the following are types of orders issued by an administrator?

    I. Stop order

    II. Cease and desist order

    III. Resume order

    IV. Criminal order

    A. I only

    B. II only

    C. I and II

    D. III and IV

14. When a registrant who is subject to a summary order requests a hearing, the hearing must occur within how many days?

    A. 15 days

    B. 30 days

    C. 60 days

    D. 365 days

15. All of the following are potential penalties for ethical and legal breaches except:

    A. Rescission

    B. Revocation

    C. Fines

    D. Imprisonment

16. **When a civil lawsuit is filed against a securities professional or firm, a guilty party may be liable for which of the following?**

    I.   Cost of the security
    II. Attorney's fees
    III. Potential earnings
    IV. Commissions

    A. I and II
    B. I and IV
    C. I, II, and III
    D. I, II, III, and IV

17. **The statute of limitations on an ethical violation from discovery is:**

    A. 30 days
    B. One year
    C. Two years
    D. Three years

18. **All of the following are possible consequences of a criminal violation of securities laws except:**

    A. Loss of licensure
    B. $50,000 fine per violation
    C. Three years in prison per violation
    D. Civil lawsuits

19. **Which of the following are true regarding rescission?**

    I.   It is offered by a client.
    II. It must be offered within 30 days of a transaction.
    III. The issuer must pay interest.
    IV. A client has 90 days to respond.

    A. II only
    B. III only
    C. I, III, and IV
    D. II, III, and IV

20. **According to the Uniform Securities Act, an interpretive opinion:**

    A. Can only be issued by a court
    B. Is used when a registrant is clearly guilty
    C. Must be issued within 30 days of an appeal
    D. Is used when no further action will be pursued by the administrator

Chapter 3 Practice Question Answers

1. **Answer: A.** Bank CDs offered to customers are not considered securities transactions that state regulators oversee. They would be regulated by the appropriate banking regulators. However, the sale of shares of ownership in a bank that will trade in the open market is considered an issuance of securities that is subject to regulation. Likewise, a corporation raising money through the sale of bonds and a small business (regardless of the size) raising money by selling ownership to the public are both considered a transaction in which securities are issued and are subject to regulation.

2. **Answer: D.** Commodities futures and insurance contracts that do not have a variable component (where a portion of the value is invested in the markets) are not considered securities. Publicly traded stocks, bonds, and options are all considered securities.

3. **Answer: D.** Registration statements contain all the relevant information regarding a security being issued, including the type of security (stock, bond, etc.), the quantity, the amount that will be raised, and the appropriate contact info.

4. **Answer: B.** When a security issuer has no previous information on file about a specific security, it must start from scratch and provide a large amount of info to a state's administrator. Registration by coordination allows a streamlined process for when securities are being issued in more than one state, while a notice filing simply lets an administrator know that a security that is not required to otherwise register is transacting in their state.

5. **Answer: C.** The list of required officers is for those owning 10% or more, not more than 1%. Financial statements, balance sheets, regulatory and legal history, and a sample security must all be provided.

6. **Answer: D.** While many foreign entities may be exempt from registration, a domestic company that only invests in foreign companies must still register. Securities of an insurance company licensed to operate in the state, U.S. government securities, and securities issued by a local municipality are all exempt.

7. **Answer: C.** Though a bank's CDs are exempt from registration requirements, securities of ownership in the bank itself are subject to registration, especially for its initial offering. Transactions by an executor, transactions among underwriters, and isolated non-issuer transactions are all generally exempt.

8. **Answer: B.** Section 402(a) focuses on exempt securities, while Section 402(b) focuses on exempt transactions.

9. **Answer: B.** A state administrator is concerned with where an offer originated and where it was directed. Where funds were mailed to or from has no bearing.

10. **Answer: D.** The state would have no jurisdiction over a foreign issuer that a resident of their state interacted with while out of that state, because the transaction did not originate in the state and was not directed to the state. Non-federally registered securities that are offered to or from individuals in their state would all fall under their jurisdiction. Additionally, any security that is being used in a fraudulent or deceptive scheme within the state, even federally registered securities, would fall under its jurisdiction.

11. **Answer: D.** State securities administrators can conduct investigations as they deem necessary to determine whether any person has violated or will violate state securities law. They do not sue registrants on behalf of the public, but allow individual clients to do that as they see fit. They do not have the power to arrest registrants, but must request the assistance of a court and law enforcement for that to occur. They are not permitted to modify the Uniform Securities Act, since it is put in place by a state's elected officials.

12. **Answer: C.** An administrator does not have the authority to issue search warrants, though it can request that information and records be made available to them. Only a court of law can issue a search warrant. An administrator can subpoena individuals, hold hearings (which is different than operating as a court of law), and review firm records.

13. **Answer: C.** Stop orders, as well as cease and desist orders, are issued by a state administrator. There is no such thing as a resume or criminal order.

14. **Answer: A.** After a hearing has been properly requested, the state administrator must set the hearing within 15 days.

15. **Answer: A.** Rescission is a remedy offered by issuers or advisers who realize they have made a mistake in dealing with a client and want to fix it before matters get worse. It is initiated by the issuer or adviser and not the administrator or courts. Having one's registration revoked, receiving a fine, and imprisonment are all possible consequences of ethical breaches, even though criminal fines and imprisonment cannot be decided by the administrator.

16. **Answer: D.** A professional or firm that is found to have financially damaged a client can be forced to pay an amount that includes the actual cost of any securities, loss due to investment advice, any attorney or court fees incurred by the client, commissions and fees paid to the party in violation, and interest (potential earnings) on those amounts.

17. **Answer: C.** The statute of limitations to bring a suit against a registrant is two years from the date the client discovers the violation, or three years from the date of the original violation itself. This question specifically asked about the statute of limitations from discovery.

18. **Answer: B.** The maximum fine per willful violation is currently $5,000, not $50,000. Someone found in willful violation can also lose his license, be subject to civil lawsuits, and receive up to three years in prison per violation.

19. **Answer: B.** An issuer pays a client the interest they would have otherwise earned on an investment had they not invested in the security or transaction that was reversed. Rescission is offered by an issuer or adviser, not a client. The person or firm offering rescission can do so at any point, but clients must respond to the offer within 30 days of when it is extended.

20. **Answer: D.** An interpretive opinion is used by the administrator when no further charges will be pursued against a registrant. It essentially says that the administrator does not interpret the registrant's actions to be a violation of the law.

CHAPTER FOUR
Communications with Clients and Prospects

(12 questions on the exam)

Unfortunately for anyone required to register under the Uniform Securities Act, arbitrators, judges, and juries tend to side with the public when it comes to disputes about what was communicated. That's because they put the responsibility on professionals to know the laws and make an effort to put things into plain English for their clients.

4.1. DISCLOSURE

The cornerstone of good and ethical communication with clients is the concept of **disclosure,** or revealing what a client needs to know to make an educated decision about your services or about an investment you're presenting them with. That doesn't mean you need to reveal every single fact about your life and career, or every tidbit of information ever generated about a potential investment, just those considered **material facts.** That means that you need to share anything that a reasonable person would want or would need to know as a part of the decision-making process. This would be a good time to reacquaint yourself with the brochure rule mentioned in Chapter One.

As part of the disclosure process it is crucial that you don't misrepresent or omit any material facts. **Misrepresentation** means that a professional doesn't accurately describe or communicate an aspect of his or her qualifications, of his or her services, or of an investment. **Omitting** means that a professional just flat out skips over even mentioning something that a reasonable person would want to know.

> 📖 **Test Note:** If the exam asks whether it is okay to omit facts when dealing with a client/investor, the answer is that it is okay to omit immaterial facts, but not okay to omit material facts. Material facts are those that are relevant to making an informed investment decision.

There are a number of situations that require proper disclosure to a client or potential client, including:

- Clients of an investment adviser or IAR who are provided with reports or investment recommendations prepared by someone else need to be notified of this fact.

- Broker-dealers that are owned by, affiliated with, or under common control of an issuer must disclose this fact to clients and prospects interested in purchasing securities of that issuer.

- Broker-dealers must, upon request, provide customers with any information they are entitled to. Broker-dealers must also respond to any formal written requests or complaints. As such, broker-dealer agents are expected to bring any written complaints to the attention of their broker-dealer.

- Compensation arrangements must be fully disclosed to clients, in addition to meeting the standards discussed in Chapter Five.

- Material conflicts of interest are only acceptable when they are clearly disclosed to the client. Conflicts of interest will be addressed in Chapter Five.

This is not a full list of situations that require disclosure; these are just some key areas where you will be expected to know that disclosure is required. Remember that all material facts should be disclosed. This includes information about:

- The people and firms making transactions or providing advice
- The securities or advice involved
- The person's role in a given transaction
- How the person is compensated

4.1.1. DELIVERY OF THE PROSPECTUS

Another important part of the disclosure process for broker-dealers and agents is the delivery of the prospectus to interested investors. The prospectus, as described earlier, is a detailed description of a securities issue, which must be provided to each investor who is interested in purchasing that security. To ensure that broker-dealers and agents live up to their obligations with regard to prospectus delivery, the SEC has established the following guidelines:

- **Prospectuses must be given for new issues only.** After an issue is no longer considered to be new, the SEC assumes that there is enough information out in the market for investors to make informed decisions, and the prospectus is no longer required.

- **What is considered a new issue?** A stock that has just had an IPO. So if *Shake Shack* goes public, and you buy shares shortly after the IPO, you will be given a prospectus. For stocks that go public on an exchange like the NYSE or the NASDAQ, the prospectus has to be given to anyone who buys up to 25 days after the IPO (after that it is no longer considered a new issue). For stocks that go public over the counter, the prospectus has to be given for up to 90 days after the IPO. There is a difference between the exchanges and the OTC because the SEC assumes that there will be more information out in market about companies that go public on an exchange than over the counter.

- **What else is considered a new issue?** An open-ended mutual fund or variable annuity also requires a prospectus. This is because shares of the mutual fund or annuity are being issued new to each investor. So anyone buying a mutual fund or variable annuity will always receive a prospectus.

- **When does the prospectus need to be given to the customer?** A prospectus must be given to a customer by the confirmation of the transaction. This means, at the time the trade confirmation is given to the customer, which can be no later than when the transaction settles (usually not later than three business days after the trade date).

To complicate matters even more, if you are one of the first investors to buy in an IPO, the broker-dealer will need to give you a preliminary prospectus at least 48 hours prior to the IPO. So this means if you were one the very first investors to buy shares in the *Shake Shack* IPO, you would receive a preliminary prospectus before your purchase.

What these requirements boil down to is the fact that a broker-dealer or agent must keep their customer apprised of all important information related to new issues. This means they must offer full disclosure, which is, in essence, what a prospectus is meant to provide. By making that document available to clients, broker-dealers and agents are performing their duties. Failure to deliver the prospectus in a timely manner will result in regulatory actions against the violating firm.

DELIVERY OF A PROSPECTUS

	Listed and NASDAQ Securities	OTCBB Securities
IPOs	Up to 25 days after offering	Up to 90 days after offering

SUMMARY

4.2. UNLAWFUL REPRESENTATIONS CONCERNING REGISTRATIONS

The financial services industry is overflowing with designations and titles consumers don't understand. In fact, financial regulators have taken steps in recent years to limit the usage of superfluous professional titles, as well as educate the public about what actually means what. This is especially true when it comes to bogus certifications that have to do with working with seniors.

Some titles and distinctions can be misleading to potential clients. For instance, though a professional might earn credentials such as a Certified Financial Planner (CFP) or Certified Financial Analyst (CFA), such distinctions are not endorsed by FINRA. Instead, they are bestowed upon a professional by an independent organization, and that should never be represented as FINRA approval or certification. To make such a claim would constitute misrepresentation and represent a violation of disclosure requirements.

As far as regulators and the exam are concerned, it is crucial that you know that misrepresenting yourself with superfluous designations, as well as misrepresenting your securities registrations or licensing exams, will land you in boiling hot water. Put simply, you are not permitted to claim you are something you are not, or that passing this exam and getting licensed represents something that it doesn't.

By passing this exam and getting registered, you've simply done those two things and nothing more. You are not approved by the SEC, FINRA, or your state's securities administrator. You're not certified as any kind of specialist in one type of securities or another. You simply have demonstrated the minimum required level of knowledge to provide investment advice or transact in securities, and you've properly notified regulators that you'll be selling them.

 Test Note: Securities, like persons, are registered with the regulatory authorities; they are not approved. To suggest otherwise is misleading, untrue, and will get you in trouble with regulators.

4.3. PERFORMANCE GUARANTEES

There are very few guarantees in the investment world. In fact, with the exception of U.S. government guaranteed securities, the word "guaranteed" cannot even be used. Even in that case, you cannot guarantee a rate of return, only that a client will receive their principal and interest should she hold a government bond to its maturity (termination) date. Investment advisers and IARs are prohibited from making guarantees about gains or losses with the advice they provide. It is also prohibited for broker-dealers to guarantee that customers will not lose money. In other words, your broker cannot offer to make up the difference on a loss.

That means securities professionals cannot make any kind of promises about any investment's potential growth, its safety, or the level of performance a client's portfolio will experience in general if the client works with that professional.

4.4. CLIENT CONTRACTS

At the core of the formal client-professional relationship, especially investment advisory relationships, is the client contract. This document outlines the services that a securities professional will provide his or her clients, spells out what the fees or commissions will be, discloses conflicts of interest, etc. Since this is such an important piece of documentation, the NASAA has put standards in place regarding the contract.

New and renewed investment advisory contracts must:

- Be in writing

- Outline all services to be provided

- Contain a term (time limit) for the contract

- Contain the advisory fee

- Include the formula for calculating the fee

- Specify the amount of the fee to be returned if the client terminates early

- Specify whether the contract grants discretionary authority to the adviser over the client's portfolio

- Include specific wording that the contract may not be assigned to another professional without the client's consent

- State that the investment adviser will not be compensated on the basis of capital gains or capital appreciation (performance-based fees)

- If the investment adviser is a partnership, notify clients if change in the partnership (a partner has been added or left) has occurred

Further, no advisory contract can be entered into or can contain language that requires a client to waive any part of his or her rights under the Investment Advisers Act of 1940.

⚡ EXERCISE

CHOOSE ALLOWED OR NOT ALLOWED

1. _____ When meeting with a new client, agent Earnest Starr fails to disclose his past work as a commercial actor.

2. _____ Abel Mann, an agent, effects a transaction in a new security. He provides a copy of the preliminary prospectus on the day that the client receives a trade confirmation and then gives his client a copy of the final prospectus one day later.

3. _____ Cindy Redd, an investment adviser, publishes an advertisement in which she notes that she has passed all of her licensing exams and is properly registered with FINRA.

4. _____ Investment adviser Serta Nement regularly promises potential clients that if they follow her advice their investments will see significant gains.

5. ____ Bill Vonn, an investment adviser, completes a contract with a new client. In the contract, Bill's fee is not listed; however, he and his client have a verbal agreement to revise the contract upon agreeing to an acceptable rate of compensation.

ANSWERS

1. **Allowed.** Starr's past career endeavors are not material facts for a client considering whether or not to use his services.

2. **Not allowed.** A final prospectus must be delivered to the client no later than the date of trade confirmation.

3. **Allowed.** It is perfectly fine to say that you are registered with FINRA as long as that is true. To state that you are approved or certified by FINRA, however, would not be allowed.

4. **Not allowed.** Promising gains is considered to be a guarantee, which is prohibited.

5. **Not allowed.** The adviser's fee must be stated in the original contract.

4.4.1. TYPES OF CLIENT ACCOUNTS

When opening new accounts with a broker-dealer, customers have several different options. There are three basic account types that are typically maintained at most broker-dealers: cash accounts, margin accounts, and option accounts. Before a client becomes involved in making transactions, she should set up an account choosing one of these methods.

Let's look at the differences between each of these account types.

A **cash account** is one that does not involve credit in any way. Simply put, the customer pays in cash for each transaction. That means each security purchased must be paid in full at the time of sale.

In a **margin account** an investor can use credit to pay for some portion of the security. Typically, the investor pays part of the price of the security and the broker-dealer loans the investor funds for the remaining amount due. The borrowed funds must be secured by the customer with money or securities that are placed in the customer's account at the broker-dealer. The SEC mandates an initial margin requirement of 50%, meaning the customer must put down at least half of the price of the stock in the margin account. Once securities have been purchased in the account, the customer must maintain 25% equity value of the securities. In order for the account to be valid, a written margin agreement must be signed by the customer promptly after the initial margin transaction.

Finally, an **options account** allows the investor to purchase options to buy or sell a specific security at a set price by a certain date. Call options allow the investor to buy securities at a certain price on or before a certain date; put options allow the investor to sell a security at a certain price on or before a given date. As options are speculative and thus inherently risky for investors, a client must provide financial information, investment objectives, and document previous investment experience before opening this type of account.

4.5. **FRAUD**

Any act, practice, or course of business that is manipulative or deceptive may be considered **fraud**. This includes misrepresenting and omitting material facts. Fraud is deemed such a tremendous violation that all *persons* are prohibited from engaging in fraudulent activity in connection with securities offers and transactions under the Uniform Securities Act. This means that even persons that don't need to register under the Act, such as federal covered advisers and out-of-state broker-dealers who only deal with institutional clients, can still have action taken against them by a state administrator if they engage in fraud in connection with a securities offer or transaction in that state.

Certain activities have been explicitly declared to be fraudulent for investment advisers:

1. Using advertising that does not comply with the standards set forth by the Investment Advisers Act of 1940

2. Taking custody of client funds or securities without meeting the necessary safekeeping requirements

3. Paying cash for client solicitations unless:

   a. the solicitor is not subject to an order from the SEC and has not been convicted of a relevant felony or misdemeanor within the past ten years,

   b. the payment is made based on a written agreement, and

   c. the compensation arrangement is disclosed to the client in writing

4. Failing to disclose to a client all material facts concerning:

   a. a financial condition that is reasonably likely to impair the adviser's ability to meet a contractual commitment to clients, if the investment adviser is subject to net capital requirements

   b. a legal or disciplinary event that is material to an evaluation of the adviser's integrity or ability to meet contractual commitments to clients

One activity that is deemed fraudulent for broker-dealers and agents is market manipulation. This is where the broker-dealer or agent engages in a transaction by deceptive means, generally with the intention of affecting the price of a security. The violation is discussed in greater detail in Chapter Five. Misrepresenting the status of a client's account, such as by telling the client that her portfolio is performing differently than it actually is, is another example of fraud.

4.5.1. COMMON CATEGORIES OF INVESTMENT ADVISORY FRAUD

Fraud is an exceptionally broad concept that may show up in any part of a securities professional's business. To avoid committing fraud, securities professionals and firms must remain honest in their dealings with clients and the public. Some common types of investment advisory fraud that have been prosecuted by the SEC are listed below (taken from an academic paper by Dimmi and Gerkin). These include:

- **Direct theft.** The adviser steals directly from clients and hides it with false statements.

- **Self-dealing.** The adviser illegally profits from his client's investments (e.g., front-running, when a professional uses knowledge of a client's intent to make a large order, to profit from a change in the price of the security).

- **Ponzi schemes.** An adviser promises high returns to new investors, but instead of investing the money, he pays the returns to the early investors. The Ponzi scheme will fall apart when the adviser can no longer find new investors.

- **Overstating assets.** An investment adviser overstates returns and account values and then charges larger fees based on these overstated values.

4.6. CODE OF ETHICS AND ACCESS PERSONS

The SEC says that registered investment advisers must adopt and enforce a **code of ethics** for all supervised persons. The purpose of this rule is to prevent fraud by reminding advisory firms of their fiduciary responsibility to their clients. Interestingly, the SEC does not require that firms adopt a specific standard of ethics, but instead, they must develop their *own* standards. That code of ethics must put a priority on protecting **material inside information** and on overseeing certain employees' personal trading.

The adviser must describe its code of ethics to clients, it must include a description of the ethics code in Form ADV Part 2A, and it must furnish a copy of its ethics code to clients upon request. This would make a great multiple choice question on an exam.

Violations of the code of ethics should be reported promptly.

An important part of this rule is the requirement that advisers monitor the personal securities transactions of access persons to prevent the misuse of nonpublic information.

Remember, **access persons** include employees, directors, officers, and fiduciaries with access to inside information about securities, gained from their work with or for an investment adviser. The investments of persons must be monitored on an ongoing basis.

Reporting requirements. Access persons must report their securities holdings to the chief compliance officer of the firm within 10 days of becoming an access person and then again at least annually. All securities are reportable with the following five exceptions:

- Government securities
- Money market instruments such as CDs
- Money market funds
- Unaffiliated mutual fund shares
- Unit investment trust securities which are invested exclusively in unaffiliated mutual fund shares

Access persons must also report to the firm any personal securities transactions within 30 days of each calendar quarter, and private placements and IPO investments by access persons must be cleared with the firm in advance. The rule does not require the firm to adopt a specific code of behavior, but it requires a minimum standard of fiduciary behavior and compliance with securities laws. The chief compliance officer must review access persons' securities transaction reports.

Firms must keep a written acknowledgment from each access person that he received the code of ethics. Records of securities transactions by access persons must be kept for at least five years. Such records must include a list of access persons, copies of the code of ethics, reports made by access persons, and any records of violations and corrective actions.

The rule specifically identifies portfolio managers as being access persons, and it states that any supervised person, including "administrative, technical and clerical personnel" who "have information about investment recommendations whose effect may not yet be felt in the marketplace" may be access persons. Any supervised person could be an access person; the determining factor is access to material nonpublic information.

Finally, the rule states that "if the firm's primary business is providing investment advice, then all of its directors, officers and partners are access persons."

No personal securities reporting is required if:

- The transactions stem from an automatic investment plan
- The securities in question are in accounts that the access person does not control or influence
- The adviser has just one access person and the firm keeps records of the access person's holdings and transactions

☝ EXERCISE

CHOOSE FRAUDULENT OR NOT FRAUDULENT

1. _____ An investment adviser fails to disclose facts about a financial condition that is not material to its effectiveness as a firm.

2. _____ An investment adviser has a written agreement that allows it to pay cash to an independent solicitor for bringing clients to the firm.

3. ____ **An adviser purchases a security for his own account in advance of purchasing a large block of the same securities for a client. He makes this purchase because he expects the price of the security to get a boost from his client's purchase.**

4. ____ **An employee of a firm reports his securities holdings to the firm's compliance office one week after first obtaining inside information.**

ANSWERS

1. **Not fraudulent.** Only financial conditions that are reasonably likely to impair an adviser's ability to meet a contractual commitment to clients must be reported.

2. **Not fraudulent.** Paying cash under a written agreement is permissible.

3. **Fraudulent.** An adviser who uses his knowledge to purchase the same securities ahead of a client (hoping to gain from a bump in the price of the security) has engaged in front-running, and this practice is not allowed.

4. **Not fraudulent.** An employee must report his or her securities holdings to a firm's compliance office within 10 days of becoming an access person.

4.7. ADVERTISING

Unless you were born into a well-connected family, clients won't likely just fall into your lap. You're going to have to market and advertise yourself and your firm to make a living. Of course, that means that your state securities administrator is going to have some standards about what you put into print and the documentation you need to provide to your clients and prospects. And keep in mind that in the securities industry, an advertisement is any communication about investment services that is addressed to more than one person. That means that websites, social media forums, emails, printed reports, and press releases are all considered to be advertisements.

As with everything else, the core of all rules about advertising and marketing comes down to two things every client and prospect is entitled to honesty and transparency.

Specifically prohibited in advertisements for investment advisers and investment adviser representatives are:

- Testimonials regarding services provided by an investment adviser or its representatives unless they are taken from an independent third-party website; these testimonials are subject to certain restrictions described below (Broker-dealers are permitted to use testimonials, which are also subject to certain restrictions.)

- References to past recommendations, unless the IA or IAR provides a list of *all* recommendations he has made for at least 12 months, as well as a statement that any past success is no guarantee of future results

- Any statements that would communicate or imply that a graph, chart, formula, or other device can by itself determine which securities are best to buy or sell, or when they should be bought or sold

- Any promises of a free report, research, or analysis, unless those items will truly be provided free of charge

- Any statements that imply directly or indirectly that an advertisement is approved by the state administrator or regulators

- Any false or misleading material statements

Broker-dealers are prohibited from publishing or circulating any kind of communication (including advertisements) that claims to report any transaction or quotation unless the broker-dealer believes that the transaction or quotation is bona fide (true). Broker-dealers also must not use advertising in a deceptive or misleading manner. This means they must avoid nonfactual data and conjecture, as well as any displays designed to detract from the effect of any prospectus or disclosure.

Offering or selling securities that are unregistered on both the state and federal level and that do not qualify for an exemption is illegal.

The state securities administrator may require that advertising intended to be distributed to prospective investors (including the clients or prospective clients of an investment adviser) be filed with the administrator.

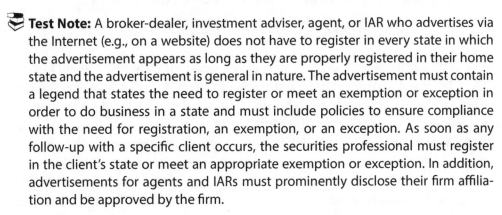 **Test Note:** A broker-dealer, investment adviser, agent, or IAR who advertises via the Internet (e.g., on a website) does not have to register in every state in which the advertisement appears as long as they are properly registered in their home state and the advertisement is general in nature. The advertisement must contain a legend that states the need to register or meet an exemption or exception in order to do business in a state and must include policies to ensure compliance with the need for registration, an exemption, or an exception. As soon as any follow-up with a specific client occurs, the securities professional must register in the client's state or meet an appropriate exemption or exception. In addition, advertisements for agents and IARs must prominently disclose their firm affiliation and be approved by the firm.

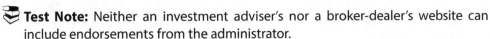 **Test Note:** Neither an investment adviser's nor a broker-dealer's website can include endorsements from the administrator.

Test Note: Investment advisers may not disclose the identity or affairs of any clients without being required to by law, unless the client consents to the disclosure.

4.7.1. TESTIMONIALS FOR INVESTMENT ADVISERS

Investment advisers and their representatives are generally prohibited from advertising testimonials or soliciting their clients for testimonials. In 2014, however, the SEC released new guidance which allows IAs and IARs to feature public testimonials on their own social media sites that have appeared on third-party social media sites, such as Yelp. This is allowed only if all testimonials about the IA or IAR on the site are included and the site is independent from the IA or IAR. In this case, the word testimonial includes both positive and negative experiences with an adviser. The IA or IAR must not have any ability to influence the commentary on the third-party site. If the IA or IAR posts commentary on the site or influences commentary in any way, posting the testimonial would be prohibited. Also, if an IA or IAR has paid for the commentary, it cannot be used. Ratings from the third-party site may also be posted as long as the third-party developed the rating system rather than the IA or IAR.

The SEC has also said that IAs may direct customers to their own social media site (i.e., "Check us out on Facebook!") and it will not be considered soliciting testimonials from customers. Additionally, lists of followers on social media sites will not be considered testimonials or endorsements as long as the firm does not suggest that these are clients or that they had favorable experiences as clients of the firm.

Also, IAs and IARs may point to a third-party website where there is public commentary about their business. They may even include the third-party's website, as long as they are independent from the website. For example, they may say "Check us out on Yelp."

The SEC has warned IAs that directing people to third-party fan pages with commentary about the IA or IAR may be viewed as directing customers to testimonials.

4.8. ELECTRONIC COMMUNICATIONS AND SOCIAL MEDIA

Electronic communications include websites, blogs, webinars, and social media sites such as Twitter and Facebook. For regulatory purposes, electronic communications can contain static and interactive content, and each have different rules associated with them. These rules were devised for broker-dealers and their agents.

FINRA defines static content as content that stays on the website until it is removed by the firm or the site's administrator. Static content is usually available to all users of the site. For instance, profiles of representatives and background information on the firm are examples of static content. Interactive content refers to real-time communications, such as instant messaging, Twitter, and interactive webinars. Communications having static content generally require approval by a registered principal prior to being posted. Interactive, real-time communications do not require prior approval by a principal in general. The exception to this rule is where interactive electronic communications recommend a specific investment product, in which case firms are urged by FINRA to have a principal approve the content prior to posting because the recommendations will trigger suitability rules.

With regard to electronic communications and social media, all firms are expected to develop and adopt policies and procedures to ensure that electronic communications with the public comply with regulations. Any third-party links on a firm's website must also comply with FINRA regulations and contain no false or misleading information. Firms must enact systems to supervise, train and educate their personnel who are permitted to use social media for business purposes.

Like other broker-dealer communications with the public, communications via electronic media must be kept on file and maintained for three years.

4.8.1. COMMON TYPES OF SOCIAL MEDIA OR ELECTRONIC COMMUNICATIONS FRAUD

As the popularity of social media increases, so do the fraudulent investment schemes that rely on social media. Social media presents an environment where information is shared and exchanged among users. Users recommend products that they like to others, creating an environment where misleading and false information can be easily passed on. In addition, people commonly reveal intimate details of their lives, presenting a situation ripe for fraud. Common forms of social media fraud include:

- **"Pump and dumps."** These schemes typically involve "pumping" up the price of a security through false or misleading information across an array of social media sites. Posts on these sites will often claim to have inside information and urge investors to purchase a stock quickly to get in early on the investment. The individuals promoting the stock then profit by "dumping" any shares they may own at an inflated value before the rest of the investors sell.

- **High-yield investment programs (HYIPs).** HYIPs are typically unregistered investments that are offered on websites promising high yields at little to no risk to investors. Individuals promoting these fraudulent offerings will often go to Twitter, Facebook, or other social media sites to tout their alleged high returns and low risk, encouraging interested parties to share the information with others and visit the HYIP website for further details. The sites often advertise, "huge," "handsome," or "guaranteed" returns. While they often draw investors, their promises of guaranteed, high performance and unregistered status make most of these sites fraudulent.

- **Misleading research opinions and touting.** When parties publish misleading information on investment newsletters about a security, it is considered fraud. This occurs when third-parties publish inaccurate research opinions, funded by an investment adviser, broker-dealer, or issuer. This also occurs when a third-party recommends or **touts** a security in exchange for a fee, but does not accurately disclose the relationship and compensation received from an issuer or broker-dealer in the advertisement.

4.9. BROKER-DEALERS OPERATING WITHIN A BANK SETTING

Many broker-dealers operate within bank settings. Because this may lead retail customers to assume that banking rules apply to broker-dealers, the NASAA has issued model rules regarding broker-dealers who operate within a bank setting.

1. The broker-dealer should offer its services in an area that is separate from the location where retail banking activities are taking place.

2. The broker-dealer's name needs to be clearly stated where the broker-dealer activity is taking place.

3. The broker-dealer needs to distinguish its services from the retail bank.

4. The broker-dealer must disclose orally and in writing that the securities purchased/sold by the broker-dealer are not insured by the FDIC, are not guaranteed by the bank, and are subject to investment risks such as loss of principal. The broker-dealer should try to get a written acknowledgment of the disclosures at the time that a client opens the account.

5. If a representative of the broker-dealer makes a reference to SIPC coverage, she must clearly explain (in written or oral form) the coverage to the client.

6. Communications with the public that include the location of the broker-dealer must include the information stated in number 4 above. The following shortened version may be used in most advertising contexts:
   » Not FDIC Insured
   » No Bank Guarantee
   » May Lose Value

4.10. INVESTMENT COMPANY COMMUNICATIONS

NASAA has certain rules regarding the communications broker-dealers and agents who are selling shares in an investment company can make to their clients. Investment companies include unit investment trusts, closed-end funds, open-end funds (mutual funds), and face amount certificates. These rules include:

- All sales charges that may be associated with purchasing, retaining, or redeeming the shares must be disclosed to clients.

- Solicitors cannot call a fund "no load" or say it has no sales charge if there is a front-end sales charge, a contingent deferred sales charge, or a marketing or service fee that exceeds 0.25% of the average assets of the fund per year (or for a closed-end fund, any underwriting fees or other offering expenses).

- All due to breakpoints need to be disclosed.

- The recommendation of a particular class of investment company shares (A-, B-, or C-shares) must be suitable for the investor.

- Solicitors should not recommend the purchase of multiple investment company funds that have the same investment objective because the client will end up paying higher fees for no more diversification.

- Solicitors should not recommend the sale of a client's current mutual fund for a new mutual fund with a similar investment objective unless it is genuinely suitable for the client (otherwise the client will incur unnecessary fees).

- Solicitors should not state a mutual fund's current yield or income without reporting the fund's average annual return for one-, five-, and ten-year periods and explaining the difference between current yield and annual return.

- Solicitors cannot imply that investing in an investment company is comparable to investing in a bank certificate of deposit without explaining the differences in risk between the two investments, and without explaining that investment company funds are not insured by the FDIC.

- Solicitors must not mention or imply insurance, credit quality, or guarantees for a security without disclosing other relevant kinds of investment risk, such as interest rate, market, political, liquidity, and exchange rate risks.

- Solicitors are prohibited from selling dividends by claiming that the customer would benefit from a dividend and using that as a reason for them to purchase a security in situations when there would be no actual benefit.

- Solicitors may not make projections of future performances or unwarranted statements. Statements based on insider information are also prohibited.

- Simply delivering a prospectus does not count as full and fair disclosure. It is the responsibility of the broker-dealer or agent involved to make sure that all material facts involving a security are described to a client in order to provide full disclosure.

- Solicitors are prohibited from emphasizing certain information in a prospectus by marking up or highlighting parts of the prospectus.

EXERCISE

ANSWER TRUE OR FALSE

1. _____ **Broker-dealers are permitted to use customer testimonials in their advertisements.**

2. ____ **Investment adviser representatives can never use references or past recommendations as part of their advertising efforts.**

3. ____ **Graphs and charts are prohibited from advertisements for investment advisers and investment adviser representatives.**

4. ____ **Third-party links provided on a broker-dealer firm's website are always subject to FINRA guidelines.**

5. ____ **Broker-dealers operating within a bank setting should always offer their services in an area distinct from where regular banking activity takes place.**

6. ____ **As long as an agent selling shares of a mutual fund delivers a final prospectus before a given sales date, full disclosure has been provided.**

ANSWERS

1. **True.** Broker-dealers may use customer testimonials; investment advisers may only use third-party testimonials in specific instances. .

2. **False.** An investment adviser representative can use references and past recommendations as long as she provides a list of all recommendations she has made for at least the past 12 months.

3. **False.** Graphs, charts, and formulas are not prohibited; however, statements or implications that would lead one to believe they are representative of a security's potential merits are not allowed.

4. **True.** Any third-party link that appears on a firm's website must be in compliance with FINRA regulations.

5. **True.** Broker-dealers operating in a bank should always make their location distinct from the place where regular banking takes place.

6. **False.** While the delivery of a prospectus is required, it alone does not represent full disclosure. A securities professional is responsible for explaining all material facts to a client. Simply handing the client a copy of a prospectus alone does not meet this requirement.

4.11. PRACTICAL APPLICATION

The past six months have been exciting for Amy Adams. After getting hired at one of the biggest firms on Wall Street, she buckled down and studied hard for all her securities licensing exams. Needless to say, after she passed, she was more than excited to email all her family members and friends and let them know that her state's securities administrator had certified and approved her to help them with their investment needs.

Her excitement was dampened a little when she received a frantic call from her firm's compliance department informing her that she needed to be extremely careful about misrepresenting her qualifications, the licensing process, and her firm. As part of the conversation, the compliance department informed Amy Adams that she would need to take a refresher course on "Communicating with the Public."

As part of the class, Amy met other professionals who had made similar novice mistakes. Brad was required to attend after using an overly simplified advisory contract that did not include the client's fee and other important information. Sarah was asked to attend after misrepresenting the safety of some corporate bonds when she told a client that the bonds were guaranteed even though they were not.

After the class and her discussions, it finally clicked for Amy. She realized that the heart of the rules about communication with clients is that full and honest disclosure helps preserve a client's ability to make an informed choice about what they're investing in or whom they're working with.

☐ Define the concept of disclosure.

☐ Why are clients and prospects entitled to proper disclosure?

☐ What is a material fact?

☐ What is the difference between misrepresentation and omission?

☐ When must a prospectus be provided for a new offering?

☐ What rule must be followed for research reports prepared by someone else?

☐ How do an issuer and a broker-dealer being affiliated affect disclosure?

☐ What can a professional not communicate regarding his or her registration?

☐ When can a professional offer a performance guarantee?

☐ What details must be included in an investment advisory contract?

☐ Under what conditions can a professional reference past recommendations?

☐ What cannot be communicated about a chart, formula, or graph?

☐ What is the state administrator's role in approving advertisements?

Chapter 4 Practice Questions

1. **Which of the following describes a material fact that would likely need to be disclosed to a customer?**

    A. That a professional is not a Certified Financial Planner
    B. The number of years a professional has been licensed
    C. The fees associated with an account
    D. That another professional at the firm has been sued for securities fraud, even though that professional won't be handling the client's account

2. **Which of the following would require disclosure to a client?**

    I. That research was prepared by a third party
    II. That a security is a new offering
    III. That a professional previously worked for a company that issues securities
    IV. That a professional has previously filed for bankruptcy.

    A. I and II
    B. II and III
    C. I, II, and III
    D. I, II, III, and IV

3. **When should a preliminary prospectus be delivered to a client?**

    A. By the time of purchase confirmation
    B. At least 48 hours prior to sale confirmation
    C. Within 48 hours of sale confirmation
    D. Within 10 business days of trade settlement

4. **Which of the following would be considered inappropriate for professionals to state about their registration?**

    A. That they've passed the Series 63
    B. That they are registered to sell securities in their state
    C. That they have never had a complaint filed against their registration
    D. That their practice is approved by their state's securities administrator

5. **Which of the following statements is true of performance guarantees?**

    A. They cannot be offered to customers
    B. They can be offered only to customers who purchase U.S. Treasury securities
    C. They can be offered only if a client signs a waiver of their rights
    D. They're permitted as long as a professional publishes a list of all his or her recommendations for the previous 12 months

6. **Which of the following details must be included in an investment advisory contract?**

    I.   The fee associated with the contract
    II. The length of time of the contract
    III. Whether the contract grants discretionary authority or not
    IV. Language prohibiting the contract from being assigned to another professional without client permission

    A. I and II
    B. I, II, and III
    C. I, II, and IV
    D. I, II, III, and IV

7. **Under what condition can a professional reference his or her previous securities recommendations?**

    A. Never
    B. Only when working with institutional clients
    C. If he or she provides the client a list of all recommendations made during the previous 12 months
    D. Only upon request of the client

8. **Professionals are prohibited from offering free research reports unless:**

    A. They are written by a third party
    B. They are part of an existing advisory contract
    C. They are free from graphs, charts, or tables
    D. They're actually free

9. **Which of the following are true of advertisements for securities, firms, and professionals?**

    I.   They must not be deceptive
    II. They must be approved by each state
    III. Prices used must represent realistic prices
    IV. They cannot show historical rates of return for an investment

    A. I only
    B. I and III
    C. I, II, and IV
    D. I, II, III, and IV

10. **All of the following are permitted in the advertising about a securities professional except:**

    A. Services offered
    B. Firm affiliation
    C. Professional designations
    D. Non-third-party testimonials for investment advisers and their representatives

Chapter 4 Practice Question Answers

1. **Answer: C.** The fees associated with an account would be material to the decision-making process for a customer and must be included. While holding an additional, non-mandatory designation such as the CFP or having worked in the industry for many years may be advantageous for a professional to mention, they are not required since they'd be unlikely to cause a potential client to find someone else. Lawsuits against professionals not working with a client's account would not be considered material and would not need to be disclosed.

2. **Answer: A.** Research prepared by a third party must be accurately represented as such and should not be passed off as the research of an investment adviser or investment adviser representative. Securities that are new offerings must be disclosed as such and purchasers must be provided with a prospectus by the confirmation due date. Previously working for a securities issuer and filing a personal bankruptcy would not require disclosure unless they somehow caused a current conflict of interest.

3. **Answer: B.** A preliminary prospectus must be delivered to clients at least 48 hours prior to the confirmation of a sale. The final prospectus must be delivered by the date of purchase confirmation.

4. **Answer: D.** It is unethical for professionals to misrepresent that they or their practice is somehow approved by the state securities administrator. Communicating that professionals have passed the Series 63, are registered to sell securities, and have never had a complaint are not unethical as long as the statements are true.

5. **Answer: A.** Performance guarantees cannot be offered to customers, since performance can never truly be guaranteed. This is different than communicating that the principal and interest payments of U.S. Treasury securities are guaranteed by the U.S. Treasury, since that makes no direct guarantees of the performance of the actual security based on the price at which it is purchased. It is unethical to ask a client to waive her rights under any of the securities acts. Professionals are permitted to share their recommendation history, not a performance guarantee, if they provide all previous recommendations for the previous 12 months.

6. **Answer: D.** All these items, in addition to numerous others, must be included in an investment advisory contract.

7. **Answer: C.** In order to reference a past recommendation, a professional must provide a list of all his or her recommendations for a minimum of the past 12 months.

8. **Answer: D.** Professionals and firms can offer free research reports, but only if they're actually free. In other words, professionals and firms cannot do a bait and switch on a client or prospect, offering them a free service but then later requiring them to pay for it or something else.

9. **Answer: B.** Above all else, advertisements must not be deceptive. Additionally, any prices used in referencing securities must use realistic prices, which should not be manipulated to make a firm or professional look better. Advertisements do not need to be approved by the state securities administrator under the USA, and historical rates of return are permitted (with proper disclosures).

10. **Answer: D.** It is unethical for an investment adviser or its representatives to use testimonials

in their advertisements unless the testimonials are provided by an independent third-party social media site and include all testimonials about the investment adviser published on that site. There is nothing unethical about discussing the services someone offers and legitimate professional designations. Firm affiliation *should* be mentioned.

CHAPTER FIVE
Ethical Practices and Obligations

(15 questions on the exam)

5.1. COMPENSATION

Compensation can be a touchy subject between professionals and their clients. No client likes paying more than they have to for the services they need, but most professionals are in this business with the intent of earning as good of a living as possible. Add to this tension the fact that compensation is one of the easiest places to cut costs or be dishonest to gain an edge. Thus, designing one's compensation structure and then fairly disclosing it to the investing public is a process that must be done with the utmost care and highest level of honesty.

Know this: your state securities administrator doesn't have a beef against professionals and firms who make a ton of money. Heck, I'd even go so far as to say that they're all for it. The only thing that they want to ensure is that you're getting paid in a way that doesn't open investors up to additional risks or unfairly limit their options, as well as making sure your compensation structures are clearly communicated in a way that allows the public to make an informed decision.

5.1.1. FEES

The most basic rule about an investment adviser's fee, but also the most nebulous, is that an adviser's fee must not be unreasonable. This means that the fee should not too greatly exceed what other advisers charge for the same services, nor should it vary too greatly from what that adviser charges his or her other clients for the same services. In addition to a fee being reasonable, there are also certain disclosures and requirements for financial professionals when working with their clients.

All conflicts of interest arising from an investment adviser's or IAR's compensation structure as it relates to a client must be disclosed to the client *in writing*. This includes situations where a securities professional is:

- Receiving fees, commissions, or compensation that are in addition to those previously communicated to the client

- Charging a client an advisory fee in addition to a commission, or vice versa

Also, recall that registered advisers are prohibited from using performance-based fees with their clients unless the clients meet certain requirements. This helps limit the exposure of unsophisticated clients who don't understand that performance-based fees can give an incentive to a professional to take greater than average risks.

5.1.2. **COMMISSIONS, MARKUPS, AND MARKDOWNS**

Unlike investment advisers, broker-dealers and agents are not paid as a percentage of assets under management. Instead, they make money through commissions, markups, markdowns, and spreads. When the firm acts as a broker, it is paid through commissions. When the firm acts as a **dealer**, it is putting its own money at risk, buying or selling securities out of its own inventory. It profits by the **spread** between what it bought the security for (bid) and what it sells it for (ask). A firm also makes money off of markups on securities that it sells and markdowns on securities that it buys.

Each of these modes of compensation must be reasonable and justifiable compared to the services performed and the market value of the securities. That means that a firm cannot charge commission fees that are substantially different from the industry's going rate. For the dealer side of the broker-dealer equation, the firm must keep its prices in line with the most recent market transactions. For example, if a dealer is selling a bond from the firm's inventory that sold the prior day for $850, it cannot charge a price of $900. That would be an unreasonable price for the security based on the market rate. Similarly, a firm could not expect to purchase the same bond from a customer for a markdown price of $800. That would also constitute an unreasonable purchase price.

Determining what is fair and reasonable with respect to markups, markdowns, and commissions has always been a challenging issue for the securities industry. In an effort to make things clearer, in 1943 FINRA published the **5% policy**, a quasi-ceiling on markups, markdowns, and commissions. Technology has lowered trading and execution costs in the decades since the 5% policy was born, and markups and spreads are much lower today. Still, FINRA has kept the 5% policy in its rules because it's a useful suggested ceiling. FINRA says markups and spreads should be based on the prevailing market price or the broker-dealer's cost if a prevailing market price is not readily available. FINRA adds the following additional considerations to help determine whether a markup or markdown is fair and reasonable:

- **Type of security**—some securities customarily carry higher markups than others

- **Availability**—the availability of a security may have a bearing on the markup

- **Price of security and amount of money involved**—both can be relevant factors

- **Disclosure**—disclosure of fees ahead of time is encouraged, and such disclosure should provide the total dollar amount and percentage

- **The pattern of markups**—a markup pattern of more than 5% may be considered unfair and unreasonable

- **The nature of the member's business**—if a broker-dealer provides additional services and facilities to the customer, a higher markup may be justified

- **Exempted securities**—securities requiring a prospectus (e.g., initial public offerings, mutual funds, variable annuities) and exempt securities (e.g., municipal securities) are generally exempt from the 5% policy

Additionally, agents and broker-dealers should not charge unfair fees for simple miscellaneous duties (making deposits, transferring securities, etc.) associated with a client's account. The NASAA has also declared it unethical for agents or broker-dealers to split or pay commissions (or any other compensation) from a transaction with anyone who is not appropriately licensed to sell that particular type of security, including clerical staff, referral sources, or even the clients themselves. The rule also says that it is a violation to split commissions with agents who do not work for the same broker-dealer or for a broker-dealer under the same common control.

5.1.3. **SOFT-DOLLAR ARRANGEMENTS**

Broker-dealers may offer free access to **soft dollar** benefits to investment advisers who direct client transactions through said broker-dealers. These products are designed to help the adviser build the business or learn more about certain products. These benefits ultimately have a value and a cost for which an investment adviser did not have to pay out of pocket. That represents an incentive to choose one broker-dealer's services over another and, in turn, a conflict of interest, since the cost for these services is ultimately reflected in the commissions paid by the investment adviser's clients.

To protect against abuse and conflicts of interest, the SEC has determined that only certain services that directly benefit a firm's clients can be accepted on a soft-dollar basis. These include:

- Research publications
- Trade execution
- Electronic services that provide market data
- Software that assists in helping to perform investment analysis
- Seminars for agents and representatives on topics appropriate to their work
- Custodial and clearing services

Additionally, certain things *cannot* be accepted on a soft-dollar basis:

- Overhead related expenses, such as office space, administrative or clerical labor, or furniture
- Compensation for referrals
- Salaries
- Cell phones and computers
- Anything that benefits the adviser but not the clients

Test Note: Investment advisers who receive soft-dollar services from broker-dealers for using them to execute trades must disclose this compensation to clients.

5.1.3.1. Compensation Disclosures

One thing to keep in mind regarding the Series 63 exam: a good general principal to go by is "Disclose, disclose, disclose." That principle applies to compensation arrangements for all securities professionals.

For investment advisers and investment adviser representatives, any fees charged as well as the formula by which those fees are determined must be included in every client contract. Without that written documentation, IAs and IARs cannot offer advice to a prospective client.

For broker-dealers and their agents, all disclosures related to compensation must be made at or before the completion of a transaction (this means by the time of settlement).

Finally, in the case of soft-dollar arrangements between a brokerage firm and an investment adviser, the latter firm must always disclose this form of compensation to clients.

Failure to comply with any of these disclosure requirements constitutes a violation of securities regulations and can lead to administrative action.

5.1.4. PAYING SOLICITORS FOR ADVISORY BUSINESS

A registered investment adviser may not make cash payments to a third-party for soliciting clients, unless all of the following conditions are met:

- The solicitor has not been subject to any outstanding SEC orders barring his activity.

- The solicitor has not been convicted of a securities-related felony or misdemeanor within the past ten years.

- The solicitor has not willfully violated federal securities law.

- The solicitor has not been barred from acting as a securities professional by a court.

- The arrangement between the investment adviser and the solicitor is in writing. If the solicitor plans on soliciting more than just impersonal advisory services, the written document must describe the activities that the solicitor will engage in.

- The client must be provided with the investment adviser's brochure (Form ADV,

Part 2) and a separate solicitor disclosure document. The solicitor disclosure document must contain the compensation arrangement between the investment adviser and the solicitor, including the amount or percentage of the advisory fee that the solicitor will receive. The investment adviser's brochure and the solicitor disclosure document cannot be presented together as one document.

- The client must sign that she has received the investment adviser's brochure and the solicitor disclosure document.

- The investment adviser is responsible for supervising the solicitor's activities.

The Investment Advisers Act of 1940 does not require solicitors to be registered as investment advisers or investment adviser representatives, as long as their activities are limited to referring clients to the investment adviser. The Uniform Securities Act, however, includes "selling investment advisory services" as part of their definition of investment adviser representative, thus requiring solicitors to register. To complicate matters further, however, the USA includes a caveat that state administrators may use their discretion to determine whether to allow unregistered solicitors to refer clients. So if an IA wishes to hire unregistered solicitors, she must check with her state administrator to determine whether registration is indeed required.

 **EXERCISE**

MATCH THE INVESTMENT PROFESSIONAL TO THE COMPENSATION ARRANGEMENT

A. Investment adviser representative
B. Agent
C. Solicitor

1. _____ **Fee based on a percentage of assets under management**

2. _____ **Markup on the price of a security purchased from a client**

3. _____ **Commissions received for effecting securities transactions**

4. _____ **A flat fee received for providing investment advice**

5. _____ **Cash payments made to a third party in return for bringing clients to a firm**

Answers: 1. A; 2. B; 3. B; 4. A; 5. C

5.2. PRACTICAL APPLICATION

One of Amy Adams's first mentors was Dianne, an industry veteran. Dianne had worked in the securities industry since the mid-1970s when the securities industry was deregulated.

With the increase in self-service brokerages offering discounted commissions and no-load mutual funds, Dianne advised Amy to create as many different sources of revenue as possible. She especially encouraged Amy to try to begin opening more fee-based advisory accounts and move away from acting only as a commission-based agent.

As Amy began to design a new marketing campaign incorporating Dianne's advice, her firm's compliance department reminded Amy that it would be unethical to charge both commissions and an investment advisory fee without providing a written disclosure to the client that she's doing so. They also reminded her that any fees she charged must be fair and reasonable considering each client's unique situation and in light of the services she actually provided.

The following week, a mutual fund representative was making a marketing visit to Amy's branch office and overheard Amy and Dianne talking about Amy's new marketing efforts. Anxious to grow sales of his mutual fund, he offered to help Amy absorb some of the cost of her marketing campaign. In addition to offering his presence and financial assistance at educational workshops, he also offered to have his assistant handle the stuffing and mailing of invitations for her upcoming workshops.

Amy was, naturally, excited to have all the additional help in building her practice. Thankfully, Dianne's years of watching other professionals make mistakes, along with making a few of her own, led her to remind Amy about the caution she needed to take with soft-dollar arrangements, in particular, that the clerical and administrative assistance offered by the mutual fund representative was not permitted on a soft-dollar basis.

5.3. CLIENT FUNDS AND SECURITIES

In the age of Bernie Madoff, Allen Stanford, and other Ponzi schemes, regulators are very serious about how you handle your clients' assets. In fact, regulators draw distinct lines in the sand when it comes to who handles client funds and securities, whether they are mixed with the assets of anyone else, and who decides to pull the trigger on transactions for clients' accounts.

At the core of the rules in this section is the idea that increased control by a professional or a firm over a client's assets *is inherently more risky* for a client than less. Thus, if more control is given away, certain protection and disclosures need to be put into place.

5.3.1. CUSTODY

It's very common for investors to give broker-dealers and investment advisers custody, or physical possession, of their securities and funds. Besides physical possession, custody includes being able to appropriate (take control of) funds and securities and being able to automatically deduct money from an account or write checks on the account. Custody also may include cases in which an adviser has an ownership stake in the broker-dealer that maintains custody or in which an adviser is a general partner in a limited partnership or a managing member of an investment LLC. Some states prohibit advisers from taking custody; check with the state administrator before acting.

Custody of client securities and money represents a huge responsibility for firms and a huge extension of trust by the public. To ensure that this trust is not misplaced and the public is protected, the SEC, NASAA, and state administrators have developed a number of model rules and standards that should be followed by investment advisers who take custody of client assets:

- Client securities and funds must be appropriately segregated, or set apart, from other securities, with proper records documenting how much each client has on deposit.

- Clients must receive regular statements (at least quarterly) of their account values. Statements should come from the qualified custodian directly or, if not, through the adviser.

- Client accounts and records must be audited at least once per year by an independent third party. The audit must be unannounced to the adviser, and the auditor must file its report with the administrator.

- No commingling, or mixing, of clients' personal assets with those of their advisers should occur.

- The custodian must not misappropriate client funds or employ them for any use (business or personal) other than what the client intends and expects.

- Clients' instructions regarding their accounts, assets, and all transactions should promptly be followed.

- Clients must be notified in writing of where and how their funds and securities will be held and must be updated on any changes in where and how their funds and securities are held.

Most advisers prefer not to have custody over client funds. In order to avoid custody, an adviser must follow these model rules. First, if securities are inadvertently sent to an investment adviser (unless he is also a broker-dealer), they must be sent back to the sender within three business days to avoid being considered in custody. Second, any investment adviser that receives a check from a customer made out to a third party (such as a mutual fund) must forward that check within three business days to avoid being considered to have taken those funds into custody.

Investment advisers have additional rules they must follow when they take custody of client funds or securities. They must notify the state securities administrator using Form ADV that they have or may have custody. They must also keep the funds and securities with a qualified custodian. The **qualified custodian** must hold the funds or securities as agent or trustee in an account either under the client's name or under the adviser's name. Qualified custodians include the types of financial institutions that clients and advisers customarily turn to for custodial services, including banks and savings associations and registered broker-dealers. Qualified custodians may be foreign financial institutions that customarily hold financial assets for their customers, provided the institution keeps advisory clients' assets in customer accounts segregated from its proprietary assets.

The SEC notes that many advisers registered with the SEC are themselves qualified custodians. These advisers may maintain their own clients' funds and securities, and as such, are required to provide account statement to their customers and abide by any custodial rules that apply. Advisers may also maintain client assets with affiliates that are qualified custodians.

The NASAA has special rules for broker-dealers who have custody of their client's securities and funds. Broker-dealer customers should not be subjected to any unreasonable or unjustifiable delays in having access to securities they've purchased or deposited or to any free credit balances (cash) they have on deposit. Broker-dealers that have custody of their customer's securities must segregate their fully paid securities from the firm's own securities and from those securities that are being used for collateral. When broker-dealers do not keep their own securities separate from their customer's securities, they are **commingling** their funds with their customers' funds, and this is a violation.

A broker-dealer must not **hypothecate** or **re-hypothecate** a customer's securities, unless the broker-dealer either has a lien on the securities or the broker-dealer receives written consent (usually through a hypothecation agreement) from the customer promptly after the initial transaction. Hypothecation is when a customer buys securities on margin and allows the broker-dealer to use these securities as collateral against the remaining amount that the customer owes the broker-dealer. When customers sign the hypothecation agreement, they allow the broker-dealer to hypothecate their securities. Hypothecation agreements usually also allow broker-dealers to use their customers' securities as collateral against the broker-dealers' own loans—this is called re-hypothecation.

Agents are prohibited from taking custody of customer assets.

Custody Requirements for Investment Advisers

- Securities and funds must be segregated from the firm's assets

- Quarterly statements of account values must be given to clients

- Unannounced third-party audit is conducted annually

- Funds may only be used for what client intends and expects

- Client instructions must be strictly followed

- Written notification of where funds and securities are held and any changes to this information must be provided

---

SUMMARY

ⵟ EXERCISE

CHOOSE PROPER OR IMPROPER

1. _____ Client funds and broker-dealer funds are held in the same account.

2. _____ Client funds are audited by an independent accountant on a scheduled date at least once a year.

3. _____ Clients receive account statements every three months.

4. _____ A broker-dealer receives written consent and then hypothecates a client's securities

ANSWERS

1. **Improper.** Commingling of funds is a violation of custody rules.

2. **Improper.** Although an annual audit by a third party is required, it must be unannounced.

3. **Proper.** Quarterly account statements must be provided to clients when advisers have custody of their accounts.

4. **Proper.** A broker-dealer with custody can hypothecate a customer's securities with previous written consent.

5.3.2. DISCRETION

There's a great old piece of wisdom that states, "Discretion is the better part of valor." In other words, choosing when to be brave (discretion) is more important than being brave itself. Nothing could be truer of the investing process. Knowing what to invest in (which security) is typically far more important than how the transaction takes place (when to invest and at what price). That doesn't mean that timing doesn't matter, but common sense says that buying the worst investment at the right time can be far more damaging than buying the right investment at the wrong time.

When a client initiates a new relationship with a securities professional, it is assumed that the client holds discretion over the types of securities that are bought in the account, the timing, and the price. In other words, a securities professional can't just begin exercising decision-making power, or discretion, over a client's account, making trades whenever he sees fit. If he does begin making trades without the client giving him the authorization to do so, he's in violation and subject to legal consequences.

A client, however, may decide to give permission to her securities professional to exercise decision-making ability (discretion) over some or all aspects of the investments in her account. Most commonly, this comes in the form of **time and price discretion**, where the client has made the final decision on which securities to buy (usually based on her professional's advice), but gives her professional the freedom to buy or sell that security when he thinks he can get the best price. This bestowing of time and price discretion can be done verbally and is unique to each transaction that is made, though it can be made for multiple future transactions that have not yet occurred as long as the transaction takes place by the end of the business day. It's important to note that this level of discretion does not permit a securities professional to decide *how much* of a security he's going to buy or sell. Only when and for what price.

If the client wishes to give her securities professional final decision-making authority over which securities to transact or how much to buy, then the professional must get this permission in writing. For investment advisers and investment adviser representatives, this written transfer of discretionary authority must be signed by the client within *10 business days* of when the first discretionary trade was made by her securities professional, assuming that the client gave verbal permission for the securities professional to exercise discretion prior to that trade. If proper written authorization is not received within this time period, the professional has committed a violation and will be subject to administrative proceedings. It would be considered illegal and unethical for a securities professional to make discretionary trades without his client's permission and then try to get her to sign a written letter of discretionary authority later. For broker-dealers and agents, written discretionary authorization is required prior to any trade in a customer's account where the broker-dealer exercises discretion beyond time and price discretion.

Even if a client provides discretion to a professional, she still has the ability to make decisions for her own account. Failing to follow the legitimate instructions of a client is never acceptable.

DISCRETIONARY TRADING AUTHORITY TIMETABLE		
	Verbal Authority Must Be Given	**Written Authority Must Be Given**
Investment adviser (or IAR)	Prior to first discretionary trade	Within 10 business days of first trade
Broker-dealer (or agent)	Not valid	Prior to first discretionary trade

5.3.3. TRADING AUTHORIZATION

As previously mentioned, discretion is when a professional is given written permission by a client to buy or sell securities in the client's account, as the professional sees fit. This stands in contrast to a non-discretionary relationship or account, where the adviser has to get verbal permission from a client prior to every transaction in the client's account.

In addition to these two options, there is a third option for designating who can initiate transactions in a client account. Under a **trading authorization**, a third party (in addition to the professional and the client) can be given permission to buy or sell securities for the client. This often occurs within families or companies, when one person manages accounts for multiple people.

For a trading authorization to occur, one very important thing must happen. Specifically, the client must sign a written authorization, naming the outside third party and outlining what type of trading authorization the third party is given. Without that written authorization, it is an ethical violation to take an order for a client account from a third party who is not the owner of the account.

One place that professionals often get into ethical hot water is taking orders from one spouse for the other spouse's account. It is not uncommon for one spouse or partner to manage the finances for the entire household, including a spouse's investment or retirement accounts. Thus, a client who is going to allow her spouse to act on her behalf must provide a written trading authorization to do so.

 **EXERCISE**

CHOOSE PERMITTED OR NOT PERMITTED

1. _____ A client gives written permission to her investment adviser representative to make trades for her one week after the first trade was made by that adviser. She gave verbal permission prior to the first trade.

2. _____ A client gives written permission to his agent to make trades one week after the first trade was made by that agent. The client gave verbal permission prior to the first trade.

3. _____ A client gives verbal permission for time and price discretion to his investment adviser prior to any trades taking place. The client then provides written permission two weeks after the first time and price discretionary transaction took place.

4. _____ A client gives written authorization for a third party to buy securities on her behalf.

ANSWERS

1. **Permitted.** Written consent for discretionary authority for an investment adviser representative must be given no later than 10 days following the first discretionary trade, and verbal permission must be given prior to the trade.

2. **Not permitted.** Written consent for discretionary authority for an agent must be given prior to any discretionary trade being made.

3. **Permitted.** For a time and price discretionary trade, only verbal authorization is required.

4. **Permitted.** Trading authorization is allowed when a client acknowledges in writing that a specified third party can trade on the client's behalf.

5.3.4. **PRUDENT INVESTOR STANDARDS**

Modern prudent investor standards are based on an older rule known as the prudent man rule. Under this rule, professionals acted as fiduciaries (trusted advisers) and were expected to show the same level of care for others' portfolios as they, or any other prudent person, would for their own. In other words, they should not subject their clients' portfolios to any more risk than the average, cautious investor would take.

Over the years, the relatively simple requirement for professionals to compare themselves to a prudent person has been spelled out and expanded into what is now called the Prudent Investor Rule (note the change from *man* to *investor*). In addition, the Prudent Investor Rule recognizes that the most cautious investment may not always be the most prudent investment, because prudent includes making money and beating inflation as well as preserving capital. Most state laws require fiduciaries to follow the principles included in this rule.

The Prudent Investor Rule is based on modern portfolio theory and outlines the following principles, which must be upheld when managing assets for a fiduciary account:

- The fiduciary should view risk and return in the context of the whole portfolio and in the context of the account owner's broader portfolio goals. For example, options may be appropriate within the context of the whole portfolio. When choosing an investment, the fiduciary should take transaction costs into consideration.

- The fiduciary should diversify investments whenever possible to avoid unnecessary unsystematic risk, unless it's not prudent to do so.

- The fiduciary should avoid unreasonable fees and transaction costs whenever possible.

- The fiduciary must balance the goal of preservation of capital with protection of purchasing power. It is usually prudent to take some risk in order to beat inflation and protect purchasing power. It is often appropriate to invest in income-producing investments (fixed-income investments) as well as investments that appreciate over time (equity investments), because equity investments have been shown to beat inflation over the long-run.

- Fiduciaries have a duty, as well as the authority, to delegate investment-making decisions when appropriate. To this end, mutual funds are acceptable investments, because a professional manages the mutual fund portfolio. In addition, hiring an investment adviser to help manage a child's UGMA account may be an appropriate expense, depending on the custodian's experience. Interestingly, fiduciaries cannot delegate all investment decisions; they must make the decisions regarding amounts and timing of distributions paid to the account holders or beneficiaries.

In addition to the principles listed above, professionals who act as fiduciaries (they hold or manage assets for other people) need to consider a client's investment objectives (including the desire to take risk to achieve growth) and ability to tolerate risk and experience losses, using careful investment selection and diversification to manage risk. No investment should be made before a client's needs and objectives are fully understood or before any potential investment is adequately assessed. Professionals should not simply park clients' money in investments until they figure out a better option. For those fiduciaries who are acting as estate executors, they must also consider the terms and conditions of the deceased's will.

5.3.5. **SUITABILITY**

While some ethical standards for securities professionals are simple black and white, do this or don't do that kinds of rules, others are a lot more gray. Suitability is one of those concepts that require professionals to make an ongoing effort to ensure that they are looking out for their clients' best interests and walking the ethical line.

Suitability is the idea that not all investments are right for all clients, due to a wide variety of factors, including an investment's cost, level of risk, expected return, and growth or income features. These factors, though they may make an investment seem attractive relative to other investments, *must be measured only in comparison to a client's financial situation, investment objectives, and risk tolerance.* A client's other security holdings, financial needs, and tax status should be considered as well.

In other words, a top-ranked mutual fund that has posted great growth for ten straight years in a row may be completely inappropriate for someone who never, ever, wants to see his investments have a negative performance year. Likewise, someone who hopes to grow her investments at a rate that exceeds inflation should not have the bulk of her money parked in low-yield savings accounts for any extended period of time. Thus, suitability involves making sure clients are taking *enough risk* to meet their goals, just as it can be about making sure clients are not taking *too much risk* to keep them from reaching those goals.

In short, determining suitability is a mix between an art and a science that requires two very important things—listening and talking. First, professionals have to listen very carefully to what their clients express as their short- and long-term goals, their ability to tolerate risky investments, and their need for immediate income from their investments or their ability to hang on for long-term growth potential. Further, when clients don't know how to express these things or do it inadequately, a professional who is focused on suitability asks questions. He sorts through what the client has to say and helps clarify exactly what the client wants and expects.

Second, a professional keeping an eye on suitability talks to his clients in full detail about all the ins and outs (risk, cost, etc.) associated with any potential investment. He ensures, through proper disclosure and accurate facts, that clients know what they are getting themselves into and have a chance to say for themselves whether an investment is suitable or not.

Further, the concept of suitability means that a professional is always keeping an eye out for whether investments that were once suitable for a client are no longer a good match. For example, clients who had invested heavily in stocks throughout their working years may find these completely unsuitable once they begin living off their nest eggs. As an investment begins to appear unsuitable for a client, an ethical professional will have a discussion about the situation with his client, outlining his concerns and making more appropriate recommendations.

5.3.5.1. **Blanket Recommendations**

A **blanket recommendation** is when a firm or financial professional makes a recommendation to all their customers or clients to buy or sell a particular security. Since a blanket recommendation does not consider whether the action is suitable for each individual customer, making such a recommendation is generally a bad idea.

5.3.5.2. **Broker-Dealer Suitability**

Broker-dealers must believe on reasonable grounds that the transactions or strategies they recommend are suitable for an individual customer. A firm may approve an account only after conducting a **suitability analysis**, based on the firm's due diligence in understanding the risks of the recommendations it makes and the customer's personal and investment profile. The firm must make reasonable efforts when opening an account to collect and maintain this information.

Specifically, FINRA recognizes three components with regard to suitability obligations:

- **Reasonable-basis obligation.** A broker-dealer must understand the complexity and risks of a security or investment strategy and consciously determine whether it is suitable for at least some investors. If a member firm or its brokers and dealers do not understand the risks and mechanics of mortgage-backed securities, for example, it is a suitability violation to recommend them to investors.

- **Customer-specific obligation.** A broker-dealer must have a reasonable basis to believe that a recommendation is suitable for the particular customer based on the customer's personal and investment profile. The suitability analysis must evaluate the customer's investment objectives, time horizon, and financial status, including current income, tax status, other investments, and liquid net worth. Personal characteristics, including age, employment, dependents, trading experience, and risk tolerance, must be examined also.

- **Quantitative suitability obligation.** A broker-dealer who has control over a customer account must have a reasonable basis to believe that a series of recommended securities transactions are not excessive.

Only after the suitability analysis has been conducted can the broker-dealer work up an investment strategy and recommend transactions. However, a broker may accept *unsolicited* orders from a client who has not provided the appropriate suitability information.

5.3.5.3. **Broker-Dealer vs. Investment Adviser Suitability**

Investment advisers have a fiduciary duty to their customers, which requires them to put their customers' interests before their own. Under the new suitability rule described above, broker-dealers are required to make recommendations that are in the best interests of their clients. This best-interest requirement prohibits broker-dealers from putting their own interests ahead of their clients.

The primary difference in the recommendation requirements between broker-dealers and investment advisers now lies in the fact that an investment adviser is obligated to recommend the best investment for a client, while a broker-dealer is only obligated to recommend a suitable investment for a client.

 **EXERCISE**

ANSWER TRUE OR FALSE

1. _____ Diversification should be considered as part of the prudent investor standard, as it tends to reduce potential risk.

2. _____ Under the suitability rule, securities professionals should always try to remove any potential for client risk.

3. _____ As long as an agent discusses in full detail a client's investment needs, wants, and expectations before engaging in any trades, the suitability requirement has been met.

4. _____ Until all relevant suitability information has been considered, a broker-dealer is prohibited from engaging in all securities transactions for a client.

5. _____ Under the suitability rule, recommendations made by broker-dealers and investment advisers are held to different standards.

ANSWERS

1. **True.** Portfolio diversification, since it reduces overall risk, is considered to be an important aspect of the prudent investor standard.

2. **False.** Suitability involves making sure clients are taking enough risks to meet their goals just as much as it does ensuring they are not subject to unnecessary risk.

3. **False.** An initial in-depth discussion of investment needs, wants, and expectations is a requirement for suitability, but so too is a continuous evaluation of changes to a client's goals and investment situation.

4. **False.** In the case of an unsolicited transaction (one made at the request of the client), a broker-dealer does not need to meet the suitability standards.

5. **True.** Broker-dealers are obligated to recommend a suitable investment for a client; investment advisers are obligated to recommend the best investment for a client.

5.3.6. **UNETHICAL TRADING PRACTICES**

The NASAA outlines a number of unethical practices relating to the purchase or sale of securities through professionals and their firms. Yet again, these prohibited practices are considered taboo because they ultimately create conflicts of interest between a client and his professional, limit a client's ability to get a fair price for his securities, and prevent him from monitoring his own account.

Most importantly, broker-dealers and agents are always expected to try to provide a price for a purchase or sale that is as close as possible to the current market price. Substantially under- or over-pricing a security, especially when the firm is selling from its own account (known as acting as a principal), would be considered a serious violation. Likewise, **front-running**, that is, buying or selling a security for your own or your firm's account prior to doing it on behalf of customers, in order to get a better price for yourself or your firm, is not permitted. Again, customers deserve to get the fairest price possible at the time of their transaction.

Because principal transactions often involve conflicts of interest, an investment adviser must give full disclosure of its role in a principal transaction and receive written permission from the client before the completion/settlement of the transaction. Broker-dealers must simply note their role on the trade confirmation.

Further, broker-dealers are prohibited from using the phrase "at the market" to describe a security's price, unless they reasonably believe that an active market for that security exists outside of their firm. In other words, if the only firm that buys or sells a security is the client's firm, it would be unethical for them to say that the security is being sold at the market price.

A related violation is when a broker-dealer offers to buy or sell a security at a particular price with no intention of actually buying or selling the security at that price. For example, if a broker-dealer gives a quote of $30.25 to $30.50 it needs to be willing to buy the security at $30.25 and sell it at $30.50. Not honoring quotes is called **backing away**.

Manipulating market prices through unnecessary trading among agents is also a violation. In this kind of manipulation, agents and/or broker-dealers agree to buy and sell securities to each other at similar prices to give the impression that a security has a more active market than it actually does. They do this in order to drive up the price of the security. This is called making **matched trades**. Another form of market manipulation is **painting the tape**. This is when a group of people trade a security back and forth among themselves to create the appearance of higher trading activity and artificially raise the price of the security.

It is also a violation for a broker-dealer or agent to manipulate the price of a security by spreading rumors about it.

Another violation is for an agent to maintain an account that contains fictitious information that is used to effect transactions that would otherwise be prohibited.

Holding back shares of a public offering that were allotted to a broker-dealer is also a violation. During a public offering, broker-dealers are allotted a certain amount of shares to be sold to investors; it is a violation for them to hold back these shares for their own accounts in the hopes that the price will rise in the future.

COMMON UNETHICAL TRADING PRACTICES

Violation	Description
Overpricing or underpricing a security	Offering a security for a price that is far above or below its market price
Front-running	Buying or selling a security for an account based on non-public information of an upcoming block trade in the security for a customer
Falsely claiming at the market	Claiming a security is being sold at market price when it is not
Backing away	Offering to buy or sell a security at a certain price with no intention of actually doing so
Making matched trades	Working with another broker-dealer or agent to buy and sell securities at a similar price, in turn creating a false sense of demand
Painting the tape	Trading a security back and forth with other securities professionals in order to create the appearance of high trade activity
Holding back shares	Holding onto shares allotted to a broker-dealer during an IPO in the hopes that their value will rise in the future

5.4. **PRACTICAL APPLICATION**

A few months into her new career, Amy Adams's firm was rocked with a big scandal. Two brothers, who were respected and admired for their apparent financial success, were accused of improper handling and use of client funds. While this came as a surprise to many of the other securities professionals, many of the clerical staff at the office had long recognized some irregularities in the way that Carl and Kevin Rook had handled client funds, securities, and supporting paperwork. Thankfully for the Rooks' clients, as well as the firm's reputation, their unethical behavior was discovered before the damage got worse.

At the core of the Rooks' behavior was the fact that they seemed to confuse their clients' assets with their own. It turns out that the brothers would often deposit client checks to their own account for two to three weeks at a time, to assist them in qualifying for large mortgages and expensive car loans. This commingling of their assets with those of their clients took a turn for the worse when one of the brothers began misappropriating client funds, using deposited cash to help cover large payments on fancy things he couldn't afford.

In an effort to cover their tracks, the brothers pursued a very active trading strategy, using both large numbers of unauthorized trades and risky recommendations, to bury their theft of client funds under a mountain of paperwork. It didn't take long for the complaints to begin coming in, given that many of the accounts they were trading in without consulting their clients did not have written discretionary agreements in place. Evidence began to mount when clients began requesting cash balances that should have been there and the brothers could not promptly process their requests.

Needless to say, the day the auditors showed up unannounced for their annual visit, the brothers found an excuse to visit some of their clients in other states. Fortunately for Amy, her firm, and their clients, these brothers were met at the airport by securities regulators, a few police officers, and a couple pairs of handcuffs.

5.5. CONFLICTS OF INTEREST AND FIDUCIARY ISSUES

This section of the study guide covers conflicts of interest and fiduciary issues. There are perhaps no greater concepts that link every topic discussed in this book or presented to you on the exam. Simply put, a conflict of interest is a scenario in which a securities professional or firm has an incentive to serve one interest at the expense of another interest or obligation. It can include serving the interest of that individual or firm over a client or serving the interest of one client over another. The rules all come back to the concept of registered investment advisers and registered investment adviser representatives being fiduciaries, or trusted third parties, whose primary duty is to watch out for the best interests of those who place their trust in them.

Individual states and the federal government require registration and regulation to protect the investing public, who generally place a great deal of trust in you and your colleagues. It's this trust, paired with a lack of training and expertise, that can place the public at enormous risk of being taken advantage of. To this end, the Uniform Securities Act and the NASAA require agents and investment adviser representatives to place their clients' best interest above their own, especially in areas and actions that may represent a direct **conflict of interest** between the two.

Again, if you can burn this concept (the protection of a public who place their trust in us) into your brain, then you'll have a strong internal compass to help you navigate the exam.

5.5.1. EXCESSIVE TRADING

There's no more classic, blatant conflict of interest and ethical violation than excessive trading. Often referred to as **churning**, this ethical violation involves a professional recommending or making trades in a customer's account simply for the sake of generating revenue. In plain English, recommending or making a trade simply to generate a commission is unethical.

At the core of this is the most basic conflict of interest in the securities industry—*the client's net worth versus the professional's net worth.* Simply put, all transactions recommended or made must be with the intent of meeting a client's investment objectives. If they are not, then they are considered excessive.

Does that mean that even one trade per year can be considered excessive? While regulators will not likely track you down over an account in which you make one trade in a year, it's possible that your registration could be acted against if the client could prove the trade was not made with the primary interest of moving his or her financial goals forward. Of course, the stories you hear in the news about excessive trading or churning usually involve hundreds of trades in a short period of time, generating thousands of dollars in commissions.

One important distinction is that excessive trading can occur in both discretionary and non-discretionary accounts. In other words, even when a broker-dealer or its agent has to get permission from the client for each and every trade (known as a non-discretionary account), they can still be guilty of excessive trading. That's because clients are relying on your expertise to tell them when is the best time to buy and sell, which is a position of power that can be easily abused.

5.5.2. LOANS TO AND FROM CLIENTS

While it might come as a surprise, one of the more common ethical is an investment adviser, IAR, or agent loaning money to or borrowing money from his or her clients. When you stop to think about it, it's not hard to imagine why this temptation is so common. Financial professionals often have intimate knowledge about the finances of their clients, including when their clients have extra money lying around or are short of much needed cash. In these situations, professionals without clear boundaries might easily see an opportunity to borrow money at a favorable rate from their clients, or lend out their money at rates better than what they'd get through other opportunities.

While this may be beneficial for the professional, and even appear beneficial for the client, it puts the client at risk of an unfair transaction and even a substantial loss. Thus, an investment adviser or IAR is not permitted to borrow from a client, unless that client is actually a broker-dealer, an affiliate of the investment adviser, or lending institution. Likewise, an IA or IAR may not loan money to a client unless the firm is a lending institution and actively engages in lending money as part of his or her business, or the loan is to an affiliate. Agents must not borrow money from or loan money to customers (though they may still borrow money normally from lending institutions). The NASAA does not prohibit broker-dealers from borrowing from or lending to customers, though they must comply with margin and lending rules.

5.5.2.1. Margin and Lending Specific Rules

When a broker-dealer does offer lending services, especially those that involve allowing clients to buy more securities than they have cash for, using their existing portfolio as collateral, certain ethical requirements are placed on firms and securities professionals. Failure to meet these requirements can result in action by a securities administrator.

- For margin accounts, a written margin agreement must be in place promptly after the first trade being executed on margin (money borrowed from the firm).

- For other loans (besides using a margin account to purchase additional securities) for which a client wishes to use his securities as collateral, a written agreement must be in place promptly after the initial transaction or the broker-dealer must have a lien on the securities.

5.5.3. **SHARING PROFITS AND LOSSES IN A CUSTOMER ACCOUNT**

One of the most important characteristics of a good securities professional is that her advice is objective and free from personal bias. To insure that, federal and state regulators generally prohibit investment advisers from linking their compensation to the profits or losses of clients. In other words, aside from a few exceptions, securities professionals are prohibited from directly sharing in the profits or losses in a client account.

When this ethical standard is violated, it usually looks like one of two things. Most commonly, it occurs when a securities professional agrees to work for a percentage of any gains they earn for their client in a specified period (e.g., 20% of the profits earned during each calendar year). The other instance is when a professional promises to limit a client's losses by reimbursing the client in the event that the account heads south.

In both of these common cases, the reason behind this prohibition against performance-based compensation has to do with the belief that it's difficult for securities professionals to focus on a client's investment objectives when they have a huge amount to gain or lose personally. If there is an incentive for them to take an above average risk or to limit their client's exposure, it's going to be hard for them to work in the best interest of their client.

There are a few notable exceptions to this rule that may show up on the exam. The reasons for these exceptions have to do with the fact that some sophisticated investors may actually prefer this type of arrangement. But it's also based on the premise that the sophisticated investors are smart enough to understand the risks associated with it.

A registered investment adviser can enter into a performance-based compensation arrangement only with the following parties:

- **High net worth individuals**—individuals with at least $1 million in assets with the professional's firm or at least $2 million in net worth, excluding their primary residence

- **Qualified purchasers**—individuals and family-owned corporations with $5 million or corporations with $25 million

- **Business development companies**—closed-end funds that invest in small or troubled businesses and are not registered under the Investment Company Act

- **Private investment companies (hedge funds)**—companies whose shares are beneficially owned by no more than 100 people and which do not make a public offering of their securities

- **Registered investment companies**—annuities, mutual funds, unit trusts, etc.

- **Certain advisory firm personnel**—key operational personnel of the investment advisory firm (officers, directors, and investment adviser representatives)

- **Non-residents of the United States**

Agents may only share in the profits or losses of a customer's account with the written authorization of the customer and the agent's broker-dealer. Moreover, according to FINRA rules, agents may only share in the profits and losses in proportion to their investment in accounts. For example, if an agent and a customer open an account together, and the agent contributes 60% of the funds and the customer contributes 40% of the funds, the agent must share in the profits and losses according to the same proportion.

5.5.4. CLIENT CONFIDENTIALITY

Few things can damage relationships like money. It can change people's motivations, undermine their trust, and call into question their intentions. That's why many clients are more apt to talk about their love lives than their financial lives.

To help protect client confidentiality, the NASAA places a high value on investment advisers keeping their clients' information under wraps. In fact, they require investment advisers and investment adviser representatives to not disclose any details including a client's name, state of affairs, or account details, unless:

- The client consents to it.
- They're required to by law.
- They're required to by a court order.

♟ EXERCISE

ANSWER TRUE OR FALSE

1. _____ **Churning cannot occur in a discretionary account.**

2. _____ **Agents generally cannot borrow money from or loan money to customers.**

3. _____ **For a margin account with a broker-dealer, a written agreement must be in place before any trades are made.**

4. _____ **An investment adviser would be allowed to enter into a performance-based arrangement with a client with $1.75 million in net worth and a private residence valued at $600,000.**

5. _____ **An investment adviser representative can only reveal confidential client information with the client's consent.**

ANSWERS

1. **False.** Churning, or excessive trading, can occur in both discretionary and non-discretionary accounts.

2. **True.** Although they may borrow money from lending institutions, agents must not borrow money from or lend money to customers.

3. **False.** For a margin account with a broker-dealer, a written agreement must be in place no later than promptly after the first trade is executed.

4. **False.** High net worth individuals are allowed to enter into performance-based arrangements with investment advisers; however, to qualify for that distinction an investor must have at least $2 million in net worth, excluding his primary residence.

5. **False.** A client's consent is one of the means by which an investment adviser can share confidential information. The others are legal requirement and by court order.

5.5.5. CYBERSECURITY AND DATA PROTECTION

Since client information is typically kept in a broker-dealer or investment advisory firm's electronic database, cybersecurity and its role in data protection are important issues for regulators. As a result, a primary duty of the investment professional and his firm is to ensure that electronic client data remains safe and unavailable to online hackers. Failure to do so constitutes a violation of client confidentiality and can subject the financial institution to SEC or FINRA regulation.

SEC **Regulation S-P** addresses client confidentiality. This regulation requires financial institutions to adopt written policies and procedures that:

- Ensure that customer records and information are kept secure and confidential

- Safeguard customer records and data against potential security threats

- Protect against unauthorized access to customer information that has the potential to harm or inconvenience the customer

The SEC's rule also requires financial institutions to properly dispose of nonpublic personal information. This requires the firms to take reasonable measures to protect against unauthorized access to or use of the disposed information.

Firms must conduct periodic reviews to detect potential problems in their databases and to ensure that data is secure from unauthorized persons

In order to comply with these provisions, FINRA suggests that broker-dealers make sure that they have taken sufficient precautions to keep client information confidential, including a well-defined system that will do so. FINRA also urges firms to provide proper training to their employees regarding the use of technology.

In addition, FINRA encourages firms to address technology used by their associates who have access to customer information and records by considering each of the following:

- Whether the firm's existing policies and procedures sufficiently address its use of technology

- Whether the firm has taken appropriate technological precautions to keep client information confidential

- Whether the firm provides proper training to its employees regarding the use of technology and has a well-defined system to ensure that customer information be kept confidential

- Whether the firm is conducting periodic reviews to detect potential problems in its databases and to ensure that data is secure from unauthorized persons.

Over the past few years, there have been many cases of firms compromising client records because they didn't have proper cybersecurity. In several of those cases, firms were forced to pay hefty fines. Be aware that failing to implement appropriate cybersecurity controls can result in serious consequences.

5.5.5.1. **Best Practices for Forming a Cybersecurity Plan**

Both the SEC and FINRA have offered guidelines for firms to follow in order to establish and implement a framework for forming a **cybersecurity plan**. Both agencies suggest that firms:

- **Define and establish a governing framework for the prevention of cybersecurity risks.** The framework should clearly describe the specific roles and responsibilities of each employee at the firm.

- **Develop a plan to prevent, detect, and respond to cybersecurity threats.** The plan should establish the best methods to control access to system and data management and user credentials, implement data encryption procedures, protect against the loss of sensitive data, enhance data back-up and retrieval, and properly respond to data-breach incidents.

- **Conduct periodic assessments to monitor and evaluate the plan.** These assessments should consider such factors as the location of all stored information the firm possesses, the vulnerability of information and technology systems, current security control processes, the potential threat of system compromise, and the overall effectiveness of the governance structure for cybersecurity risk.

- **Implement a system of guidance for officers and employees.** This should be done by establishing written policies, procedures, and a formal training system, each of which considers potential threats and measures to prevent cybersecurity breaches.

5.5.5.2. **FTC Red Flags Rule**

The Federal Trade Commission's (FTC) Red Flags Rule requires broker-dealers, investment advisers, and investment companies to establish and maintain identity theft programs. The programs should detect the warning signs—or red flags—of identity theft in their day-to-day operations. Identity theft is the fraudulent acquisition and use of a person's private identifying information, usually for financial gain. An identity theft program can help businesses spot suspicious patterns and prevent the costly consequences of identity theft. The FTC Red Flags Rule tells businesses how to develop, implement, and administer an identity theft prevention program. Such a program must include four basic elements:

- **Reasonable policies and procedures to identify the red flags of identity theft that may occur during day-to-day operations.** Red flags are suspicious patterns or practices or specific activities that indicate the possibility of identity theft. For example, if a customer has to provide some form of ID to open an account, an ID that doesn't look genuine is a red flag.

- **A design that will detect the identified red flags.** If fake IDs are identified as a red flag, for example, procedures must be in place to detect possible fake, forged, or altered identification.

- **Appropriate actions to take when red flags are detected, including escalation procedures.** For instance, a representative should know to contact her manager when a red flag is detected, and the manager should know when to inform legal or compliance.

- **How the program will be kept current to reflect new threats.**

The identity theft programs would apply to covered accounts. Covered accounts apply to retail brokerage accounts, credit card accounts, margin accounts, and checking and savings accounts. Identity theft red flags are not meant to be different from the already existing FinCEN Red Flags, but they are expected to be tailored to the business model of the specific member firm. Examples of red flags that might signal identity theft are:

- Alerts received from consumer reporting agencies

- Suspicious documents that look altered or forged

- A suspicious address change

- Notice from victims of identity theft

Member firms are also expected to develop policies that assign specific oversight responsibility to a designated principal. Broker-dealers must issue periodic compliance reports and update policies as needed.

🏋️ EXERCISE

ANSWER TRUE OR FALSE

1. **Keeping a client's electronic data out of public view is a primary responsibility for all investment professionals.**

2. **Under the SEC's cybersecurity regulations, firms must periodically review databases used to store client information.**

3. **FINRA guidelines require only a firm's management to have defined roles and responsibilities as part of a cybersecurity plan.**

4. **As long as reasonable policies and procedures to identify the red flags of identity theft are in place, a firm has satisfied its SEC requirement to maintain an identity theft program.**

ANSWERS

1. **True.** Client confidentiality extends to data stored electronically and online. Therefore, its protection is a key responsibility for all investment professionals. The SEC has mandated policies to ensure that all firms and employees maintain high standards in order to keep this information confidential.

2. **True.** Firms must periodically review databases to ensure that client information remains secure from unauthorized persons.

3. **False.** Both FINRA and the SEC suggest that all individuals employed by the firm have defined roles and responsibilities as part of a cybersecurity plan.

4. **False.** While establishing reasonable policies and procedures to identify red flags is a key part of any identity theft program, there are additional requirements.

5.5.6. INSIDER TRADING

What do Martha Stewart and Michael Douglas's character from *Wall Street* have in common? They both went to jail for insider trading. It'd be in your best interest to not find this in common with them.

To avoid joining the elite club of inside traders, you need to avoid doing certain things. You need to avoid using information that is unavailable to the investing public to buy or sell securities in order to make a profit or avoid a loss. Likewise, you need to avoid knowingly participating in or helping your clients use information that is unavailable to the investing public to buy or sell securities to make a profit or avoid a loss.

The rationale behind this rule is that the marketplace needs to be fair for all investors, and it is not ethical for one person to take advantage of many others based on information that the masses didn't have access to. Most often, such situations occur with the officers and directors of publicly traded companies, who know the big happenings within the company before anyone else, including regulators and the news media. But it also often occurs with investors and professionals who know and work with these corporate insiders, especially when their firm is providing underwriting and investment banking services.

Insider trading is subject to a civil penalty of treble damages (three times the amount of the benefit obtained by the violation). "Benefit obtained" means profit gained or loss avoided. For more severe instances, the Justice Department may bring criminal charges, carrying maximum penalties of a $5 million fine for each willful violation and 20 years in prison. The statute of limitation on insider trading is 6 years.

Investment advisers and broker-dealers also are required to establish, maintain, and enforce internal written policies and procedures designed to prevent the misuse of material, nonpublic information. Failure to do so is considered a serious breach of ethics.

To sum up, insider trading involves the trading of securities based on material, nonpublic information. It is unlawful for anyone who gains insider information and knows it to be confidential to trade on such information. It is also unlawful for anyone to pass on inside information that is then traded on. Both the actions of the person trading on the information and the person who revealed the information are considered to be illegal insider trading.

SUMMARY

Maximum Penalty for Insider Trading	
Civil charges	Treble damages—three times the amount of the benefit obtained by the violation
Criminal charges	$5 million fine for each willful violation and 20 years in prison

5.5.7. SELLING AWAY

If you'll recall from the section on agents of broker-dealers, they are only permitted to be employed by one firm at a time. This means that any securities services they provide away from the primary firm that employs them are technically illegal. In particular, being part of the investment sales process for securities that are not sold through an agent's firm represents an ethical violation known as **selling away**.

To avoid selling away violations, agents need to be extra cautious engaging in any outside business activities, especially private placements of investor funds that could be viewed as selling away. The best way to avoid this is to properly notify one's broker-dealer of all outside business and investment activities. Once a firm is notified of an agent's wish to sell outside securities, it is authorized to allow the sale if it chooses to do so. In that case, the firm is required to give written authorization, document the sale in its records, and supervise all transactions involving the security.

5.5.8. OUTSIDE BUSINESS ACTIVITIES

Under FINRA rules, an agent who wishes to engage in outside business activities (activities that are outside of their employment with their broker-dealer) for compensation must give prior written notice to the member broker-dealer. The broker-dealer must review the notice and give an evaluation of the activity, imposing limitations or prohibiting the activity if necessary.

5.5.9. PERSONAL OUTSIDE INVESTMENT ACCOUNTS

Agents are allowed to open personal investment accounts at other broker-dealers as long as both the agent and the outside firm with which the agent is trading provide sufficient documentation. That documentation must include the following from the outside firm:

- Written notification to the agent's employer of the agent's intent to open or maintain an account with the firm

- The transmission of copies of confirmations, statements, and any other information related to the outside account if requested by the employer firm

- Notification to the agent of having met the above requirements

The agent is also responsible for notifying his or her employing firm that she intends to open an account with an outside firm. Additionally, she must notify the outside firm of her status as an employee of a different brokerage firm.

5.5.10. MARKET MANIPULATIONS

Make no mistake about it—regulators are happy for you and your clients to make a ton of money in the securities markets. What they don't like, though, is professionals and their clients manipulating the markets deliberately through any of a variety of recognized taboo tricks. In other words, feel free to ride the roller coaster; just don't make any attempts to drive it.

For the average investor, manipulating the stocks of the Dow Jones Industrial Average may be virtually impossible due to the sheer number of trades taking place each day and the large number of analysts covering each company. But rather substantial swings in the prices of thinly traded penny stocks can be accomplished with a much smaller volume or a well-timed rumor.

This doesn't mean that professionals or their clients need to be overly concerned about accidentally manipulating the market through their transactions or casual discussions. It just means that they need to avoid all attempts of doing these things in the hope of affecting the price of a security. Regulators want the markets to operate freely, based on honest supply and demand. The moment that gets interfered with and someone introduces artificial forces to affect prices, they've got a problem.

Four particular situations the exam may ask you about are:

- Taking part in a buy or sell transaction that doesn't really involve any true transfer of ownership (i.e., a fake purchase or sale)

- Intentionally entering identical and opposite trades as someone else for the same security and amount (you buy 100 shares of XYZ and your partner sells 100 shares at the same time) with the intention of creating a false sense of trading activity or volume

- Buying or selling a security in a series of transactions with the intent of driving the price up or down and tempting other investors to buy or sell in response (also known as painting the tape)

- Using false information to open and trade in an account

5.5.11. **PERFORMING DUE DILIGENCE**

Broker-dealers and their associates have an obligation to perform reasonable diligence on the products that they sell. This means that they need to understand the nature of the securities (especially complex products) that they are recommending, including their risks and rewards. They also should be reasonably sure that the securities they are selling would be suitable for at least some customers. This is often referred to as the reasonable-basis suitability obligation.

FINRA has reminded broker-dealers that certain products require more due diligence because of their high level of risk. Regulation D private placements are one such product because they are usually illiquid, risky, and often little is known about the issuer. In addition, because they are exempt from registration, they often lack a prospectus and the extensive disclosures that come with it. For these reasons, FINRA requires broker-dealers and their agents to do the following when recommending private placements:

- Disclose to customers when they lack material information about the issuer or its securities

- Do not rely solely on an issuer for information concerning a company in lieu of reasonable investigation

- Take a high degree of care in investigating and verifying an issuer's claims

- Conduct a standard suitability analysis. Such an analysis should include an investigation of an issuer's management, its business prospects, assets, and any claims held against that issuer.

If each of these requirements is met and properly documented, a broker-dealer has fulfilled its due diligence obligations for private placements. It is interesting to note that while private placements are mostly sold to sophisticated investors, FINRA still requires broker-dealers and their agents to perform reasonable diligence on these products as well as any other products that they sell.

5.5.12. OTHER CONFLICTS OF INTEREST

While the conflicts of interest outlined thus far are the big ones you're likely to see on the exam, you very well may see a question or two about any of the following actions. Again, if you're stuck between a couple of possible answers, remember that the heart of the law is protecting clients' best interests over that of their professional or their firms. If it seems that the client is getting the shaft when you choose an answer, then it is probably the wrong one.

5.5.12.1. Acting as Both Principal and an Investment Adviser

While broker-dealers regularly sell their customers securities that they themselves actually own (known as acting as a principal), it is far less common for an investment adviser to do the same thing. Since an investment adviser is not registered as a dealer, selling a customer securities out of the firm's account requires special written consent from the customer by the date the transaction is complete.

5.5.12.2. Acting as Agent to Both Parties (Agency Cross Transactions)

Underlying the very concept of being an investment adviser for a client is the idea that you are working in his or her best interest. Naturally, it creates a conflict of interest when you are representing both sides of a transaction (the buyer and the seller), since to work in one person's best interest is to potentially do harm to the other.

If an investment adviser acts as broker/agent for two parties, it may only advise the buyer or the seller to make the trade, not both. In order for an adviser to effect an agency cross transaction for a client, it must have its client's written consent after having provided the client with full disclosure surrounding the agency cross transaction. The adviser must send the client a written confirmation at or before the completion of each transaction. The adviser must annually disclose in writing the number of agency cross transactions it has made on the client's behalf and the amount of commissions generated from them.

5.5.12.3. Recommending Securities the Professional Trades In

Anytime an investment adviser recommends a security that she owns, the adviser must disclose this to the client. Advisers must also disclose if they are acting against the recommendations they provide to clients. This limits unethical professionals' abilities to drive up or down the price of an investment by telling their clients to buy or sell, and then doing the opposite themselves.

5.5.12.4. Duty of Best Execution

An investment adviser must try to get best execution on securities transactions for clients. **Best execution** means more than just seeking low trading commissions for clients. Instead, the SEC says that an adviser must look at the full range of a broker's services and consider total cost, quality, execution capability, commission rate, financial responsibility, responsiveness to the adviser, and the value of any research services (soft dollars) provided. The obligation to seek best execution on trades stems from the adviser's fiduciary role, as stated in the Investment Advisers Act and other legislation. An adviser must always put a client's interests above its own interests or the interests of anyone else.

Broker-dealers and agents are required to make reasonable efforts to find as favorable a price as possible for a customer's transaction given the prevailing conditions of the market. Trade execution is not instantaneous; quoted prices are for a specific number of shares; the market may be illiquid or volatile.

In deciding how and where to execute a trade, a broker-dealer is expected to consider these factors: (1) the character of the market for the security, including its price, volatility, and liquidity; (2) the size and the type of transaction; (3) the number of markets checked; (4) the accessibility of the quotation; and (5) the terms and conditions of the transaction, as communicated to the broker-dealer.

Interpositioning is the practice of inserting a third party between a broker-dealer and the best available price in the market when it results in a higher price to the customer than would otherwise have been necessary. For example, suppose a broker-dealer passes a customer order to another broker-dealer to purchase the security from the market. Each broker-dealer charges a commission for the service, passing the extra cost on to the customer, which the two broker-dealers will split as profit. This is interpositioning, and it is prohibited.

From time to time, a member firm cannot execute directly with a market but must necessarily employ a second broker to execute a customer order. For instance, this might occur if a member firm believes market prices will respond unfavorably if its identity in the market were known. FINRA places the burden of showing just cause for using a third party upon the member firm.

5.5.13. **INDIRECT VIOLATIONS**

Investment advisers and IARs are prohibited from engaging in an act indirectly or through another person if the act would have been unlawful for the IA or IAR to do directly. Essentially, if you ask someone or hire someone to do something for you that you would be prohibited from doing by securities law, you are still committing a violation.

 **EXERCISE**

MATCH EACH TERM TO THE APPROPRIATE SECURITIES VIOLATION

A. Insider trading
B. Selling away
C. Improper outside business activity
D. Market manipulation
E. No violation occurred

1. ____ Two agents who work at the same firm enter an agreement in which one agent buys 100 shares of a security at $100, while another agent sells 100 shares of the same security at $100.

2. ____ A client is made aware of material non-public information about a specific security and, as a result, buys shares of that security the following day.

3. ____ An agent sells securities to a client that are not are not sold by his firm outside his firm's knowledge.

4. ____ An agent makes trades in an account with another firm without notifying her employing firm.

5. ____ An officer of a publicly-traded company tells an investment adviser that the production of a much publicized product may not occur as originally planned.

ANSWERS

1. **D.** Intentionally entering identical and opposite trades for the same security in order to create a false sense of trading activity is a mode of market manipulation.

2. **A.** Engaging in a securities transaction based on non-public material information is considered to be insider trading.

3. **B.** Selling securities that are not sold through an agent's firm (outside of the firm's knowledge) constitutes selling away.

4. **C.** When making trades with another firm, an agent must notify his employing firm in writing and must ensure that the outside firm does the same.

5. **E.** As long as no trade took place involving securities related to this inside information, there is no violation.

5.6. PRACTICAL APPLICATION

Back when Amy was finishing her first year in business, she had built a reputation as a solid professional who consistently looked out for the best interests of her clients. As such, she was asked to come speak to her firm's newest class of recruits about the biggest fiduciary mistakes that trusted advisers make early in their careers.

When she began to talk, an ambitious young professional suggested that the only professionals who get in ethical and legal trouble are the ones who are crooked from the start. He explained further that everything she would be discussing would be a non-issue for most people in the training class, because they were all upstanding professionals.

Amy, having once felt the same way, told the young professional that his clear sense of right and wrong was comforting and admirable. But she went on to explain that one of the hardest ethical boundaries to navigate is the one between a client's need to make money and a professional's need to make money. Unlike clear-cut situations such as commingling or misappropriating client funds, avoiding subtle conflicts of interest took a very deliberate ongoing effort. Not willing to back down, Amy shared a cautionary tale about another idealistic professional from her own training class.

Kelly, who was about ten years older than Amy, already had a family of four when she began working at Amy's firm. Unlike Amy, who was single, Kelly could not suddenly ask her family to begin eating Top Ramen and microwave burritos while she struggled to earn her first commissions and fees. To compensate, Kelly worked extra long hours and jumped at every opportunity to open new accounts.

Unfortunately, Kelly's efforts didn't result in nearly enough revenue, even though she was the branch leader in establishing new client relationships. As the months went by, Amy noticed that Kelly was making more and more questionable decisions regarding the advice and recommendations she gave her clients.

It started with Kelly shifting her investment philosophy from "buy and hold" to "active trader." While Amy was not opposed to that philosophy, she overheard Kelly joking at the office Christmas party, in front of the other professionals' dates, about how she had become an expert at talking her clients into larger than average trades. She even mentioned clients by name, poking fun at a client who was also a well-known business owner, which was a breach of client confidentiality.

As the months progressed, Amy explained that Kelly began to trade in small penny stocks, not only for her clients, but also for herself. Often times, Kelly would even spread rumors about these stocks around the office, in hopes of talking other professionals into buying or selling the stocks and, in turn, driving the price up or down.

Though Kelly's strategy seemed to be paying off for her, all her ethical violations came to a head and her career came to an end when she began soliciting unqualified clients to participate in performance-based compensation arrangements. The firm, upon review of the previous few months of Kelly's activities, fired her for "substantial violations of her fiduciary responsibility and engaging in numerous conflicts of interest." As was required by law, her firm also reported her to securities regulators, resulting in both a civil suit and criminal charges against Kelly.

☐ What constitutes an unreasonable fee?

☐ What compensation conflicts of interest must be disclosed to a client in writing?

☐ With whom can a professional not split fees or commissions?

☐ What is the rule concerning charging fees for miscellaneous services?

☐ What is a soft-dollar arrangement?

☐ What services can be received under a soft-dollar arrangement?

☐ What services are prohibited on a soft-dollar basis?

☐ Define custody.

☐ Define discretion.

☐ Define commingling.

☐ What type of discretion needs a written authorization?

☐ When must a written authorization giving discretion be on file?

☐ What is a trading authorization and who might it be given to?

☐ What are the prudent investor standards?

☐ What is suitability?

☐ What is the general difference between the prudent investor standard and suitability?

☐ What constitutes an unethical trading practice?

☐ Define front-running.

☐ Define conflict of interest.

☐ Define excessive trading.

☐ How many trades does it take to be considered excessive?

☐ What is another name for excessive trading?

☐ Who can loan money to their clients?

☐ Who can borrow money from their clients?

☐ Which clients are eligible for a performance-based compensation arrangement?

☐ Which client information must a professional keep confidential?

☐ When can client confidentiality be broken?

☐ Define insider trading.

☐ What is non-public information?

☐ Define selling away.

☐ Define market manipulation.

☐ What are some common ways professionals manipulate the market?

☐ What is an agency cross transaction and how does it need to be handled?

☐ What is the conflict of interest in acting as an agent to both parties to a transaction?

☐ When are professionals permitted to recommend securities that they themselves also own?

Chapter 5 Practice Questions

1. **If a professional is registered as both an agent and an investment adviser representative, which of the following is true regarding agent commissions and investment advisory fees:**

   A. The professional may charge both to the same client at the same time.

   B. The professional may charge both, but not to the same client at the same time.

   C. The professional must charge whichever results in the lowest overall cost to a client.

   D. The professional may not charge both, but has to choose if he is going to operate as an investment adviser representative or agent.

2. **A good measure of whether or not a fee is reasonable is:**

   A. Whether or not a client feels it is fair

   B. What fees are charged to other similar clients

   C. What portion of the fee a professional keeps

   D. How long the client has been with the professional

3. **Which compensation-related conflicts must be disclosed to a client in writing?**

   I.   Receiving bonuses from their firm based on their level of revenue

   II. Splitting compensation with another licensed professional

   III. Splitting compensation with an unlicensed professional

   IV. Receiving compensation related to an account that is in addition to what was initially disclosed to a client

   A. IV only

   B. I and IV

   C. I, II, and III

   D. II, III, and IV

4. **Soft-dollar arrangements can best be defined as:**

   A. Those in which the client's fees or commission are based on volume

   B. Those in which a broker-dealer provides products or services to a professional or firm without charging them

   C. Those in which a client's commissions are counted toward their investment advisory fee

   D. Those in which securities professionals trade their services for services their clients can offer

5. **Which of the following soft-dollar services can be ethically accepted by a professional or his firm?**

    I.   Research services
    II. Investment analysis software
    III. A laptop computer to run investment software
    IV. Subscriptions to electronic data services that provide quotes and news headlines

    A. I only
    B. I and II
    C. I, II and IV
    D. I, II, III, and IV

6. **Which of the following types of compensation can result in a conflict of interest for a securities professional?**

    I.   Soft-dollar arrangements
    II. Commissions
    III. Investment advisory fees
    IV. A $50 annual account maintenance fee

    A. I only
    B. I and II
    C. I, II, and III
    D. I, II, III, and IV

7. **Which of the following would constitute custody over client assets?**

    A. A professional who can initiate trades in a client's account at the client's broker-dealer of choice.
    B. A professional who accepts a check from a client, made payable to a mutual fund company, to be submitted with his or her application to open an account with that mutual fund.
    C. A professional who accepts prepayment of a client's advisory fees.
    D. A professional who stores a client's stock and bond certificates in his or her firm's safe.

8. **All of the following are true of discretionary authority for an investment adviser except:**

    A. It shifts responsibility for determining suitability off of the professional and on to a client.
    B. A written discretionary agreement must be on file with the professional's firm within 10 days of the first trade.
    C. Discretionary authority can initially be granted verbally, until paperwork can be properly signed.
    D. Discretionary authority can be revoked at any time by a client.

9. **When an investment adviser or broker-dealer has custody over a client's assets, those assets must be:**

   A. Segregated
   B. Commingled
   C. Invested promptly
   D. Audited quarterly

10. **Which of the following would represent an unethical action on the part of a professional?**

    I.   Depositing client funds to their personal bank account
    II. Withdrawing a client's advisory fee from the client's account
    III. Using client funds to pay for a business luncheon with that client
    IV. Pooling all his or her clients' cash balances and paying his or her firm's legitimate operating expenses out of those balances

    A. I only
    B. I, II and III
    C. I, III, and IV
    D. I, II, III, and IV

11. **When a client gives an agent of a broker-dealer permission to buy 100 shares of XYZ Corporation, but leaves the purchase price and the timing up to the agent, that agent has been given:**

    A. Full discretion
    B. Time and price discretion
    C. Custody
    D. Third-party trading authorization

12. **When a customer wishes to buy or sell a security, a broker-dealer:**

    A. Is obligated to get them the lowest or highest price of the day, respectively
    B. Is obligated to get the client a fair price, as close to the agreed-upon price as possible
    C. Cannot buy or sell the security for its own account during the same day
    D. Does not have any obligations relative to price; investing is inherently risky

13. **All of the following are true for investment advisers holding custody over client assets except:**

    A. They must provide regular statements of account.
    B. They must provide prompt access to free credit balances.
    C. They must conduct quarterly audits of each account.
    D. They must properly segregate client assets.

14. A fiduciary is best defined as:

    A. Someone who works for someone else

    B. Someone who is expected to make a profit for someone else, to the best of their ability

    C. Someone who gets paid to give advice to someone else

    D. Someone who is placed in a position of trust and expected to act in the best interest of someone else

15. All of the following would be considered clear conflicts of interest except:

    A. Recommending a security for purchase that is owned by the adviser's other clients

    B. Recommending a security also owned by the adviser

    C. Recommending securities from an issuer that employs the adviser's spouse

    D. Receiving a free Wall Street journal subscription from a mutual fund company whose products you sell to your clients

16. All of the following are true regarding an investment professional's obligations toward client confidentiality except:

    A. Firms are responsible for ensuring that clients' electronic data is secure from online hackers.

    B. Client records must be kept confidential in all cases.

    C. Firms must ensure that customer records and information are kept secure.

    D. Periodic reviews of firm databases in which customer information is stored must take place.

17. Which of the following would constitute someone sharing inside information?

    A. A CEO talking to his barber about last year's annual report for his company

    B. A securities professional sharing a stock tip with someone who is not a customer

    C. A CEO's spouse telling his mother about an upcoming merger that will be announced the following week

    D. A stockholder telling a non-stockholder what was discussed in that year's annual stockholder's meeting

18. Which of the following clients may enter into a performance-based compensation arrangement with an investment adviser?

    I. Registered investment companies

    II. An individual with over $500,000 in net worth

    III. A business development company

    IV. An investment adviser's secretary

    A. I only

    B. I and III

    C. II and III

    D. I, II, and IV

19. Selling away is best defined as:

    A. Selling investments not offered by an agent's firm

    B. Selling securities to individuals who are not clients

    C. Selling a firm's securities at a better price than their client's securities

    D. Churning a customer's account

20. An agency cross transaction performed by an investment adviser:

    A. Is unethical and not permitted

    B. Is unethical and not permitted if the adviser is receiving a fee or commission from both parties

    C. May be ethical and does not represent a conflict of interest

    D. May be ethical and requires a signed consent form from any involved clients

Chapter 5 Practice Question Answers

1. **Answer: A.** A firm or professional may theoretically charge both to a client, but this fact needs to be disclosed to them in writing. Professionals are not required to choose the compensation arrangement that results in the lowest overall cost, as long as the compensation arrangement chosen is in the client's best interest.

2. **Answer: B.** While it is not the only measure that should be used to determine if a fee is fair, a client that is being charged substantially more than other similar clients is likely being charged an unreasonable fee. Since most clients would always prefer a lower fee, their opinion of their fee is not a great measure of its reasonableness. Likewise, the portion of a fee the IAR or agent keeps after his or her firm takes their cut and the length of a relationship are not good measures of whether or not a fee is ultimately fair and reasonable.

3. **Answer: A.** Receiving compensation related to an account that wasn't initially disclosed to a client requires a new disclosure of that fact in writing. Neither receiving broad-based bonuses that do not create conflicts of interest nor sharing compensation with another licensed professional would require a separate written disclosure. Splitting compensation with an unlicensed professional is prohibited in general, regardless of a disclosure being made.

4. **Answer: B.** Anytime a professional receives services from a broker who also provides services to her clients, it is considered a soft-dollar arrangement and can result in a conflict of interest.

5. **Answer: C.** Research services, software for analysis, and electronic data subscriptions are all acceptable for soft-dollar arrangements. Computer hardware, furniture, and clerical services are all prohibited in soft-dollar arrangements.

6. **Answer: D.** Any compensation, commission, or fees charged by a firm or their professionals can create a conflict of interest. Even an account maintenance fee, which can represent a large amount of money when multiplied across thousands of accounts on an annual basis, can create a conflict of interest.

7. **Answer: D.** Having physical possession over a client's securities definitely constitutes custody. If an investment adviser who is not also a broker-dealer receives securities, they must be returned to the sender within three days to avoid it constituting custody. Being able to initiate trades in an account held at another broker-dealer simply constitutes a trading authorization. Passing along a check made out to another firm or investment company would not constitute custody, as long as the investment adviser or investment adviser representative forwards it on to the proper custodian within three business days. Prepaid fees are simply that, prepaid fees.

8. **Answer: A.** Since the professional has been given the highest level of freedom to buy and sell in a customer's account without the customer authorizing each trade, there is even more responsibility than before to determine suitability placed on the adviser. Discretionary authority can be revoked at any time by a customer. Discretionary authority for investment advisers and investment adviser representatives can be initially granted verbally, and must be evidenced by a written agreement within 10 days of the initial discretionary trade.

9. **Answer: A.** Assets should be segregated, or separated, from a professional's or firm's assets. If they are not, it is considered commingling and is unethical. Client assets should only be

invested after a professional has determined suitability, which may take a while. Client accounts should be audited at least yearly.

10. **Answer: C.** Depositing client funds to a professional's personal account is commingling and is highly unethical. Likewise, using client assets to pay any expenses (business luncheons, firm expenses, etc.) is misappropriation and is also unethical. Withdrawing the fee outlined in an account agreement or advisory contract, however, is permissible.

11. **Answer: B.** This type of discretion occurs when a client gives instructions to buy or sell a security but leaves the actual time and price of that trade up to the professional's expertise. No written authorization is needed for this level of discretion, assuming the trade takes place by the end of the business day. Full discretionary authority, when a professional is free to buy what he wants, when he wants, requires a written authorization from the client.

12. **Answer: B.** Broker-dealers and agents should always attempt to get a client a price that is as close as possible to the agreed-upon price (or the market price, if that is what the client wished to transact at). There is no way a firm could reasonably get someone the highest or lowest price of the day. Firms and professionals can buy and sell for their own accounts on the same day, but they need to ensure that their client is not having to get in line for a good price after the firm. Clients' needs and their right to fair transactions should always come before a professional's or firm's desires.

13. **Answer: C.** Client accounts must be audited by an independent third party annually, not quarterly. Additionally, clients must be provided with regular statements (at least quarterly), have access to their free credit balances promptly, and have their assets segregated from the firm's general assets and a professional's personal assets.

14. **Answer: D.** At its core, a fiduciary is a trusted professional expected to give advice and act in a way that is in the best interest of her client. Simply working for someone else or getting paid to give advice does not make someone a fiduciary. Rather it is a unique expectation that is placed on financial professionals, defined by the fact that trust is placed in a person, regardless of how or if she is compensated. Lastly, fiduciaries are not expected to make as much profit as possible for each client, but rather to do what is most in line with each client's objectives and risk tolerance.

15. **Answer: A.** Simply recommending a good thing to multiple clients is not a conflict of interest; more likely it is an expectation of a good investment adviser. However, recommending securities that the professional owns does create a conflict of interest, as does receiving a Wall Street Journal subscription paid for by a mutual fund vendor or recommending securities issued by a spouse's employer. It's important to note, however, that conflicts of interest do not by themselves prohibit a professional from acting, but rather require proper disclosure to the client or prospect.

16. **Answer: B.** Client records may be released by client request, legal requirement, or court order.

17. **Answer: C.** Due to the fact that the merger has not been announced yet, sharing this information with anyone outside the company, even a spouse or partner, could be considered the illegal sharing of non-public information. A CEO talking about last year's annual report is talking about information that is already public, as is a stockholder sharing information learned in a stockholder's meeting. A stock tip from a professional is not unethical by itself, unless it is actually based on info that is considered non-public.

18. **Answer: B.** Performance-based compensation contracts are available only to clients that likely have the ability to understand the risk and conflicts of interest associated with them. Those clients include registered investment companies (mutual funds) and business development companies. Individual investors must have over $2 million in net worth, excluding their primary residence (or $1 million in assets with the professional's company), not $500,000. Lastly, senior personnel and securities professionals at investment advisory firms can hire other investment advisers and IARs on a performance-basis, but not a firm's rank and file employees such as secretarial staff.

19. **Answer: A.** Selling securities not offered through one's broker-dealer represents an ethical violation if done without the broker-dealer's approval. Churning a customer account and getting a better price on the same securities when transacting at the same time as a customer are ethical violations, but aren't classified as selling away. Selling to individuals who aren't clients does not necessarily represent an ethical violation, since they'd arguably become clients the moment you sell to them.

20. **Answer: D.** An agency cross transaction is one in which the broker or agent is acting on behalf of both the buyer and seller in the same transaction. For investment advisers acting as brokers, this presents a natural conflict of interest since the adviser is supposed to work in the best interest of each individual party. However, these types of transactions are permitted if the adviser only recommends the trade to one side of the transaction (the buyer or the seller, not both), the adviser provides the client with full disclosure regarding the agency cross transaction and obtains the customer's written consent, the adviser sends the client a written confirmation at the completion of each transaction, and the adviser annually discloses to the client in writing how many agency cross transactions have been made on the client's behalf and the amount of commissions generated from them.

CHAPTER SIX
Federal Securities Acts

(There are not any exam questions specifically designated to test material in this section. Instead, this chapter provides necessary background information to help you answer other questions.)

The laws that govern the securities industry at the federal level include the Securities Act of 1933, the Securities Exchange Act of 1934, and other key pieces of legislation. The framework for these laws was created after the greatest stock market crash in U.S. history, because individual investors lost an enormous amount of wealth that had been invested in a largely unregulated stock market, by a largely unregulated industry of issuers, broker-dealers, and investment advisers.

More than anything else, the regulations contained in these acts are in place to protect investors by ensuring four key things. The first is to ensure that securities sold to consumers are properly registered before they hit the shelves for sale. Proper registration means that the issuers of the securities must disclose all relevant information about the securities. This brings us to our second point, which is that investors need to have all the information at hand to make an informed decision about the security before they invest. The third is that investment professionals and broker-dealers must meet standardized requirements prior to opening up shop. The final goal is to outline key ethical standards and practices clearly, so that no professional, firm, or securities issuer can claim it didn't know better.

6.1. THE SECURITIES ACT OF 1933

One of the first pieces of legislation to come out of the most devastating U.S. stock market crash of all time was the Securities Act of 1933. At the core of this act is the belief that investors have a right to make informed decisions about the securities they're purchasing or own. To that end, the Securities Act of 1933 requires the vast majority of securities offered to U.S. investors to go through a registration and disclosure process.

The initial step in this process is the filing of a registration statement, which contains key information about the security being issued, the details of its actual issue process (price, date, etc.), and information about the issuer itself. Usually, this form is filed by the company issuing the securities with the help of an investment banker (also known as an underwriter), who is a special type of broker-dealer that focuses on helping companies issue their securities to the public.

When this registration is filed, the security begins a 20-day cooling-off period. During this period, regulators examine the registration filing and the issuer to make sure the legal requirements are met. This usually means checking to make sure that all the necessary information is there for investors to make an informed decision for themselves. When the SEC determines that the security has met the registration requirements, it is not approving the security. During this cooling-off period, no sales may be made for the security.

During the cooling-off period, a tombstone ad may be published, which announces the basic details of the offering without discussing its investment merits or offering it for sale. The underwriter or issuer may take indications of interest, however. An indication of interest is nothing more than that—an investor saying he might be interested in purchasing the security, without the investor actually committing to it, depositing any type of money, etc. Financial professionals need to be careful that they don't promise their clients the ability to obtain a security before it is issued, much less take a deposit for the purchase of the security. Doing so could lead to a violation of the Securities Act of 1933. Anyone providing an indication of interest must be given a copy of the preliminary prospectus, also known as the red herring.

If all goes as planned, the security is released to the public by regulators on the issue date chosen by the issuer in its registration statement, which must be at least 20 days after the filing time. If the issuer decides not to offer the security immediately, and instead holds it for a later date when the market is more favorable, it is referred to as a shelf offering, since it is being registered and put back on the shelf for later use.

Buyers in the initial public offering receive the security at its public offering price, or POP. This first time it is sold is in the primary market, but then it trades freely in the secondary market with the price being driven by investor demand.

6.1.1. EXEMPTIONS TO THE SECURITIES ACT OF 1933

If a security is deemed exempt from the Securities Act of 1933, it means the issuer does not need to register the security on the federal level. However, the issuer may be required to register the security at the state level, depending on each state's laws and procedures.

Securities exempt from registration under the Securities Act of 1933 include:

- Federal government securities (U.S. Treasury bonds, U.S. savings bonds, and U.S. agency bonds, such as mortgage-backed securities and collateralized mortgage obligations)
- Municipal securities (issued by city, county, and state governments)
- Bank securities such as certificates of deposit (CDs)
- Commercial paper (fixed-income securities that mature less than 270 days from issuance)
- Securities issued by charitable and non-profit organizations

Additionally, certain offerings and transactions (not just the security, as above, but how the security is offered or sold) are exempt from the Securities Act of 1933. These include:

- **Regulation A offerings, also known as circular offerings.** An issuer can issue and sell up to $50,000,000 worth of securities within any 12 month period with a reduced registration filing requirement.

- **Regulation D offerings, also known as private placements.** These are sales of securities to accredited investors or 35 or fewer non-accredited investors, though paperwork must still be filed. The securities issued under a private placement are restricted and cannot be resold without meeting specific requirements laid out in Rule 144. This kind of stock is often referred to as legend stock because of the prohibition printed on the stock itself.

- **Rule 147 offerings.** These offerings allow an issuer to register its securities with its own state and not federal regulators if the issuer's main operations are located within that state, 80% of its income is generated in the state, and 80% of its assets are located within the state. The issuer must agree to sell to state residents only. Buyers of the stock additionally must agree not to resell to non-residents for at least nine months.

6.2. THE SECURITIES EXCHANGE ACT OF 1934

Right after the Securities Act of 1933 was passed, legislators and regulators recognized the need to also regulate those who sell securities to the public for a living, not just the securities themselves. It turns out that securities don't have as great a tendency as people do to act unethically. Under this act, broker-dealers and agents or representatives acting on their behalf are required to register with regulators.

To meet its objectives, the Securities Exchange Act of 1934 (also referred to as the Exchange Act or the 1934 Act) defines a broad set of guidelines to govern securities trading. Five major pieces of information about the Exchange Act are important to remember:

- It contains important trading laws—including laws on insider trading.w

- It gave the Federal Reserve Board the power to regulate margin requirements.

- It created the Securities and Exchange Commission (SEC) to be the body primarily responsible for the creation and enforcement of securities laws.

- It allows securities exchanges to regulate themselves (e.g., New York Stock Exchange)—under the condition that they register with the SEC and devise a set of rules consistent with the Act's specific guidelines.

- It allows broker-dealers to regulate themselves—under the condition that they register with a national securities association. Like the exchanges, the association would register with the SEC and devise its own rules under SEC guidelines.

This last point came in a 1938 amendment to the Exchange Act, known as the Maloney Act. The over-the-counter market was not initially included in the 1934 Act, because the market was considered too spread out and ill-defined to be effectively regulated. Under the Maloney Act, the OTC market would be regulated by a national securities association, which would regulate and enforce the federal securities laws and SEC regulations.

Today the Financial Industry Regulatory Authority (FINRA) is the entity that regulates the OTC market. Broker-dealers who do business in the securities industry must register with FINRA, except for bank dealers and those who deal exclusively in exempt securities, such as municipal securities.

The 1934 Act is often referred to as the People Act because it regulates the people, such as broker-dealers, who work in the securities industry.

Because the exchanges and national securities associations are allowed to regulate themselves, they are called self-regulatory organizations (SROs). Besides the New York Stock Exchange, SROs include NASDAQ, FINRA, the MSRB, and the Chicago Board Options Exchange. FINRA remains the only fully registered national securities association.

 EXERCISE

MATCH THE ACT TO THE CORRECT STATEMENT

A. 1933 Act
B. 1934 Act

1. _____ This Act regulates the primary markets for securities.

2. _____ This Act requires the registration of all nonexempt securities.

3. _____ This Act regulates secondary markets for securities.

4. _____ This Act established the SEC.

5. _____ This Act requires broker-dealers to register.

6. _____ This Act allows the exchanges to regulate themselves.

Answers: 1. A; 2. A; 3. B; 4. B; 5. B; 6. B

6.3. TRUST INDENTURE ACT OF 1939

While the aftermath of the stock market crash of 1929 was immediately apparent to investors who owned stocks, it took another five to ten years for bondholders to feel the full effect of the economic implosion. Companies that were initially able to hang on by a thread and make interest payments eventually began defaulting in greater and greater numbers. In response, the U.S. government instituted the Trust Indenture Act of 1939. Under the Trust Indenture Act, companies issuing more than $5 million worth of bonds over a one-year period are required to enter into a contractual relationship with a trustee. The trustee's job is to ensure that investors receive what they are promised under the bond issue (interest and principal) and to pursue legal action on behalf of the bondholders if an issuer fails to pay what was promised.

6.4. INVESTMENT COMPANY ACT OF 1940

Many people claim that the Investment Company Act of 1940 created mutual funds, but this is incorrect. Mutual funds, along with other types of pooled investments, were available even before the 1929 stock market crash. The Investment Company Act of 1940, instead, began regulating these investments and their issuers. Also covered under the act are unit investment trusts (UITs), which are simplified investment pools for which a preset portfolio is constructed and a limited amount of investment units are sold, and face value certificates, which are essentially unit investment trusts that promise to pay back investors a certain amount on a certain date.

The main purpose of this act is to require the same types of disclosures for mutual funds, UITs, and face value certificates (collectively referred to as investment companies), as were already required for other types of securities. It is important to not confuse this act with the Investment Advisers Act of 1940, which regulates the professionals who might recommend or manage these investments.

The Investment Company Act of 1940 protects those who invest in investment company securities by requiring that all investment companies:

- Register with the SEC

- Prepare a prospectus stating the company's investment objectives and financial conditions

- Submit annual reports to the SEC and semiannual reports to shareholders (the reports must include a balance sheet, an income statement, a list of securities owned, and a statement of recent changes in the portfolio)

- Obey other operating and governance rules specific to the type of fund.

An investment company must be a domestic corporation and at least 40% of its board of directors must not be interested persons of the investment company.

6.5. INVESTMENT ADVISERS ACT OF 1940

As mentioned earlier, the Investment Advisers Act of 1940 requires the registration of people and companies giving investment advice to the public for a fee. This stands in contrast to the Securities Exchange Act of 1934, which regulates firms and individuals acting as broker-dealers and earning their revenue through commissions and markups.

Whether an adviser must register under the Investment Advisers Act of 1940 comes down to whether or not the adviser answers yes to all three of the following questions:

- Does it provide investment advice? First and foremost, does someone give advice relating to the purchase, sale, or management of investments?

- Is the adviser actually in the business of providing advice? Incidental advice, given in the course of offering other non-investment advice, does not require someone to register. The act specifically notes that lawyers, accountants, engineers, or teachers who are giving this advice as part of a broader job description are exempt from registration.

- Is the adviser compensated for giving investment advice? If someone is compensated for providing investment advice, as opposed to receiving compensation for primarily providing another service, it would indicate the need for registration.

Specifically exempted from registration under the Investment Advisers Act of 1940 are:

- Broker-dealers whose advice is incidental to the conduct of their business, with no additional fees or compensation added to pay for the advice
- Banks
- Advisers dealing only in government securities
- Publishers of general investment newsletters and books

Advisers with $110 million or more in assets under management must register on a federal level (with the SEC). Advisers with less than $100 million under management must register at the state level. Investment advisers with assets under management of at least $100 million but less than $110 million can choose where they register—state or federal.

To register, advisers must file a **Form ADV**, which includes their background information, the nature of their business, their education, etc.

☐ The Securities Act of 1933 was created to provide reliable information to investors about the securities they invest in. In the Act, how is this goal attained?

☐ How many days is the cooling-off period and what is permitted during the cooling-off period?

☐ Name five major exemptions to the Securities Act of 1933.

☐ What part of the securities industry does the Securities Exchange Act of 1934 regulate?

☐ What national securities association regulates broker-dealers, agents, and the OTC market?

☐ What is the responsibility of the trustee in the Trust Indenture Act of 1939?

☐ Which federal securities legislation regulates pooled investments, also known as investment companies?

☐ Name four legal requirements of investment companies under the Investment Company Act of 1940.

☐ Publishers are exempted from which landmark securities legislation?

Chapter 6 Practice Questions

1. **The primary purpose of the Securities Exchange Act of 1934 was to regulate:**

   A. Issuers of securities

   B. Investment companies

   C. Broker-dealers, agents, and the exchanges

   D. Investment advisers

2. **All of the following would be exempt from registration under the Investment Advisers Act of 1940 except:**

   A. Broker-dealer charging a fee for investment advice

   B. Publisher charging a fee to write a column about investments

   C. Lawyer giving investment advice as part of his oversight of a client's estate

   D. Teacher paid for instructing students on the proper way to construct a portfolio

3. **Under the Investment Advisers Act of 1940, advisers must register if all of the following are true except:**

   A. They provide investment advice.

   B. They are in the business of providing advice.

   C. They are compensated for giving investment advice.

   D. They buy and sell securities.

4. **Bond investors are protected by what piece of legislation?**

   A. The Securities Exchange Act

   B. The Trust Indenture Act

   C. The Investment Company Act

   D. The Investment Advisers Act

5. **Which of the following exceptions to the Securities Act permits up to 35 non-accredited investors:**

   A. Regulation D offerings

   B. Rule 147 offerings

   C. Regulation A offerings

   D. Cooling-off offerings

Chapter 6 Practice Question Answers

1. **Answer: C.** The Securities Exchange Act of 1934 was designed to regulate broker-dealers, individuals selling securities on behalf of broker-dealers, and the exchanges the trades take place on. Issuers of securities are primarily regulated under the Securities Act of 1933. Investment companies are primarily regulated under the Investment Company Act of 1940. Investment advisers are primarily regulated under the Investment Advisers Act of 1940.

2. **Answer: A.** Broker-dealers are regulated under the Securities Exchange Act of 1934 and are exempt under the Investment Advisers Act as long as they do not charge a fee for giving investment advice that is incidental to the provision of their commission- or markup-based services. Publishers, lawyers, teachers, and engineers are all exempt if their advice is incidental to their primary job description.

3. **Answer: D.** Buying and selling securities—in other words, serving as a securities broker-dealer—does not require investment adviser registration under the Investment Advisers Act of 1940.

4. **Answer: B.** Under the Trust Indenture Act, companies issuing more than $5 million of bonds over a one-year period are required to enter into a contractual relationship with a trustee. The trustee's job is to ensure that investors receive what they are promised under the bond issue and to pursue legal action if an issuer fails to pay what was promised.

5. **Answer: A.** Regulation D offerings, also known as private placements, are sales of securities to accredited investors or 35 or fewer non-accredited investors. The securities issued under a private placement are restricted and cannot be resold without meeting specific requirements laid out in Rule 144. This kind of stock is often referred to as legend stock, due to the prohibition printed on the stock itself.

    Regulation A offerings, also known as circular offerings, allow an issuer to issue and sell up to $5,000,000 worth of securities with a reduced registration filing requirement.

    Rule 147 offerings allow an issuer to register its securities with its own state and not federal regulators if the issuer's main operations are located within that state, 80% of its income is generated in the state, and 80% of its assets are located within the state.

    Cooling-off offerings exist only in the imagination of the writer of this question.

Practice Exam #1

1. **An employee of an investment advisory firm who provides advice and solicits new customers must be registered as a(n):**

   A. Investment adviser
   B. Investment adviser representative
   C. Broker-dealer
   D. Agent

2. **All of the following may result in mandatory federal registration for an investment adviser except:**

   A. Operating as a mid-sized investment adviser with clients in 39 states
   B. Working as a pension plan consultant with $25 million in employee accounts
   C. Serving as an adviser to registered investment companies
   D. Sharing an office with an affiliated SEC-registered adviser

3. **All of the following are true of an investment adviser's registration except:**

   A. It expires one year after it was filed.
   B. It becomes effective 30 days after filing.
   C. They must file a consent to service of process.
   D. They must meet net capital requirements.

4. **Which of the following would not meet the definition of an investment adviser representative?**

   A. An employee under the direct supervision of the investment adviser
   B. Clerical or ministerial staff
   C. An investment adviser representative with fewer than five clients in the state where they have their office
   D. An agent of a broker-dealer who receives a fee for telling a client to not purchase any investments at the current time

5. **All of the following must be filed on behalf of an investment adviser representative at the appropriate time except:**

   A. Form ADV
   B. Form U4
   C. Form U5
   D. Notice of Termination

6. **All of the following are true of an investment adviser representative's registration except:**

   A. It is effective 45 days after filing.
   B. It expires December 31 of each year.
   C. It can be suspended for filing an incomplete application.
   D. It can be revoked for failing to meet continuing education requirements.

7. **Which of the following must be completed within 30 days for an investment adviser representative assuming there are no administrative orders against the application or pending proceedings?**

   I.   Registration after application has been submitted
   II.   Notice of Transfer
   III. Notice of Conditions
   IV.   Withdrawal after application has been submitted

   A. I and II
   B. II and III
   C. I and IV
   D. III and IV

8. **An agent is excluded from the definition of a broker-dealer because:**

   A. Agents work for investment advisers.
   B. Agents and broker-dealers are the same thing.
   C. Agents do not ever act in a dealer capacity; only in a brokerage capacity.
   D. Agents are considered employees of broker-dealers or issuers.

9. **All of the following are excluded from the definition broker-dealer except:**

   A. Investment advisers who offer in-house brokerage services
   B. An international banking institution not offering brokerage services
   C. Issuers
   D. Agents

10. **Two broker-dealers can transact with one another:**

    A. Regardless of their registration status with a state
    B. Only if both broker-dealers are registered
    C. As long as one broker-dealer is registered
    D. As long as the broker-dealer initiating the transaction is registered in that state

11. **All of the following are exceptions to the definition of a broker-dealer except:**

    A. An institutional investor
    B. An issuer
    C. A credit union that only offers CDs
    D. An agent

12. Which of the following are customers that would potentially exempt a firm from having to register as a broker-dealer in a state in which the firm has no office?

I. An insurance company
II. A pre-existing customer that is only temporarily in another state
III. A private investor with more than $1,000,000 in assets
IV. An investment company

A. I and II
B. II and III
C. I, II, and IV
D. I, II, III, and IV

13. All of the following banks would be required to register as a broker-dealer under the 1956 Uniform Securities Act except:

A. A bank that leases out a portion of its space to an otherwise unrelated broker-dealer
B. A bank whose employees receive a flat fee for referring customers to the bank's affiliated broker-dealer
C. A bank that offers broker-dealer services under an identical name
D. None of these would be required to register

14. Which of the following activities are permitted for foreign broker-dealers wishing to remain exempt from registration?

I. Directly effecting transactions for institutional investors
II. Effecting transactions for retail investors through a registered broker-dealer
III. Effecting unsolicited securities transactions
IV. Soliciting transactions for a foreign client who is vacationing in the United States.

A. I and II
B. II and III
C. III and IV
D. I and IV

15. Which of the following can only occur in an Office of Supervisory Jurisdiction?

A. Creation of sales literature
B. Solicitation of customer orders
C. Initial completion of client paperwork
D. Order execution

16. Agents working for a foreign broker-dealer operating in a state:

A. Are exempt from registration
B. Are exempt only if their broker-dealer is also exempt
C. Only need to register if they are U.S. citizens
D. Do not need to register

17. **All of the following would be considered an agent except:**

    A. Someone who only offers to complete a transaction but does not follow through on it

    B. Someone who receives incentive compensation for helping an issuer sell his or her securities

    C. Someone who only receives a commission for a transaction that was incidental to their primary role

    D. Someone who is the director of a broker-dealer

18. **Which of the following conditions would most likely result in someone acting as an agent being exempt from state registration as such?**

    A. Selling mutual funds that only invest in government securities

    B. Working for a broker-dealer that is also exempt from state registration

    C. Having fewer than five clients in their state of residence

    D. Holding another credential such as the CFP or CIMA designation

19. **Which of the following actions would not result in someone needing to be registered as an agent in a state?**

    I.   Helping an issuer repurchase its own securities

    II. Helping an issuer sell its securities to employees of the issuer without receiving a commission or incentive compensation

    III. Purchasing an issuer's securities for your own account

    IV. Selling AA rated commercial paper for a broker-dealer

    A. I and II

    B. I and III

    C. I, II, and III

    D. I, II, III, and IV

20. **All of the following are means by which a state securities administrator can act against an agent's registration except:**

    A. Withdrawal

    B. Restriction

    C. Revocation

    D. Suspension

21. **A state securities administrator has cancelled the registration of an agent who has demonstrated legal problems until the end of his next licensing period. This is known as:**

    A. Renewal

    B. Suspension

    C. Conditions

    D. Revocation

22. **If an agent becomes newly registered on August 1, 2016, her license must be renewed no later than:**

    A. January 31, 2017
    B. June 1, 2017
    C. August 1, 2017
    D. December 31, 2016

23. **Someone acting on behalf of a registered broker-dealer or issuer would not need to register in any of the following situations except:**

    A. They work for a broker-dealer and only work with institutional investors.
    B. They only sell an issuer's securities on a commission basis.
    C. They only help an issuer repurchase its own securities.
    D. Their only work involves helping customers pledge their securities for a loan.

24. **Which of the following is/are true of someone who works exclusively as an agent, as opposed to an investment adviser representative?**

    I.   Someone working solely as an agent can receive a fee for providing investment advice.
    II. Someone working solely as an agent can receive a commission for helping to effect a transaction.
    III. Someone working solely as an agent can sell securities not offered through their broker-dealer without notifying the broker-dealer.
    IV. Someone working solely as an agent must meet certain net asset requirements.

    A. I only
    B. II only
    C. III and IV
    D. II, III, and IV

25. **Agents and investment adviser representatives are both subject to which of the following requirements?**

    A. Providing consent to service of process
    B. Maintaining a minimum level of net capital
    C. Not using testimonials
    D. Filing a Form ADV as part of the registration process

26. **All of the following are true of a private company that proposes to issue a security except:**

    A. It is considered an issuer, even though no security has been issued.
    B. It must have its securities approved by their state securities administrator.
    C. The individuals selling the securities will need to be registered as agents.
    D. The officers and directors of their company will not need to register as agents.

27. Securities requiring state registration under the Uniform Securities Act include:

  I.   Stock in private companies
  II. Bonds issued by a municipality
  III. Commodities
  IV. Fixed annuities

  A. I only
  B. I and II
  C. I, III, and IV
  D. II, III, and IV

28. One of the primary documents used to register new securities is:

  A. Form 3
  B. Form 144
  C. The registration statement
  D. The Fair Disclosure document

29. Which of the following are Section 402(b) exemptions from registration?

  I.   A transaction between an issuer and an underwriter
  II. A sale to a private, non-institutional investor
  III. An isolated non-issuer transaction
  IV. An unsolicited purchase through a broker-dealer

  A. III only
  B. I and II
  C. I, II, and IV
  D. I, III, and IV

30. All of the following are exceptions to the definition of an offer except:

  A. Stock dividends paid to shareholders without them having to pay anything additional.
  B. Communication to securities holders about a legitimate corporate action
  C. An underwriter re-selling shares it received as compensation during an IPO
  D. Pledging of securities as collateral for a loan

31. If someone charged with a violation requests a hearing in writing, the hearing must be held within:

  A. 10 days
  B. 15 days
  C. 45 days
  D. 60 days

32. If a registrant is found to be in criminal violation of securities laws, he or she may be subject to a maximum of:

    I. $5,000 fine per violation

    II. $10,000 fine per violation

    III. Three years in prison per violation

    IV. Five years in prison per violation

    A. I only

    B. II only

    C. I and III

    D. II and IV

33. The statute of limitations for civil suits is:

    A. Two years from the date of discovery, three years from the date of violation

    B. Two years from the date of violation, three years from the date of discovery

    C. Three years from the date of discovery, five years from the date of violation

    D. Three years from the date of violation, five years from the date of discovery

34. In handling a potential securities violation, an administrator may engage in all of the following actions except:

    A. Issuing subpoenas

    B. Issuing arrest and search warrants

    C. Demanding records from registrants

    D. Communicating investigative results to the public

35. All of the following are true of interpretive opinions except:

    A. They are issued primarily by the SEC, not state administrators.

    B. They are used to terminate investigative proceedings.

    C. They are issued in circumstances where the administrator finds no wrongdoing.

    D. They are based on the laws and code of a state.

36. If a hearing is requested by a professional or firm that has received an administrative order, the administrator must set a date within:

    A. 15 days

    B. 30 days

    C. 60 days

    D. 90 days

37. **Which of the following is true regarding the assignment of an investment advisory contract to another professional?**

    I. The client must give his or her consent.
    II. An explanation that it cannot be transferred without client consent must be included in the advisory contract.
    III. The adviser can transfer it to whoever they deem appropriate in the event of their own incapacity.
    IV. Someone can consent to assignment of their spouse's individual retirement account.

    A. I and II
    B. I, II, and III
    C. I, III, and IV
    D. I, II, III, and IV

38. **A client may waive her rights under the Investment Advisers Act of 1940:**

    A. If the rights being waived are specifically outlined in the advisory contract
    B. If the rights being waived are not also found in the Uniform Securities Act
    C. If the investment adviser is also serving as the client's broker-dealer
    D. Under no circumstances

39. **All of the following would likely be things a client has a right to know under the concept of disclosure except:**

    A. Previous material actions against a registrant by its state
    B. Average rate of return for all of the adviser's clients
    C. Relationships between the adviser and employees of an issuer it is recommending
    D. The termination fee for the advisory contract

40. **An investment advisory contract must contain which of the following?**

    I. The expected increases to the advisory fee after the initial term is up
    II. The amount of the fee to be returned upon early termination of the contract
    III. The target rate of return of the investment contract
    IV. An explanation of the level of trading authority granted with the contract

    A. I and III
    B. II and IV
    C. I, III, and IV
    D. II, III, and IV

41. **Advertisements for securities professionals:**

    A. Must be approved by the state securities administrator
    B. Must not offer free research reports
    C. Must be kept on file by the professional and his firm
    D. Must not include formulas or strategies of any kind

42. If professionals choose to reference their past recommendations, all of the following must occur except:

A. They must provide potential customers with a list of everyone to whom the recommendations were made.

B. They must provide potential customers with a list of all recommendations made within the last 12 months.

C. They must include wording that any past success is no guarantee of future results.

D. They must use accurate historical prices related to their recommendations, if prices are referenced.

43. If a broker-dealer and an investment adviser are affiliated or under shared ownership, which of the following are true?

I. They cannot act in both capacities for the same client.

II. They must disclose this fact to their clients.

III. They must offer their clients the lower cost relationship of the two.

IV. They may not recommend securities they also own in their own account.

A. I only

B. II only

C. II, III, and IV

D. I, II, III, and IV

44. Which statement best describes a professional's duty of disclosure?

A. He must answer any question posed by a client or potential client regarding his firm or his own career.

B. He is only required to provide material information to a client or potential client when directly asked.

C. He must provide a client or potential client with all the material details regarding their relationship, even if not asked.

D. He must only provide clients or potential clients with the information required in an investment advisory contract.

45. Which of the following is prohibited in advertisements offered by investment advisers?

A. Offering prospective clients an informational brochure that includes testimonials from former clients

B. Listing the performance of all past stock picks for the past twelve months

C. Offering free services with the intention of delivering those services

D. All of the choices are prohibited

46. Which of the following must be stated in an investment advisory contract?

    I.   Formula for computing the advisory fee

    II. The amount of return expected to be produced for the client

    III. A statement of commitment to diversification

    A. I only

    B. II and III only

    C. I and III only

    D. I, II, and III

47. The primary standard used in the NASAA Model Rules regarding fees charged by securities professionals is that they must be:

    A. Nominal

    B. Reasonable

    C. Appropriate

    D. Uniform

48. Which of the following are permissible compensation and revenue arrangements under the Uniform Securities Act?

    I.   Soft-dollar arrangements

    II. Administrative fees

    III. Commissions

    IV. Investment advisory fees

    A. I only

    B. II and III

    C. II, III, and IV

    D. I, II, III, and IV

49. All of the following can be accepted by a professional or firm on a soft-dollar basis except:

    A. Research

    B. Electronic market data

    C. Software used to perform investment analysis

    D. Temporary employment help

50. Which of the following situations must be disclosed to a client in writing?

    A. If a professional is receiving both commissions and fees

    B. If a professional has been granted time and price authority over a security purchase

    C. If a professional has had a complaint filed against him by another client

    D. If a professional has acquired an additional professional designation since the start of the client relationship

51. If someone else is legally choosing the securities that are traded in a customer's account, which of the following would allow this?

   I.   A third-party trading authorization has been signed by the client

   II. Full discretion has been given to a securities professional in writing

   III. They are the person's spouse, which grants them authority to trade on their behalf

   IV. The client could not be reached and would have lost a substantial amount of money had their professional not acted

   A. I and II

   B. I and III

   C. I and IV

   D. I, II, III, and IV

52. Client accounts held in custody by an investment adviser must be all of the following except:

   A. Segregated

   B. Audited

   C. Subject to regular statements

   D. Properly insured

53. If a client gives full authority to an investment adviser over the phone:

   A. It is invalid; full discretionary authority must be in writing.

   B. It is invalid; professionals may only exercise time and price discretion.

   C. It is valid if followed up by a written authorization within 10 days from the first trade.

   D. It is valid only in the event that the client will be traveling out of the country or incapacitated.

54. Regarding their free credit balances, customers have a right to:

   A. Access without an unreasonable delay

   B. A fair rate of interest

   C. Monthly statements

   D. No fees unless trading activity actually occurs

55. All of the following may violate the Prudent Investor and Suitability standards except:

   A. Taking too much risk

   B. Not taking enough risk

   C. Recommending the same type of investment to all clients

   D. Using diversification to reduce non-compensated risk

56. Investment advisers must disclose to a client anytime they recommend a security that:

   A. Another client owns

   B. They currently or previously have owned

   C. They or their firm currently own

   D. They, their firm, or any representative at their firm currently owns

57. The definition of churning most likely includes all of the following except:

    A. A professional recommending purchases of securities to generate a commission

    B. A professional recommending sales of securities to generate a commission

    C. A professional with discretionary authority over an account who is trading simply to generate a commission

    D. A professional trading in his or her own account to generate a commission

58. Which of the following would be most likely be considered substantial conflicts of interest for a professional?

    I. Owning securities her clients own

    II. Charging a high-maintenance client a more substantial fee

    III. Being involved in outside business dealings with a client

    IV. Borrowing money from a client's family member

    A. I and II

    B. I and III

    C. II and IV

    D. III and IV

59. A signed margin agreement must be in place no later than:

    A. The date an account is opened

    B. Promptly after the first purchase on margin in the account

    C. 10 days after the first purchase on margin in the account

    D. The date of the first sale of a security purchased on margin

60. All of the following are exceptions listed in the Uniform Securities Act, for which performance-based compensation is acceptable except:

    A. Individuals with a net-worth over $500,000

    B. Registered investment companies

    C. Certain firm personnel

    D. Business development companies

61. Client confidentiality can be broken under which of the following circumstances?

    I. The client requests it

    II. A court order is issued

    III. It is required by law

    IV. At the client's death

    A. I only

    B. I and II

    C. I, II, and III

    D. I, II, III, and IV

62. An investment adviser that was otherwise uninvolved in one of its representatives committing insider trading could be found in violation of the law if it did not:

A. Fire the employee upon discovery of the actions

B. Willingly reimburse investors for damages

C. Have process and procedures in place to prevent insider trading

D. Perform background checks on its customers

63. All of the following would likely constitute selling away except:

A. Switching firms and inviting your previous clients to move their accounts

B. Helping one's brother sell partnerships in his small storage unit business

C. Inviting one's customers to invest funds in a private company that they would not otherwise have access to

D. Helping a client purchase a security that is not offered by your firm, even though it is offered by most others

64. Which of the following actions would likely be considered market manipulations by regulators?

I. Using false information to open and trade in an account

II. Buying or selling a security in regular intervals (dollar-cost averaging)

III. Engaging in a sale between related parties with the intent of creating activity in security

IV. Intentionally entering into identical and opposite trades

A. I only

B. I and II

C. I, II, and III

D. I, III, and IV

65. For an investment adviser to act as agent to parties on both sides of a transaction:

A. Is unethical

B. The clients need to be related

C. The investment adviser must have the client's consent and send the client an annual written disclosure statement

D. Nothing additional needs to occur; he is fulfilling his capacity as an agent

Practice Exam #1 Answers

1. **Answer: B.** An employee of an investment advisory firm would register as an investment adviser representative. Someone working as an employee of a broker-dealer would register as an agent, though someone could technically be registered as both, if she works for a firm that is both an investment adviser and a broker-dealer.

2. **Answer: B.** Pension plan consultants do not need to register on a federal level unless they have $200 million in assets. Operating as a mid-sized investment adviser with clients in 15 or more states would require someone to register federally, as would serving as an adviser to registered investment companies or sharing a principal office with an affiliated SEC-registered investment adviser.

3. **Answer: A.** Investment adviser registration expires on December 31 of each year, so an adviser registering late in the year will only have a few months before he needs to reregister.

4. **Answer: B.** Staff members performing basic secretarial or customer service duties do not need to be registered. Direct supervision does not remove the need for registration. An investment adviser representative must always register in his or her primary state. Giving someone advice to not buy a security still constitutes providing investment advice that could require someone to register.

5. **Answer: A.** Form ADV is filed by an investment adviser to register itself, not an investment adviser representative. All the other mentioned forms must be filed for an IAR.

6. **Answer: A.** Registrations for IARs become effective 30 days after they are filed unless the state's administrator intervenes.

7. **Answer: C.** Registration and withdrawal must be completed within 30 days after the application is filed, assuming there are no administrative orders against the application or pending proceedings.

8. **Answer: D.** Agents are employees of a broker-dealer or issuer and thus do not need to register as a broker-dealer.

9. **Answer: A.** An investment adviser offering brokerage services under the same name must register as a broker-dealer. All the other options are exempt.

10. **Answer: A.** Broker-dealers can always transact with one another, regardless of their registration status in a state.

11. **Answer: A.** Most broker-dealers are in fact considered institutional investors. All the other options are exceptions to the definition of a broker-dealer: an agent and an issuer are both their own exceptions, while a credit union falls under the exception for a bank, savings institution, or trust company.

12. **Answer: C.** There is no exemption for broker-dealer registration for working with individual clients with more than $1,000,000.

13. **Answer: D.** A bank is an exception to the definition of a broker-dealer under the 1956 Uniform Securities Act.

14. **Answer: C.** Foreign broker-dealers can perform a list of prescribed functions and still avoid registration. Those functions include effecting transactions for U.S. institutional investors through a registered broker-dealer; effecting unsolicited transactions; and effecting and soliciting transactions for foreign clients temporarily in the U.S., American citizens resident outside of the U.S., certain international organizations, and agencies or branches of U.S. persons located outside the U.S. Foreign broker-dealers may not effect solicited transactions for American retail investors who are based in the U.S.

15. **Answer: D.** Any location where order execution takes place requires proper supervision by a principal and is considered an Office of Supervisory Jurisdiction (OSJ). The other activities listed can take place outside of an OSJ.

16. **Answer: B.** If a foreign broker-dealer operating in the state is exempt, then so are its agents.

17. **Answer: D.** Officers and directors are not considered agents unless they would otherwise come within the definition of an agent. Offering to complete a transaction (even though it was never completed) still requires registration. Receiving a commission, regardless of the setting, generally requires registration.

18. **Answer: B.** Working for a broker-dealer that is also exempt generally leads to their agents being exempt. Selling a mutual fund that invests in government securities is not the same as the exemption for those who only sell government securities for the government agency. Everyone must register in their home state unless they meet an exemption or can register on a federal level.

19. **Answer: C.** Helping an issuer repurchase its own securities, as well as helping it sell its securities to its own employees on a non-commission basis, does not require registration as an agent. Purchasing for your own account never requires registration. Representing a broker-dealer in a securities transaction, however, does generally require registration.

20. **Answer: A.** Withdrawals are initiated by registrants, not by the state securities administrator as all the other options are.

21. **Answer: B.** Suspension means that the registrant is not permitted to operate in the state for a temporary period.

22. **Answer: D.** All registrations expire on December 31 of each year.

23. **Answer: B.** If someone sells an issuer's securities on a commission basis, then he needs to be registered.

24. **Answer: B.** Someone working solely as an agent can receive a commission for a transaction. She cannot receive a fee for advice or sell away from her firm (sell securities not offered by their broker-dealer without notifying the firm). She is not subject to net asset requirements.

25. **Answer: A.** Both must provide consent to service of process. Agents and IARs do not need to meet net capital requirements, but agents can use testimonials. Advisers, not agents or IARs, must file a Form ADV.

26. **Answer: B.** The state securities administrator does not approve securities and it is important to never give that impression. Generally, individuals selling securities of an issuer need to register as agents, but officers and directors of a company do not. A company is considered an issuer the moment it proposes to offer a security, even though one has not been issued yet.

27. **Answer: A.** Stock in private companies generally requires registration. Municipal bonds, commodities, and fixed annuities do not need registration.

28. **Answer: C.** The registration statement is the primary document used to register a security in a state. Form 3 is filed by corporate insiders with the SEC and Form 144 is filed with the SEC as notice of the proposed sale of restricted securities.

29. **Answer: D.** Transactions between an issuer and their underwriter, as well as isolated non-issuer transactions and unsolicited purchases through broker-dealers, are exempt. Sales to a private investor are not.

30. **Answer: C.** Selling securities in the open market would constitute a valid offer of securities.

31. **Answer: B.** Once a written request for a hearing has been submitted, a hearing must occur within 15 days.

32. **Answer: C.** Registrants found in criminal violation of the law can be fined up to $5,000 per violation and imprisoned for up to 3 years per incident. These fines are not determined by the state's administrator, but must be imposed by a state's judicial system.

33. **Answer: A.** The statute of limitations for civil suits is two years from the date of discovery and three years from the date of violation.

34. **Answer: B.** State securities administrators have no police power. These issues must be handled by local law enforcement if a court deems them necessary. All other options are within the scope of an administrator's power.

35. **Answer: A.** Administrative opinions are issued by the state as a way to terminate an investigation when the administrator finds no incidence of wrongdoing.

36. **Answer: A.** If a hearing is requested, the administrator must set a date within 15 days.

37. **Answer: A.** Clients must be advised that a contract cannot be transferred without their consent and must in fact give consent prior to assignment of a contract. Advisers and spouses cannot assign or consent to assignment without the account owners' consent.

38. **Answer: D.** There are no circumstances under which clients may waive their rights.

39. **Answer: B.** Average rate of return for an adviser's clients is outside the scope of what is practical for most advisers to track and report and does not need to be disclosed to all potential clients. Previous material administrative actions, relationships that create a conflict of interest, and the termination fee for an advisory contract all need to be disclosed.

40. **Answer: B.** The amount of the fee to be returned upon early termination of a contract and an explanation of the level of trading authority must be disclosed in the advisory contract. Expected increases after a contract expires and target rates of return do not need to be included in a contract.

41. **Answer: C.** All advertisements must be kept on file by a professional and his or her firm. Advertisements are not approved by state securities administrators and must specifically not contain any implication that they are. Free research reports can be offered, as long as they truly are free. Formulas can be included in advertisements, but it must not be implied that they are the sole basis for security selection.

42. **Answer: A.** Providing a list of everyone to whom the recommendations were made would be a violation of those clients' confidentiality. A professional must, however, provide a list of all recommendations made in the last 12 months and use accurate historical prices in doing so.

43. **Answer: B.** They must disclose to their clients that they are affiliated or under shared ownership, although they are free to act in both capacities with a client's consent. They are under no obligation to offer the lowest cost arrangement and are not restricted from recommending securities they also own.

44. **Answer: C.** Clients have a right to all material information they might need to make a decision about entering into a relationship with a professional or their firm. They do not need to answer every question asked by their clients, as long as the question or its answer is not material.

45. **Answer: A.** Investment advisers can only use testimonials that appear on an independent third-party website. They can do so if all testimonials related to their firm that appear on the site are presented to clients. Testimonials provided on materials issued by the investment adviser, such as informational pamphlets, are strictly prohibited. Investment advisers can list the performance of past stock picks as long as they list all of them that they have made over the past twelve months. Investment advisers can also promise free services to clients as long as they actually deliver upon that promise.

46. **Answer: A.** An investment advisory contract must include in writing, among other items, the services to be provided, the term of the contract, the advisory fee, and the formula for computing the fee. The expected return is not an item that is required, or typically found, in an investment advisory contract. There is no such statement as a commitment to diversification statement that is required, or typically found, in an investment advisory contract.

47. **Answer: B.** Fees must be reasonable when compared to the services provided.

48. **Answer: D.** All are permissible compensation arrangements under the Uniform Securities Act.

49. **Answer: D.** Clerical help and other overhead expenses cannot be provided on a soft-dollar basis. Research, electronic market data, and investment analysis software can all be provided on a soft-dollar basis.

50. **Answer: A.** If a professional is being compensated as both an agent and an investment adviser representative, this must be disclosed in writing. Time and price discretion does not require written authorization. New complaints do not need to be disclosed, especially prior to the administrator making a ruling, nor do professional designations.

51. **Answer: A.** Authority to choose which securities to transact in for a client's account, whether given to a professional or an unregistered third party, must be in writing. Spouses are not automatically granted authority to trade on each other's behalf simply by being married. Professionals cannot act on a client's behalf without permission, even if they believe it to be a great opportunity or to avoid a loss.

52. **Answer: D.** Accounts must be segregated, audited at least once per year, and statements must be provided to their owners at least quarterly. They are not required to be properly insured under the Uniform Securities Act.

53. **Answer: C.** Phone authorization is valid for an investment adviser or IAR as long as it is followed up with a written authorization in 10 days.

54. **Answer: A.** Customers should be able to access their free credit balances without undue delay. Firms are not under an ethical obligation to provide a competitive rate of interest on their client accounts and are permitted to charge reasonable account fees even if no trading occurs. When an investment adviser takes custody of client assets, statements need to be issued at least quarterly, not monthly.

55. **Answer: D.** Non-compensated risk is risk that an investor isn't paid to take. If an investor does not use diversification, he is subject to greater risk, but his expected return does not increase. Thus a prudent investor should always use diversification if possible. Taking too much risk or failing to take enough, as well as blanket recommending the same investment to all clients regardless of their risk tolerance, would all be violations of suitability and prudent investor standards.

56. **Answer: C.** Investment advisers must advise a client of anytime they are recommending a transaction in a security they or their firm owns. They do not need to advise clients of securities they've previously owned or are owned by representatives at their firm.

57. **Answer: D.** A professional trading in his or her own account to generate a commission would not generally be considered churning, since he or she is aware of the financial consequences of the excessive trading. All the other instances, since they are executed in a client's account, would be considered churning.

58. **Answer: D.** Being involved in outside business dealings with a client as well as borrowing money from a client's family members would both be considered major conflicts of interest. Owning securities that clients own happens frequently and rarely represents a direct conflict of interest. Charging a high-maintenance client more is appropriate as long as the fees fairly represent the amount of work required by the firm and professional.

59. **Answer: B.** A margin agreement must be in place promptly after any trading on margin occurs. It does not need to be in place when the account is opened, since many accounts start as non-margin (cash) accounts and are later converted.

60. **Answer: A.** To enter into a performance-based contract with an individual client, the individual must have at least $1 million under management with the client's firm or $2 million in net worth, excluding the value of his or her primary residence. Registered investment companies; advisory firms' officers, directors, and representatives; and business development companies can all enter into performance-based contracts.

61. **Answer: C.** Client confidentiality can be broken if ordered by a court, if permitted by law (such as under the Patriot Act), or if the client requests it. A client is still entitled to confidentiality at death, with confidential information only being released to the appropriate heirs and individuals handling the estate.

62. **Answer: C.** All investment advisers are expected to have policies and procedures in place to help curtail insider trading. Employees do not necessarily need to be fired and firms are not expected to do background checks on their customers. While firms may be required to reimburse investors after a civil suit, this is not expected until such a suit is brought.

63. **Answer: A.** Switching firms is not unethical by itself. Selling away specifically has to do with being part of the sales process for securities not offered by one's firm. It's important to note that this most often happens with securities and ownership interests in small businesses and local investments whose owners have ties to a professional.

64. **Answer: D.** Using false information to open an account and trade, creating false activity, and entering into identical and opposite trades are all considered forms of market manipulations. Buying securities at regular intervals (such as dollar-cost averaging) does not constitute market manipulation unless it is done with the intent to raise or lower prices.

65. **Answer: C.** If an investment adviser acts as a broker or agent for both sides of a transaction (known as an agency cross transaction), it must have its client's written consent after having provided full disclosure about the transaction. The adviser must also send the client an annual written disclosure statement that shows how many agency cross transactions have been done for the client and how much the adviser has earned in commission from those transactions. Note that an investment adviser may only act as an adviser for one side of the agency cross transaction—for the other side they must be acting solely in a broker/agent capacity.

Practice Exam #2

1. **An investment adviser is someone who:**

   A. Provides trading services for a fee
   B. Provides investment advice for a fee
   C. Assists customers with transactions for a commission
   D. Assists customers with transactions for a fee

2. **Which of the following would be considered providing investment advice?**

   A. Publishing a newsletter that discusses the gas and oil industries
   B. Publishing a newsletter that gives money-saving tips for families
   C. Publishing a newsletter that includes recommendations based on an individual's investment situation
   D. Publishing a newsletter where investments are mentioned on an incidental basis

3. **All of the following are exempt from state registration as an investment adviser except:**

   A. Federal covered advisers
   B. Advisers working only with institutional investors
   C. Out-of-state advisers with fewer than 25 clients in the state
   D. Anyone exempted by amendments to the law

4. **An investment adviser representative:**

   A. Must meet net capital requirements
   B. Should never receive a commission for their services
   C. Is not subject to licensing examinations
   D. Must be re-registered every year

5. **Which of the following are possible net capital requirements for different investment advisers, depending on the nature of their business?**

   I. $50,000
   II. $35,000
   III. $10,000
   IV. A positive net worth

   A. I and II
   B. I and III
   C. I, II, and III
   D. II, III, and IV

6. **Employees of a federally registered investment adviser do not need to register in the state if:**

   A. They have fewer than 10 clients in the state.
   B. They do not have an office in the state and do not provide investment advice for compensation.
   C. They only publish investment-based newsletters.
   D. They only advise investors on bonds securities.

7. **An investment adviser representative whose registration is accidentally incomplete may be subject to:**

   I. Delayed registration
   II. Denial of registration
   III. Withdrawal of registration
   IV. Criminal penalties

   A. I and II
   B. II and III
   C. II and IV
   D. III and IV

8. **A broker (as opposed to a dealer) is best defined as someone who:**

   A. Creates securities for purchase by the public
   B. Effects securities transactions for the account of others
   C. Receives a commission for providing investment advice
   D. Sells securities it has previously purchased

9. **The primary difference between a broker and a dealer is that:**

   A. A dealer acts as a go-between for two unrelated buyers.
   B. A dealer acts a go-between for an issuer and a buyer.
   C. A dealer buys or sells for its own account.
   D. A dealer buys or sells for the accounts of others.

10. **If a broker-dealer has no office in a state and its only dealings within that state are with an issuer in the issuer's securities, the broker-dealer:**

    A. Must register
    B. Must register only if the issuer plans on later selling directly to customers in the state
    C. Must register if any of the broker-dealer's officers are also officers of the issuer
    D. Does not need to register

11. **All of the following would be considered institutional customers for a broker-dealer except:**

    A. A domestic bank
    B. An international bank
    C. A company with at least $5,000,000 in assets
    D. An employee pension plan with at least $10,000,000 in assets

12. An institutional investor includes which of the following?

    I.   Broker-dealer

    II.   Insurance company

    III.   Mutual funds

    IV.   Profit-sharing trusts with at least $1 million in assets

    A.   I and III

    B.   II and III

    C.   I, III, and IV

    D.   I, II, III, and IV

13. A Canadian broker-dealer with offices and customers (who are residents) in a state:

    A.   Must register with the state

    B.   Must only register if greater than 50% of their customers are not Canadian

    C.   Does need to register unless transacting with citizens of that state

    D.   Does not need to register

14. Which of the following is not true of the requirements for broker-dealers supervising agents?

    A.   A broker-dealer is required to have a written set of procedures governing the activities of all agents.

    B.   A broker-dealer must ensure that periodic inspections take place in order to check on compliance procedures.

    C.   A broker-dealer must require its agents to attend quarterly compliance meetings.

    D.   A broker-dealer must maintain an Office of Supervisory Jurisdiction (OSJ).

15. To register, a broker-dealer must file:

    A.   Form BD on the SRO system

    B.   Form BD on the CRD system

    C.   Form ADV on the SRO system

    D.   Form ADV on the IARD system

16. For how many years are broker-dealers required to keep most records on file?

    A.   One year

    B.   Two years

    C.   Three years

    D.   Five years

17. Which of the following orders may only be issued with prior notice, opportunity for a hearing, and written findings of fact?

    A.   Cease and desist order

    B.   Stop order

    C.   Summary suspension

    D.   Summary postponement

18. **Broker-dealers may be subject to audits by their licensing state(s):**

    A. No more than once every two years
    B. No more than annually
    C. No more than quarterly
    D. At any time

19. **All of the following would be considered limits on association for agents and broker-dealers except:**

    A. Employing someone whose registration is suspended by the state administrator
    B. Employing someone who is not properly registered in the state
    C. Working as an investment adviser representative while also working as an agent
    D. Working as an independent agent between working for registered broker-dealers

20. **All of the following may be considered an agent under the Uniform Securities Act except:**

    A. Investment adviser representatives
    B. Broker-dealers
    C. Directors of broker-dealers
    D. Officers of issuers

21. **Someone whose job description is limited to processing distributions, deposits, and customer complaints for a broker-dealer would:**

    A. Need to register as an agent
    B. Need to register as an investment adviser representative
    C. Be considered a clerical or ministerial employee
    D. Need to register as an agent if they receive any form of bonus

22. **Jim is an agent for XYZ brokerage with an office in Maine. If Jim wishes to effect a transaction for Sally, who is vacationing in Florida, which of the following conditions must be met?**

    I. Sally has been a client of Jim's with an account at XYZ for more than 30 days prior to leaving for her vacation.
    II. Sally has been in Florida for 30 days or less.
    III. The transaction involves exempt securities.
    IV. The transaction must be unsolicited.

    A. I and IV only
    B. I and II
    C. II and III
    D. II and IV

23. Under the Uniform Securities Act, a representative of an issuer would be required to register as an agent for which of the following transactions:

A. Transactions between an issuer and the underwriter of the security
B. Transactions involving only municipal securities
C. IPOs
D. Private placements

24. Which of the following forms would need to be filed when someone is hired as an agent of the broker-dealer?

I. Form U4
II. Form U5
III. ADV
IV. ADV-W

A. I only
B. IV only
C. I and II
D. I and III

25. Unless challenged by a state's security administrator, applications for registration of an agent automatically become effective in:

A. 10 days
B. 30 days
C. 60 days
D. 90 days

26. All of the following are true of an agent's renewal of registration except:

A. It must be filed by the agent by December 31.
B. Association with a broker-dealer or issuer is required to renew a registration.
C. Failure to pay filing fees can result in a denial of one's application.
D. Applicants must submit to an initial background check.

27. Who must notify the administrator when an agent begins or terminates employment with a broker-dealer or issuer?

A. The agent only
B. The broker-dealer or issuer only
C. Both the agent and the broker-dealer or issuer
D. Neither the agent nor the broker-dealer or issuer

28. If a state administrator wishes to challenge an agent's application before it becomes effective, it must:

A. Issue a denial order or initiate a proceeding within 30 days of the application filing

B. Initiate a hearing within 90 days of the application filing

C. Notify the agent within 10 days of receipt of the application

D. Notify the agent's broker-dealer within 10 days of receipt of the application

29. A prospectus for a new issue must be delivered to a potential investor if he has previously not received one and which of the following occur(s)?

I. Public advertising begins.

II. He is offered the security by an agent.

III. He receives a confirmation for the purchase of the security.

IV. The security is delivered to him.

A. II only

B. I and III

C. II and III

D. III and IV

30. All of the following securities are exempt from registration except:

A. A CD from an FDIC-insured bank

B. A security that is not traded on a major exchange

C. A security issued by a non-profit organization

D. A security issued by an insurance company authorized to operate in the state

31. Which of the following are powers held by a state security administrator?

I. Initiate investigations

II. Collect evidence for investigations

III. Create securities laws

IV. Arrest offending parties

A. I and II

B. II and III

C. I, II, and III

D. II, III, and IV

32. Orders issued by the state administrator are effective:

A. Immediately

B. After 10 days

C. After 30 days

D. Only if unchallenged by the recipient

33. All of the following are administrative actions available to an administrator when a person or company violates securities laws except:

A. Revoke the person or company's registration

B. Suspend the person or company's registration

C. Issue a cease and desist order

D. Require registrants or issuers to compensate investors for losses

34. Which of the following are damages an investor can sue for in civil courts?

I. The cost of the securities

II. Fees and commissions paid

III. Legal costs

IV. Interest that could have been earned

A. I and IV

B. II and IV

C. I, II, and III

D. I, II, III, and IV

35. A rescission offer must be accepted within:

A. 10 days

B. 20 days

C. 30 days

D. 60 days

36. Which of the following companies would be most likely to register a security using Registration by Filing?

A. A foreign company issuing shares in the U.S. for the first time

B. A large, well-established company

C. A smaller, less well-known company

D. A private domestic company that is going public

37. Which of the following are required to be disclosed to a client?

I. When a client's broker-dealer is owned by or owns an issuer of a security that is being sold to the client

II. When an investment adviser representative works for multiple firms

III. When a securities report has been prepared by someone else than the adviser providing it to the client

IV. When a securities issue being recommended has been previously owned by the professional recommending it

A. I and III

B. I and IV

C. I, II, and III

D. I, II, and IV

38. If an adviser fails to disclose an important fact about a securities issue, it would most likely be a case of:

A. Misrepresentation

B. Fraud

C. Omission

D. Disclosure

39. What is the latest that a broker-dealer is allowed to deliver a final prospectus to a client who is investing in a new securities issue?

A. 48 hours prior to sale confirmation

B. On the day the trade confirmation is delivered

C. 48 hours after purchase confirmation

D. 10 days after the transaction is made

40. Which of the following is not true of a margin account?

A. It is an arrangement in which an investor pays part of a security's price and receives the remaining amount in the form of a loan from a broker-dealer.

B. The SEC requires that the customer must put down at least half of the value of the price of securities when opening such an account.

C. A written margin agreement must be in place before any transactions are made in such an account

D. Once securities have been purchased, the customer can maintain as little as 25% of the equity value of his securities in the account.

41. All of the following terms would be considered a misrepresentation of a registrant's status except:

A. Certified

B. Approved

C. Endorsed

D. Registered

42. An investment advisory contract must contain which of the following?

I. The investment advisory fee

II. Explanation of how the investment advisory fee is calculated

III. Clarification on whether or not the contract grants discretionary authority

IV. Clarification on which of the adviser's employees may take orders from the client

A. I, II, and III

B. I, II, and IV

C. I, III, and IV

D. I, II, III, and IV

43. The advertisements placed in local newspapers by a broker-dealer cannot include:

A. Testimonials

B. Charts or graphs

C. Historical data

D. Hypothetical prices

44. All of the following are true of performance guarantees except:

A. The word "guaranteed" can never be used.

B. Professionals cannot promise to reimburse a client should a loss occur.

C. Professionals should never promise clients a rate of return.

D. Professionals should never promise clients that an investment strategy is risk-free.

45. Which of the following would most likely be considered incidences of misrepresentation?

I. Telling a client that your firm is registered as an investment adviser in your state

II. Referring to you and your unregistered assistant and intern as a client's team of advisers.

III. Claiming that a newly registered professional has never received a complaint if it is disclosed that the professional is newly registered

IV. Explaining that a mutual fund that only invests in government-guaranteed securities is no-risk

A. II and IV

B. I, III, and IV

C. II, III, and IV

D. I, II, and III

46. All advisory contracts must contain:

A. A term (time limit) for the contract

B. A minimum rate of return

C. An adviser's educational background

D. An option to renew the contract and the new fee that will be charged

47. Employees, or access persons, in an advisory firm are required to disclose all of the following to their compliance officer on a regular basis except:

A. Securities holdings they own

B. Securities transactions

C. The name of the broker, dealer or financial institution through which the security is held or transacted

D. Mutual fund investments

48. **All of the following soft-dollar compensation arrangements are prohibited except:**

    A. Cell phones and computers
    B. Continuing education of a firm's personnel
    C. Paying overhead expenses for a professional
    D. Referral bonuses

49. **A securities professional charging commissions:**

    I. Must be registered as an agent of a broker-dealer unless an exemption is met
    II. Must be registered as a representative of an investment adviser unless an exemption is met
    III. Must disclose his or her commission structure to clients
    IV. May split his or her commissions with other registered agents at the same firm

    A. I only
    B. I, II, and II
    C. I, III, and IV
    D. I, II, III, and IV

50. **If investment advisers receive commissions or fees other than those that were initially disclosed to a client, they:**

    A. Have no obligation to disclose if no conflict of interest is created
    B. Must disclose only if the compensation is soft-dollar in nature
    C. Must disclose only if the compensation comes from an issuer that is under shared ownership with their firm
    D. Must always disclose in writing

51. **Investment adviser clients must receive statements from anyone holding custody of their assets at least:**

    A. Monthly
    B. Quarterly
    C. Semi-annually
    D. Annually

52. **Which of the following, by themselves, would constitute custody of a client's assets by an investment adviser:**

    I.   Receiving a client's security in the mail and returning it to the client within one week
    II. Receiving a client's check made payable to a mutual funds company and forwarding within three business days
    III. Receiving cash for a customer
    IV. Having discretionary authority over a client's account held at an unaffiliated broker-dealer

    A. III only
    B. I and III
    C. I, III, and IV
    D. I, II, and IV

53. **Which of the following require the written consent of a client?**

    I.   Allowing a spouse to make trades in his or her account
    II. An agent or adviser exercising time and price authority in the purchase of a security
    III. An investment advisory contract
    IV. Third-party trading authorization

    A. III only
    B. I and III
    C. I, III, and IV
    D. I, II, III, and IV

54. **Mixing a client's funds with the private assets of a professional or their firm would be known as:**

    A. Custody
    B. Misappropriation
    C. Churning
    D. Commingling

55. **All of the following are true of trading authorizations except:**

    A. They can only be granted by the client in writing.
    B. They can only be granted to registered professionals.
    C. They can be revoked at any time.
    D. Spouses need one to trade in each other's individual accounts.

56. **When considering the suitability of an investment, a professional should take into account a client's:**

    I.   Risk tolerance
    II. Financial situation
    III. Investment objectives
    IV. Relationship to the adviser

    A. I and III
    B. I, II, and III
    C. I, III, and IV
    D. I, II, III, and IV

57. **The concept that no professional should subject a client's investments to more risk than a cautious person would take to achieve the same goal is best described as:**

    A. Suitability
    B. Risk tolerance
    C. Prudent Investor Standard
    D. Fiduciary responsibility

58. **An investment adviser or investment adviser representative may not engage in borrowing from a client except:**

    A. If the client is also an employee of the professional's firm
    B. When the client is an established acquaintance of the professional
    C. When the client is engaged in the business of lending money or is a broker-dealer or an affiliate of the adviser
    D. When the client signs a waiver acknowledging the conflict of interest

59. **An investment adviser may enter into a performance-based compensation arrangement with which of the following:**

    I.   Qualified individual purchasers with more than $5,000,000 in assets
    II. Qualified corporate purchasers with more than $20,000,000 in assets
    III. Private investment companies
    IV. Officers of the advisory firm

    A. I and III
    B. I, II, and IV
    C. I, III, and IV
    D. I, II, III, and IV

60. **Insider trading is best defined as:**

    A. Stock purchases or sales by the officers of an advisory firm
    B. Stock purchases or sales by the officers of a corporation
    C. Trading in a way to unfairly take advantage of fluctuations in stocks price
    D. The use of non-public information to derive personal gain or limit potential loss

61. **An agent enters into a verbal agreement with one of his clients to purchase IBM stock, leaving the timing and purchase price of the stock up to the agent. The agent buys and sells IBM from time to time, but does not own any currently. Which of the following are true?**

   I.   The agreement to purchase IBM should have been in writing.
   II. The leaving of time and price discretion up to the agent did not require a written agreement.
   III. The agent should have disclosed the fact that he or she had previously owned IBM.
   IV. The agent was guilty of front-running.

   A. II only
   B. I and III
   C. II, III, and IV
   D. I, II, III, and IV

62. **All of the following should be considered in determining if an adviser is inducing excessive trading in a client's account except:**

   A. The client's investment objectives
   B. The client's financial situation
   C. Whether the trade was recommended by the adviser or not
   D. Whether the adviser is trading as heavily in his or her own account

63. **When a customer wishes to use his or her securities as collateral for a non-securities loan and the broker-dealer does not have a lien on the securities, a written agreement:**

   A. Does not need to be used
   B. Must be in place prior to the transaction
   C. Must be in place promptly after the transaction
   D. Must be in place within 30 days

64. **If an existing agent also registers as an investment adviser representative with her current employer, which of the following would be true?**

   I.   The agent's employer is registered as an investment adviser.
   II. The agent has met net capital requirements.
   III. The agent has passed the required exams for her state.
   IV. The agent has been an agent for at least 90 days.

   A. I and II
   B. I and III
   C. I, II, and III
   D. I, II, III, and IV

65. Initiating trades with the intent of creating a false sense of overall market volume of a security is known as:

A. Churning

B. Front-running

C. Painting the tape

D. Selling away

Practice Exam #2 Answers

1. **Answer: B.** Someone who assists customers with transactions or receives a commission for the purchase or sale of a security would be considered an agent. Someone who provides investment advice for a specified fee is an investment adviser.

2. **Answer: C.** Since this newsletter specifically advises clients based on their investment situations, it would likely constitute investment advice. The newsletter discussing the oil and gas industries does not appear to specifically recommend certain stocks. Money-saving tips and incidental investment advice do not constitute someone providing investment advice as part of his or her business.

3. **Answer: C.** Out-of-state advisers may have no more than five non-institutional clients in a state to avoid registration, unless they meet another exemption.

4. **Answer: D.** Investment adviser representatives must be re-registered each year. They are not required to meet net capital requirements, may receive commissions if also registered as an agent, and must pass the appropriate licensing exams.

5. **Answer: D.** An adviser with custody over client assets must show a minimum net worth of $35,000, while an adviser with discretionary authority but without custody must show a net worth of $10,000. Investment advisers who accept prepayments of more than $500 per client and six or more months in advance must show a positive net worth.

6. **Answer: B.** These employees are not giving investment advice for compensation in that state, so they would be exempt from registration. The *de minimis* number of clients for registration is five, not ten. Investment-based newsletters may still require registration, as does someone advising customers on bonds.

7. **Answer: A.** Filing an incomplete registration can subject someone to a delayed or denied registration. It would not be withdrawn, since that can only be done by the firm or individual for someone already registered. Criminal penalties are not assessed for non-willful (accidental) violations.

8. **Answer: B.** Brokers help investors buy and sell securities from other investors. Dealers buy and sell from their own inventory.

9. **Answer: C.** A dealer buys or sells for its own account. A broker or agent helps investors buy and sell from each other.

10. **Answer: D.** As long as the broker-dealer is not dealing directly with non-exempt customers in the state, there is no need to register. Who the issuer deals with in unrelated transactions is irrelevant.

11. **Answer: C.** A company with $5,000,000 in assets would not typically be considered an institutional investor, unless it was an institutional investor for some other reason (e.g., if it was a bank or insurance company).

12. **Answer: D.** All of the choices are considered to be institutional investors that would avoid causing a broker-dealer to have to register in a state.

13. **Answer: A.** If a Canadian broker-dealer has offices and customers in a state, it would need to

register. The exceptions for Canadian broker-dealers are built around the basic premise that they do not have offices in that state and customers who call that state their residence or that the customers are making transactions in a self-directed tax advantaged retirement plan held in Canada.

14. **Answer: C.** Agents are required to attend annual, and not quarterly, compliance meetings. Each of the other answers represents a supervisory requirement for broker-dealers.

15. **Answer: B.** To register, a broker-dealer must file Form BD on the CRD system. There is no such thing as the SRO system and Form ADVs are filed for investment advisers.

16. **Answer: C.** Broker-dealers must keep most of their records on file for three years. Investment advisers, however, must keep their records on file for five years.

17. **Answer: B.** Stop orders, as well as lasting orders against a person's registration, require prior notice to the affected parties, opportunity for a hearing, and written findings of fact and conclusions of law. Cease and desist orders and summary postponements or suspensions (which last until the final determination of a proceeding against a person's registration) do not have these requirements.

18. **Answer: D.** All broker-dealers are subject to audits in the states in which they are licensed. These audits can occur at any time following their registration.

19. **Answer: C.** There is no prohibition from working in both capacities as long as all parties are properly registered.

20. **Answer: B.** A broker-dealer can never be an agent. Being an investment adviser representative does not preclude someone from being an agent as well, as long as he or she is acting in both of those capacities. An officer, director, or partner of a broker-dealer or issuer is an agent if and only if they act in an agent capacity.

21. **Answer: C.** Since they're not actually helping to buy or sell a security, they would not need to be registered as an agent. Since they're not providing investment advice, they would not need to be registered as an investment adviser representative.

22. **Answer: B.** In order for an agent to sell securities to a client on vacation in a different state from that in which he is registered, there are two main conditions. The first is that the client must have been affiliated with the agent prior to leaving on her vacation and have had an account at the agent's firm that existed for at least 30 days. The second requirement is that the client has been on vacation for no more than 30 days when the transaction occurs. As long as these requirements are met, it does not matter whether the securities traded are exempt or not.

23. **Answer: C.** A representative of the issuer would be considered an agent in an IPO. Certain transactions are exempt under the Uniform Securities Act, including transactions between an issuer and an underwriter and private placements to no more than ten non-institutional buyers (and any number of institutional buyers). Agents of issuers selling only exempt securities, such as municipal securities, are also exempt from registration.

24. **Answer: A.** A Form U4 must be filed when an agent or investment adviser representative is initially registered. The Form ADV is used to register an investment adviser. The Form U5 is used for the withdrawal of an agent's registration or investment adviser representative's registration, while the Form ADV-W is used to withdraw an investment adviser's registration.

25. **Answer: B.** Applications for registration of an agent automatically become effective in 30 days unless they are challenged by a state's security administrator.

26. **Answer: A.** Renewal of registration for agents must be submitted by their sponsoring broker-dealer, not the agent themselves.

27. **Answer: C.** When an agent begins or ends engaging in the activities that make him an agent, both the agent and the broker-dealer or issuer he works for must promptly notify the state's administrator.

28. **Answer: A.** If a state administrator wishes to challenge an agent's application before it becomes effective, it must issue a denial order or initiate a proceeding within 30 days of the application filing.

29. **Answer: D.** A prospectus must be delivered by the time the first of the following occurs—confirmation of the purchase of the security or delivery of the security. Public advertising does not require a prospectus to be delivered since there is no one specific to deliver it to.

30. **Answer: B.** Most likely, a security not traded on a major exchange would need to be registered. CDs from FDIC-insured banks, securities issued by non-profits, and those issued by insurance companies licensed in the state are all exempt.

31. **Answer: A.** Securities administrators can initiate investigations and collect evidence. Securities laws are created by state and federal legislators, while arrests have to be initiated by the courts and law enforcement.

32. **Answer: A.** Orders issued by an administrator are immediately enforceable.

33. **Answer: D.** Registrants can only be required by a civil court to reimburse investors for losses or damages.

34. **Answer: D.** All of these are permissible damages that can be sought in a civil suit against a professional or firm.

35. **Answer: C.** Rescission offers must be accepted within 30 days.

36. **Answer: B.** Registration by Filing may be used by established companies that have already registered a security with the SEC. A foreign company that has not issued shares in the U.S. before could not use Registration by Filing, and neither could a private company.

37. **Answer: A.** When a client's broker-dealer is affiliated with an issuer or a securities report has been created by someone else, this needs to be disclosed to a client or potential client. Working for multiple firms and previously owned securities are not grounds for required disclosure.

38. **Answer: C.** Omission is the leaving out of a material fact, whereas misrepresentation is explaining it incorrectly. Fraud is the willful attempt to deceive someone for gain.

39. **Answer: B.** The final prospectus must be delivered to investors who are purchasing the new securities later by the day that the trade confirmation is delivered. The preliminary prospectus, not the final prospectus, is due 48 hours prior to the sale confirmation.

40. **Answer: C.** In a margin account a customer obtains credit from a broker-dealer which helps him to make transactions. Under the terms of the account, an investor pays part of the value of securities purchased; a broker-dealer then loans the investor the remainder of the purchase

price. When opening a margin account, an investor must put down at least half of the value of securities purchased. However, once transactions have been made, that requirement is reduced to 25% of the total equity value of securities purchased. The written margin agreement, which is a requirement for a margin account, does not need to be signed until after the first transaction has taken place.

41. **Answer: D.** A registrant may be registered with the state securities administrator. She is in no way certified, approved, or endorsed.

42. **Answer: A.** Investment advisory contracts must contain the fee, its method of calculation, and whether or not the contract is discretionary in nature. No clarification is required on whether or not employees can accept orders.

43. **Answer: D.** Advertisements should never use hypothetical prices, only real historical prices. Advertisements, subject to certain restrictions, can use charts, graphs, testimonials, and historical data.

44. **Answer: A.** The word "guaranteed" can be used, but only when explaining that U.S. Treasury backed securities are guaranteed to pay their stated interest at the promised intervals and their face value at maturity. Professionals cannot promise to reimburse clients for losses, promise a rate of return, or refer to investment strategies as risk-free.

45. **Answer: A.** Referring to unregistered personal as advisers and a mutual fund as no risk would both be untrue statements and thus a misrepresentation.

46. **Answer: A.** All investment advisory contracts must have a set term to them (usually one year). Minimum rates of return, an adviser's educational background, and an option to renew are not required to be included.

47. **Answer: D.** Ownership of mutual funds is not required to be disclosed to the chief compliance officer, unless the mutual funds are advised (managed) by that same advisory firm. However, access persons are required to disclose all material information related to most securities transactions.

48. **Answer: B.** Continuing education may be provided through a soft-dollar arrangement. Paying for cell phones, computers, or overhead expenses or providing referral bonuses is prohibited.

49. **Answer: C.** A securities professional that is receiving a commission must register as an agent unless an exemption is met, disclose his or her commission structure to clients, and may split commissions with other registered personnel at the same firm (but not at different firms).

50. **Answer: D.** If an investment adviser or investment adviser representative begins receiving an additional type of compensation than was originally disclosed, this must be made known to the client in writing.

51. **Answer: B.** Clients of investment advisers must receive statements from anyone holding custody of their assets at least quarterly.

52. **Answer: B.** If an investment adviser wants to avoid being in custody of client securities, they must be returned within three days, not one week. Receiving cash obviously constitutes custody. Having authority to trade in an account elsewhere does not constitute custody (unless the professional can withdraw funds), since the firm holding the account is the custodian.

53. **Answer: C.** Allowing a spouse to initiate trades on your behalf, entering into an advisory

contract, and giving trading authorization to a third-party all require the written consent of the client. Allowing an agent or adviser to decide when and what price to buy a security (without actually having discretion over which security they purchase) can be granted verbally.

54. **Answer: D.** When assets are mixed, they are considered commingled. Misappropriation is when they are spent or invested in a way that the client would not approve of.

55. **Answer: B.** Trading authorizations can theoretically be granted to any adult, regardless of whether or not they are registered as a securities professional. Discretion, on the other hand, would typically require the recipient of those powers to be registered.

56. **Answer: B.** A client's relationship to the adviser should have no bearing on what investments are deemed appropriate or inappropriate. Their individual risk tolerance, financial situation, and objectives should be considered.

57. **Answer: C.** The heart of the Prudent Investor Standard is the comparison to what other investors would be expected to do. Suitability measures investment choices against what is appropriate for that investor only.

58. **Answer: C.** Investment advisers and IARs may only borrow money from clients that are broker-dealers, affiliates of the adviser, or established lending institutions. Simply being an acquaintance does not make it okay.

59. **Answer: C.** Qualified corporate purchasers must have over $25,000,000 in assets to enter into a performance-based contract. All the others listed may enter into such an agreement.

60. **Answer: D.** Insider trading involves profiting or avoiding a loss by using information the public did not have access to. Transactions by officers of a corporation or firm do not constitute insider trading unless they are using inside information.

61. **Answer: A.** Since the client consented to the purchase of IBM stock, no discretionary agreement is needed. Giving time and price discretion to an agent can be done verbally. The agent would not be required to disclose that he has previously owned IBM stock and is not involved in front-running based on the facts in this scenario.

62. **Answer: D.** What the adviser is doing in his or her own account is irrelevant, since excessive trading is measured by each client's individual situation, objectives, and risk tolerances.

63. **Answer: C.** While it may seem a little nebulous, this is the standard for non-security related loans. For margin transactions, the written margin agreement also needs to be in place promptly after the transaction.

64. **Answer: B.** To register as an IAR, someone must work for an investment adviser (which also may be a broker-dealer, as in this case). Additionally, they must pass the appropriate exams required for their state. There are no net capital requirements or waiting periods before an agent can become an IAR.

65. **Answer: C.** Creating fake volume in a security is known as painting the tape. Churning is when commissions are generated through excessive trading, while front-running involves getting a more advantageous price on a trade than a customer. Selling away involves selling securities or investments one's firm does not otherwise sell.

Appendixes

Appendixes

Model Rule 102(a)(4)-1

Model Rule 102(a)(4)-1
Adopted 4/27/97, amended 4/18/04, 9/11/05

Rule 102(a)(4)-1 Unethical Business Practices Of Investment Advisers, Investment Adviser Representatives, And Federal Covered Advisers

[Introduction] A person who is an investment adviser, an investment adviser representative or a federal covered adviser is a fiduciary and has a duty to act primarily for the benefit of its clients. The provisions of this subsection apply to federal covered advisers to the extent that the conduct alleged is fraudulent, deceptive, or as otherwise permitted by the National Securities Markets Improvement Act of 1996 (Pub. L. No. 104-290). While the extent and nature of this duty varies according to the nature of the relationship between an investment adviser or an investment adviser representative and its clients and the circumstances of each case, an investment adviser, an investment adviser representative or a federal covered adviser shall not engage in unethical business practices, including the following:

(a)   Recommending to a client to whom investment supervisory, management or consulting services are provided the purchase, sale or exchange of any security without reasonable grounds to believe that the recommendation is suitable for the client on the basis of information furnished by the client after reasonable inquiry concerning the client's investment objectives, financial situation and needs, and any other information known by the investment adviser.

(b)   Exercising any discretionary power in placing an order for the purchase or sale of securities for a client without obtaining written discretionary authority from the client within ten (10) business days after the date of the first transaction placed pursuant to oral discretionary authority, unless the discretionary power relates solely to the price at which, or the time when, an order involving a definite amount of a specified security shall be executed, or both.

(c) Inducing trading in a client's account that is excessive in size or frequency in view of the financial resources, investment objectives and character of the account in light of the fact that an investment adviser or an investment adviser representative in such situations can directly benefit from the number of securities transactions effected in a client's account. The rule appropriately forbids an excessive number of transaction orders to be induced by an adviser for a "customer's account."

(d) Placing an order to purchase or sell a security for the account of a client without authority to do so.

(e) Placing an order to purchase or sell a security for the account of a client upon instruction of a third party without first having obtained a written third-party trading authorization from the client.

(f) Borrowing money or securities from a client unless the client is a broker-dealer, an affiliate of the investment adviser, or a financial institution engaged in the business of loaning funds.

(g) Loaning money to a client unless the investment adviser is a financial institution engaged in the business of loaning funds or the client is an affiliate of the investment adviser.

(h) Misrepresenting to any advisory client, or prospective advisory client, the qualifications of the investment adviser or any employee of the investment adviser, or misrepresenting the nature of the advisory services being offered or fees to be charged for such service, or to omit to state a material fact necessary to make the statements made regarding qualifications, services or fees, in light of the circumstances under which they are made, not misleading.

(i) Providing a report or recommendation to any advisory client prepared by someone other than the adviser without disclosing that fact. (This prohibition does not apply to a situation where the adviser uses published research reports or statistical analyses to render advice or where an adviser orders such a report in the normal course of providing service.)

(j)   Charging a client an unreasonable advisory fee.

(k)   Failing to disclose to clients in writing before any advice is ren-
       dered any material conflict of interest relating to the adviser, or
       any of its employees which could reasonably be expected to impair
       the rendering of unbiased and objective advice including:

    (1.)   Compensation arrangements connected with advisory services
           to clients which are in addition to compensation from such
           clients for such services; and

    (2.)   Charging a client an advisory fee for rendering advice when
           a commission for executing securities transactions pur-
           suant to such advice will be received by the adviser or its
           employees.

(l)   Guaranteeing a client that a specific result will be achieved (gain
       or no loss)   with advice which will be rendered.

(m)   [Alternative 1] Publishing, circulating or distributing any adver-
       tisement which does not comply with Rule 206(4)-1 under the Invest-
       ment Advisers Act of 1940.

(m)   [Alternative 2] (1.) Except as otherwise provided in subsection
       (2.), it shall constitute a dishonest or unethical practice within
       the meaning of [Uniform Act Sec. 102(a)(4)] for any investment
       adviser or investment adviser representative, directly or indi-
       rectly, to use any advertisement that does any one of the following:

    (i.)   Refers to any testimonial of any kind concerning the
           investment adviser or investment adviser representa-
           tive or concerning any advice, analysis, report, or
           other service rendered by such investment adviser or
           investment adviser representative.

    (ii.) Refers to past specific recommendations of the invest-
           ment adviser or investment adviser representative
           that were or would have been profitable to any person;
           except that an investment adviser or investment
           adviser representative may furnish or offer to furnish
           a list of all recommendations made by the investment
           adviser or investment adviser representative within
           the immediately preceding period of not less than one
           year if the advertisement or list also includes both
           of the following:

(A) The name of each security recommended, the date and nature of each recommendation, the market price at that time, the price at which the recommendation was to be acted upon, and the most recently available market price of each such security.

(B) A legend on the first page in prominent print or type that states that the reader should not assume that recommendations made in the future will be profitable or will equal the performance of the securities in the list.

(iii.) Represents that any graph, chart, formula, or other device being offered can in and of itself be used to determine which securities to buy or sell, or when to buy or sell them; or which represents, directly or indirectly, that any graph, chart, formula, or other device being offered will assist any person in making that person's own decisions as to which securities to buy or sell, or when to buy or sell them, without prominently disclosing in such advertisement the limitations thereof and the difficulties with respect to its use.

(iv.) Represents that any report, analysis, or other service will be furnished for free or without charge, unless such report, analysis, or other service actually is or will be furnished entirely free and without any direct or indirect condition or obligation.

(v.) Represents that the [Administrator] has approved any advertisement.

(vi.) Contains any untrue statement of a material fact, or that is otherwise false or misleading.

(2.) With respect to federal covered advisers, the provisions of this section only apply to the extent permitted by Section 203A of the Investment Advisers Act of 1940.

(3.) For the purposes of this section, the term "advertisement" shall include any notice, circular, letter, or other written communication addressed to more than one person, or any notice or other announcement in any electronic or paper publication, by radio or television, or by any medium, that offers any one of the following:

(i.) Any analysis, report, or publication concerning securities.

(ii.) Any analysis, report, or publication that is to be used in making any determination as to when to buy or sell any security or which security to buy or sell

(iii.) Any graph, chart, formula, or other device to be used in making any determination as to when to buy or sell any security, or which security to buy or sell.

(iv.) Any other investment advisory service with regard to securities.

(n) Disclosing the identity, affairs, or investments of any client unless required by law to do so, or unless consented to by the client.

(o) Taking any action, directly or indirectly, with respect to those securities or funds in which any client has any beneficial interest, where the investment adviser has custody or possession of such securities or funds when the advisor's action is subject to and does not comply with the requirements of Rule 102e(1)-1. and any subsequent amendments.

(p) Entering into, extending or renewing any investment advisory contract, unless such contract is in writing and discloses, in substance, the services to be provided, the term of the contract, the advisory fee, the formula for computing the fee, the amount of prepaid fee to be returned in the event of contract termination or non-performance, whether the contract grants discretionary power to the adviser and that no assignment of such contract shall be made by the investment adviser without the consent of the other party to the contract.

(q) Failing to establish, maintain, and enforce written policies and procedures reasonably designed to prevent the misuse of material nonpublic information contrary to the provisions of Section 204A of the Investment Advisers Act of 1940.

(r) Entering into, extending, or renewing any advisory contract contrary to the provisions of Section 205 of the Investment Advisers Act of 1940. This provision shall apply to all advisers and investment adviser representatives registered or required to be registered under this Act, notwithstanding whether such adviser or representative would be exempt from federal registration pursuant to Section 203(b) of the Investment Advisers Act of 1940.

(s) To indicate, in an advisory contract, any condition, stipulation, or provisions binding any person to waive compliance with any provision of this act or of the Investment Advisers Act of 1940, or any other practice contrary to the provisions of Section 215 of the Investment Advisers Act of 1940.

(t) Engaging in any act, practice, or course of business which is fraudulent, deceptive, or manipulative in contrary to the provisions of Section 206(4) of the Investment Advisers Act of 1940, notwithstanding the fact that such investment adviser or investment adviser representative is not registered or required to be registered under Section 203 of the Investment Advisers Act of 1940.

(u) Engaging in conduct or any act, indirectly or through or by any other person, which would be unlawful for such person to do directly under the provisions of this act or any rule or regulation thereunder. The conduct set forth above is not inclusive. Engaging in other conduct such as non-disclosure, incomplete disclosure, or deceptive practices shall be deemed an unethical business practice. The federal statutory and regulatory provisions referenced herein shall apply to investment advisers, investment adviser representatives and federal covered advisers to the extent permitted by the National Securities Markets Improvement Act of 1996 (Pub. L. No. 104-290).

Dishonest or Unethical Business Practices of Broker-Dealers and Agents

[Adopted May 23, 1983]

Appendix B: Dishonest or Unethical Business Practices of Broker-Dealers and Agents

[HIGH STANDARDS AND JUST PRINCIPLES.] Each broker-dealer and agent shall observe high standards of commercial honor and just and equitable principles of trade in the conduct of their business. Acts and practices, including but not limited to the following, are considered contrary to such standards and may constitute grounds for denial, suspension or revocation of registration or such other action authorized by statute.

1. BROKER-DEALERS

   a. Engaging in a pattern of unreasonable and unjustifiable delays in the delivery of securities purchased by any of its customers and/or in the payment upon request of free credit balances reflecting completed transactions of any of its customers;

   b. Inducing trading in a customer's account which is excessive in size or frequency in view of the financial resources and character of the account;

   c. Recommending to a customer the purchase, sale or exchange of any security without reasonable grounds to believe that such transaction or recommendation is suitable for the customer based upon reasonable inquiry concerning the customer's investment objectives, financial situation and needs, and any other relevant information known by the broker-dealer;

d. Executing a transaction on behalf of a customer without authorization to do so;

e. Exercising any discretionary power in effecting a transaction for a customer's account without first obtaining written discretionary authority from the customer, unless the discretionary power relates solely to the time and/or price for the executing of orders;

f. Executing any transaction in a margin account without securing from the customer a properly executed written margin agreement promptly after the initial transaction in the account;

g. Failing to segregate customers' free securities or securities held in safekeeping;

h. Hypothecating a customer's securities without having a lien thereon unless the broker-dealer secures from the customer a properly executed written consent promptly after the initial transaction, except as permitted by Rules of the Securities and Exchange Commission;

i. Entering into a transaction with or for a customer at a price not reasonably related to the current market price of the security or receiving an unreasonable commission or profit;

j. Failing to furnish to a customer purchasing securities in an offering, no later than the due date of confirmation of the transaction, either a final prospectus or a preliminary prospectus and an additional document, which together include all information set forth in the final prospectus;

k. Charging unreasonable and inequitable fees for services performed, including miscellaneous services such as collection of monies due for principal, dividends or interest, exchange or transfer of securities, appraisals, safekeeping, or custody of securities and other services related to its securities business;

l. Offering to buy from or sell to any person any security at a stated price unless such broker-dealer is prepared to purchase or sell, as the case may be, at such price and under such conditions as are stated at the time of such offer to buy or sell;

m. Representing that a security is being offered to a customer "at the market" or a price relevant to the market price unless such broker-dealer knows or has reasonable grounds to believe that a market for such security exists other than that made, created or controlled by such broker-dealer, or by any such person for whom he is acting or with whom he is associated in such distribution, or any person controlled by, controlling or under common control with such broker-dealer;

n. Effecting any transaction in, or inducing the purchase or sale of, any security by means of any manipulative, deceptive or fraudulent device, practice, plan, program, design or contrivance, which may include but not be limited to;

   (1) Effecting any transaction in a security which involves no change in the beneficial ownership thereof;

   (2) Entering an order or orders for the purchase or sale of any security with the knowledge that an order or orders of substantially the same size, at substantially the same time and substantially the same price, for the sale of any such security, has been or will be entered by or for the same or different parties for the purpose of creating a false or misleading appearance of active trading in the security or a false or misleading appearance with respect to the market for the security; provided, however, nothing in this subsection shall prohibit a broker-dealer from entering bona fide agency cross transactions for its customers;

   (3) Effecting, alone or with one or more other persons, a series of transactions in any security creating actual or apparent active trading in such security or raising or depressing the price of such security, for the purpose of inducing the purchase or sale of such security by others;

o. Guaranteeing a customer against loss in any securities account of such customer carried by the broker-dealer or in any securities transaction effected by the broker-dealer or in any securities transaction effected by the broker-dealer with or for such customer;

p. Publishing or circulating, or causing to be published or circulated, any notice, circular, advertisement, newspaper article, investment service, or communication of any kind which purports to report any transaction as a purchase or sale of any security unless such broker-dealer believes that such transaction was a bona fide purchase or sale or such security; or which purports to quote the bid price or asked price for any security, unless such broker-dealer believes that such quotation represents a bona fide bid for, or offer of, such security;

q. Using any advertising or sales presentation in such a fashion as to be deceptive or misleading. An example of such practice would be a distribution of any nonfactual data, material or presentation based on conjecture, unfounded or unrealistic claims or assertions in any brochure, flyer, or display by words, pictures, graphs or otherwise designed to supplement, detract from, supersede or defeat the purpose or effect of any prospectus or disclosure; or

r. Failing to disclose that the broker-dealer is controlled by, controlling, affiliated with or under common control with the issuer of any security before entering into any contract with or for a customer for the purchase or sale of such security, the existence of such control to such customer, and if such disclosure is not made in writing, it shall be supplemented by the giving or sending of written disclosure at or before the completion of the transaction;

s. Failing to make a bona fide public offering of all of the securities allotted to a broker-dealer for distribution, whether acquired as an underwriter, a selling group member, or from a member participating in the distribution as an underwriter or selling group member; or

t. Failure or refusal to furnish a customer, upon reasonable request, information to which he is entitled, or to respond to a formal written request or complaint.

2. AGENTS

Engaging in the practice of lending or borrowing money or securities from a customer, or acting as a custodian for money, securities or an executed stock power of a customer;

Effecting securities transactions not recorded on the regular books or records of the broker-dealer which the agent represents, unless the transactions are authorized in writing by the broker-dealer prior to execution of the transaction;

Establishing or maintaining an account containing fictitious information in order to execute transactions which would otherwise be prohibited;

Sharing directly or indirectly in profits or losses in the account of any customer without the written authorization of the customer and the broker-dealer which the agent represents;

Dividing or otherwise splitting the agent's commissions, profits or other compensation from the purchase or sale of securities with any person not also registered as an agent for the same broker-dealer, or for a broker-dealer under direct or indirect common control; or

Engaging in conduct specified in Subsection 1.b, c, d, e, f, i, j, n, o, p, or q.

[CONDUCT NOT INCLUSIVE.] The conduct set forth above is not inclusive. Engaging in other conduct such as forgery, embezzlement, nondisclosure, incomplete disclosure or misstatement of material facts, or manipulative or deceptive practices shall also be grounds for denial, suspension or revocation of registration.

Glossary

5% Policy – a standard for determining pricing fairness that states that markups, markdowns, and commissions for broker-dealers should hover in the neighborhood of 5% of sales.

access persons – employees, directors, officers, and fiduciaries with access to inside information about securities gained from their work with or for an investment adviser.

agency cross transaction – Acting as the agent for both parties in a transaction.

agent – any individual other than a broker-dealer who represents a broker-dealer or issuer in effecting or attempting to effect purchases or sales of securities.

assets – a firm's resources. They include cash, securities, property, inventory, and office equipment.

backing away – failing to honor a firm quote.

Best Execution – the requirement that brokers evaluate customer orders and determine which markets offer the most favorable terms of execution.

blanket recommendation – When a firm or financial professional makes a recommendation to buy or sell a particular security to all of their customers or clients.

bond – promise by the issuer to pay the bond purchaser a specific amount of money in the future and also to pay periodic interest along the way.

branch office – any location where one or more associated employees is in the business of soliciting or effecting (but not executing) the purchase or sale of any security. An office responsible for supervising the activities of employees at one or more non-branch locations of the member firm is also designated a branch office.

brochure rule – investment advisers subject to federal or state registration must provide certain basic information about their services to prospective and existing clients prior to entering into or renewing an advisory contract.

broker – a firm that serves as an agent or go-between for the buyer and the seller.

broker-dealer – a firm or an individual that buys and sells securities for others or its own account.

cash account – an account where the customer must pay for all purchases made in the account (as opposed to a margin account).

cease and desist order – an order from the Administrator to stop illegal or suspicious activities.

churning – An ethical violation that involves a professional recommending or making trades in a customer's account, simply for the sake of generating revenue

clerical acts – secretarial acts that do not require registration.

code of ethics – A standardized set of rules that must be adopted and enforced by all investment advisory firms in order to prevent fraud. The code of ethics is meant to remind advisory firms of their fiduciary responsibility to their clients.

commercial paper – a short-term promissory note issued by a corporation. They may have maturities of up to 270 days, but average around 30 days. Commercial paper is exempt from registration.

commingling – mixing of a client's personal assets with those of a broker-dealer or advisory firm.

commission – A form of compensation where a professional or firm is paid for helping a client conduct a transaction.

commodity – a physical good that is traded over exchanges or markets similar to how a stock or bond is traded. Examples might include grain, cotton, and precious metals.

conflict of interest – a situation in which a professional or firm's actions in its own interest or in the interest of another party may be detrimental to a client. Conflicts of interest must be disclosed to the client.

consent to service of process – a document filed by a prospective securities professional or firm that allows a state administrator to receive legal papers (summons, notice of lawsuits, etc.) on behalf of the applicant.

contumacy – When a person who is subject to an investigation ignores a subpoena or refuses to supply the required information.

credit union securities – securities issued or guaranteed by a federal credit union or a state-supervised credit union or similar association.

custody – physical possession or actual control over movement and access to clients' securities and funds.

cybersecurity plan – A plan that should be put in place by a securities firm to address the threat of an unauthorized third-party having access to the firm's digital files.

de minimis rule – a Latin term that refers to "little things" or "trifles." In the case of the Uniform Securities Act, it refers to the rule that investment advisers and investment adviser representatives are exempt from registration in a state if they've had no more than five non-institutional clients within that state over the last 12 months. There is also a separate de minimis rule that applies to capital gains taxes on bonds sold at a small discount.

dealer – a firm that puts its own money at risk, buying or selling securities out of its own inventory.

denial – an action taken by a state securities administrator in which an application for registration is denied outright.

disclosure – revealing what a client would need to know to make an educated decision about your services or about an investment you are presenting to them.

discretion – when a client gives permission to his or her securities professional to exercise decision-making ability over some or all aspects of purchasing or selling a security.

employee benefit plan investment contracts – investment contracts issued in connection with an employee benefit plan if the administrator is notified in writing 30 days before the inception of the plan.

exchange – an organized institution that exists to facilitate the trading of stocks, bonds, commodities, or other investments.

exchange-traded securities – securities approved for trading on the NYSE, AMEX, Chicago, or other major exchanges

exempt securities – securities that are not required to be registered.

exemption – a clause that allows a person or security to avoid the need for registration.

federal covered adviser – an investment adviser registered on a federal level under the Investment Advisers Act of 1940.

federal covered security – a security registered on a federal level under the Securities Act of 1933.

federal registration – a term that refers to a firm or issuer being permitted or required to register on a federal level (permitting operation in all 50 states) as opposed to a state-by-state level.

fee – a form of compensation where a professional or firm is most commonly paid a pre-agreed-upon dollar amount or percentage of a client's invested amount for investment advice or securities service, over a period of time.

fiduciary responsibility – an ethical requirement that recognizes a professional or firm is put in a position of trust over a client's assets and should always act in their best interest.

final order – A state securities administrator's decision on what final action to take on an initial order. The final order can come in one of three forms: a vacated order, a finalized order, or a modified order.

Financial Industry Regulatory Authority (FINRA) – a self-regulatory organization that provides oversight of all U.S. broker-dealer firms and professionals. It also conducts market surveillance, not only of NASDAQ and over-the-counter trading, but also of ten U.S. securities and options exchanges, including the NYSE.

foreign government securities – securities (usually bonds) issued or guaranteed by a foreign government or its political subdivisions, with which the United States maintains diplomatic relations, as long as the security is recognized as a valid obligation by the issuer or guarantor.

Form ADV – The registration form that must be filed by an investment adviser through the federally run Investment Adviser Registration Depository system (IARD). Form ADV includes general information about the adviser, as well as more specific information that would be relevant to a potential client.

Form BD – a form that a firm must file with both FINRA and the SEC when applying for membership. It identifies the type and nature of the applicant's business and in what states it will operate.

Form U4 – a form containing detailed personal information that must be filed for all registered employees of a member firm.

Form U5 – a form that must be filed when a registered person is terminated from a member firm. The form specifies whether the termination is full or partial.

fraud – Any act, process, or course of business that is manipulative or deceptive.

front running – Effecting transactions in a sequenced manner, for both a client and oneself or one's firm in a way that results in the professional or firm getting a better price.

FTC Red Flags Rule – A rule established by the Federal Trade Commission that requires broker-dealers, investment advisers, and investment companies to establish and maintain identity theft programs. Under the terms of the rule, these programs should be set up to detect the warning signs of identity theft present in a firm's day-to-day operations.

high-yield investment program – A form of social media or electronic communications fraud typically involving unregistered investments that are offered on websites with the promise of high yields at little to no risk to investors.

hypothecation – securitizing a debt by pledging securities as collateral for a loan. In a hypothecation agreement, the lender agrees to a loan and a borrower pledges collateral. Margin agreements typically include a hypothecation agreement.

incorporation by reference – when a document filed about the same security or issuer within the previous five years can simply be referenced in a new filing, without having to include a copy of the previous filing.

insider trading – the buying or selling of securities based on one's access to confidential or proprietary information that is not available to the general public.

insolvency – When a firm is unable to meet its current financial obligations, which can result in a revoked or suspended registration.

institutional investor – an account of a bank, savings and loan association, insurance company, registered investment company, registered investment adviser, or individual with total assets of at least $50 million.

institutional investor – any of the following:

- **A bank, savings and loan association, insurance company or registered investment company**

- **An investment adviser registered either with the SEC under Section 203 of the Investment Advisers Act or with a state securities commission (or any agency or office performing like functions)**

- **Any other person (whether a natural person, corporation, partnership, trust, or otherwise) with total assets of at least $50 million**

- **Governmental entity or subdivision thereof**

- **Employee benefit plans or qualified plans that meet the requirements of Section 403(b) or Section 457 of the Internal Revenue Code, or are defined under the Exchange Act, and in the aggregate have at least 100 participants, but does not include any participant of such plans**

- **Member or registered person of such a member**

- **Person acting solely on behalf of any such institutional investor**

insurance company securities – securities issued or guaranteed by an insurance company authorized to operate in the state.

interpositioning – the practice of inserting a third party between a broker-dealer and the best available price in the market, when it results in a higher price to the customer than would otherwise have been necessary.

interpretive opinion – A procedure in which a state administrator ends an initial order against a person, firm, or issuer short of issuing a final action. An interpretive opinion is typically issued due to a lack of evidence against the alleged violator.

investment adviser (IA) – From the USA: "any person who, for compensation, engages in the business of advising others, either directly or through publications or writings, as to the value of securities or the advisability of investing in, purchasing, or selling securities, or who, for compensation and as a part of a regular business, issues or promulgates analyses or reports concerning securities."

investment adviser representative (IAR) – an individual employed by an investment adviser who makes recommendations, manages client accounts, determines which advice should be given, sells investment advisory services, or supervises employees who perform any of the foregoing.

Investment Advisers Act of 1940 – major legislation that was created to regulate the activity of investment advisers.

Investment Company Act of 1940 – an act of Congress intended to protect investment companies' clients from unscrupulous practices. It requires strict financial disclosures and imposes restrictions on the operations and governance of investment companies.

isolated non-issuer transactions – transactions between two private parties that do not occur frequently.

issuer – a person that issues or proposes to create a new security.

JOBS Act – An act passed by Congress in 2012 with the intent of stimulating the economy by removing some of the restrictions that had previously been in place for small businesses.

limitation – an action taken by a state securities administrator in which the registration of an investment adviser, investment adviser representative, broker-dealer, or agent may be restricted to operate only in certain settings and capacities.

loan association securities – securities issued or guaranteed by a U.S. savings and loan association or a similar association that is authorized to do business in the state.

margin – the option given to customers to borrow money to buy additional securities, using their existing securities as collateral for the loan. Also refers to the amount of equity contributed by a customer to a margin account, expressed as a percentage of the total market value of the securities in the account.

markdown – a discount in the cost of a security purchased for a dealer's inventory.

market manipulation – when an individual or firm uses deceptive techniques in an effort to change the price of a security. Market manipulation is prohibited.

markup – an increase in the cost of a security sold out of a dealer's inventory.

matched trades – When agents and/or broker-dealers agree to buy and sell securities to each other at similar prices in order to give the impression that those securities have a more active market than is actually the case. The goal of professionals making matched trades is to drive up the prices for those securities.

material fact – Any piece of information that a reasonable person would want or need to know as part of his decision-making process.

ministerial acts – procedural or supervised acts that do not require registration.

misrepresentation – when a professional or firm doesn't accurately describe or communicate an aspect of their qualifications, services, or an investment.

NASAA – the North American Securities Administrators Association. The NASAA is a coalition of state, provincial, and territorial securities administrators that work together to help standardize laws and protect investors.

National Securities Markets Improvement Act (NSMIA) of 1996 – Legislation passed by Congress that created the class of "federal covered securities" exempt from state registration. The act also prohibited states from enacting licensing qualifications for securities professionals that exceed federal requirements related to net capital, bonding, and recordkeeping.

net capital requirement – a requirement that a broker-dealer or investment adviser have more assets than liabilities to operate in a state or on the federal level, often set at a certain dollar amount.

non-issuer distributions – any transaction not directly or indirectly for the benefit of the issuer.

Non-issuer Transaction – a transaction between two parties, neither of which is the original issuer of the security.

nonprofit securities – securities issued by a nonprofit religious, educational, benevolent, fraternal, charitable, social, athletic, or reformatory organization or a chamber of commerce or trade or professional association.

notice filing – when a federal covered adviser informs a state's administrator that they will be doing business in the state or when a securities issuer informs the state's administrator that a federally covered security will be offered for sale in their jurisdiction.

offer – 1. any attempt to invite another party to engage in a purchase or sale transaction, which includes advertisements for securities. 2. see ask.

Office of Supervisory Jurisdiction (OSJ) – an office that demands special supervisory attention, either because FINRA deems that the activities conducted there have particular regulatory significance, or because the member firm itself believes it prudent or necessary based on certain FINRA guidelines.

omission – when a professional or firm skips mentioning something that a reasonable person would want to know.

option – a security that gives the owner the right to buy or sell a security or asset at a specified price.

options account – A type of account held by a client of a broker-dealer that allows the client to purchase options to buy or sell a specific security at a set price by a certain date.

"painting the tape" – When a group of people trade a security back and forth among themselves to create the appearance of higher trading activity and in hopes of artificially raising the price of the security.

performance guarantee – a promise about an investment's rate of return, safety, or effectiveness. Making performance guarantees to customers is prohibited, though government bonds are guaranteed to pay a specified level of interest and principal if held to maturity.

person – a legal entity. Includes individuals, companies, trusts, organizations, and governments.

Ponzi schemes – a fraudulent investment scheme in which an adviser promises high returns to new investors, but instead of investing the money, he pays the returns to the early investors. The Ponzi scheme will fall apart when the adviser can no longer find new investors.

post-registration requirements – requirements that must be met after a person, firm, or issuer has completed their registration, such as ongoing financial reporting or continuing education.

principal – 1. see dealer. 2. a supervisor acting as a dealer. 3. the initial investment amount. 4. the remaining amount owed on a loan. 5. the par value of a bond.

private placement – an offering of securities to a small group of selected investors. Private placements are subject to the provisions of the Securities Act of 1933, but if the offering meets certain conditions stated within the Act, the offering may be exempted from traditional registration requirements. Most private placements are issued under the set of rules stated in Regulation D of the Act.

prospectus – a document that provides investors with enough detailed information about the issuer of the security to make an informed investment decision about the investment.

prudent investor standard – the requirement that a professional consider a client's investment objectives (including the desire to take risk to achieve growth) and ability to tolerate risk and experience losses, using careful investment selection and diversification to manage risk.

public utility securities – securities issued or guaranteed by a railroad, common carrier, public utility, or holding company that is regulated by the United States, an individual state, Canada, or a Canadian province.

"pump and dumps" – A form of social media and electronic communications fraud that involves individuals "pumping" up the price of a security through false or misleading information across an array of social media sites in hopes of generating investment. The individuals promoting the stock then profit by "dumping" any shares they may own at an inflated value before the rest of the investors sell.

purchase – See *sale*.

put – 1. an option that grants the holder the right to sell a security or asset at a specified price; 2. to sell a security or asset through use of a put option.

qualified custodian – A financial institution

that is allowed to hold funds and securities for investors who grant custody to an investment advisory or broker-dealer firm. Qualified custodians typically include banks, savings associations, registered broker-dealers, and foreign financial institutions.

qualified purchasers – individuals with investments worth at least $5 million and institutions with investments worth at least $25 million.

reasonable-basis obligation – the obligation of the broker-dealer to fully comprehend the liabilities of security or investment and decide whether or not it is advisable for some clients.

registration – the process of an issuer, professional, or firm meeting regulatory requirements to be able to operate in a state or at the federal level.

registration by coordination – used to coordinate both the state and federal filings of a securities issue. This most commonly occurs with larger issuers who would like their securities to be made available to investors in multiple states.

registration by filing – also known as Registration by Notification, this is a registration option for issuers that have registered a security federally. It allows issuers who meet certain conditions to register on the state level by providing the state with certain basic information and documentation.

registration by qualification – when an issuer registers a security, starting from scratch in proving that their security meets the basic regulatory requirements to protect the public. This means that they need to provide a registration statement to their state securities administrator containing a boatload of information.

registration statement – the central document that must be filed for most securities issues, which contains all the relevant information about that security and its issue.

Regulation A – an SEC rule that permits smaller issues to avoid standard registration requirements. As long as a business does not want to raise more than $50 million in equity over a one-year period, the business can raise money under a Regulation A exemption. Regulation A is open to non-reporting U.S. and Canadian issuers that have a legitimate business plan. Regulation A is not open to investment companies or disqualified issuers. Under Regulation A, a business does not have to file a complete registration statement. Instead it may file an offering circular on Form 1-A with the SEC. Regulation A provides two tiers of offerings: Tier 1 allows a business to raise up to $20 million in a 12-month period and Tier 2, which has additional requirements, allows a business to raise up to $50 million in a 12-month period. Regulation A is frequently called Regulation A+ due to recent changes.

Regulation D – a federal regulation that allows for private placements. Under Regulation D, companies can offer securities to a limited group of individuals or institutions that meet certain requirements. Regulation D is open to both U.S. and foreign issuers and can be used for both equity and debt securities. To protect the public from private placement investments that have not gone through the traditional rigorous SEC review, no public advertising is permitted for Regulation D offerings.

Regulation S-P – a federal regulation that protects investors from potential identity theft by placing strict requirements on how their private information may be used.

rehypothecation – using the collateralized securities in the margin account as collateral for a loan.

rescission – when a professional or issuer offers a client the right to undo advice they were given or a security that they purchased, returning their original investment to them along with a reasonable rate of interest.

restriction – see limitation.

241

revocation – an action taken by a state securities administrator to permanently take away the registration of an investment adviser, investment adviser representative, broker-dealer, or agent to operate in that state.

Rule 147 – a registration exemption for intrastate offerings.

sale – The actual exchange of securities for some type of compensation or a contract to do so in the future.

Section 402(a) Exemptions – blanket registration exemptions given under the Uniform Securities Act to specific types of securities.

Section 402(b) Exemptions – Registration exemptions allowed under the Uniform Securities Act to securities that are bought and sold in certain types of transactions.

Securities Act of 1933 – a law that was enacted to make sure that investors have enough information about a security to make an informed decision.

Securities and Exchange Commission (SEC) – a federal government agency tasked with regulating the securities industry and protecting investors. It was created under the Securities Exchange Act of 1934.

Securities Exchange Act of 1934 – a law that established the rules and regulations outlining the requirements for market participants.

self-dealing – a process in which an investment adviser or investment adviser representative illegally profits from its clients' investments.

selling away – when an associated person buys or sells a security that is not a product of his or her member firm.

senior securities transactions – transactions involving securities senior in rank to the issuer's common stock in terms of both payments and priority given in liquidation proceedings.

soft-dollar arrangement – When compensation is paid in some form other than cash or securities, usually in the form of paying an expense for a firm or professional.

solicitor – A third party that solicits clients on behalf of an investment adviser.

state securities administrator – The regulator of securities activities in a given state.

stock – a security that represents a partial or fractional ownership in a company.

stop order – 1. a request by the state securities administrator to not proceed with issuance of a security. 2. see stop loss order.

subscription form – the Administrator may require that securities registered by qualification or coordination be sold using a specific form called a subscription or sale contract form.

suitability – the concept that not all investments are right for all clients, due to a wide variety of factors including an investment's cost, level of risk, expected return, and growth or income features.

suspension – an action taken by a state securities administrator that temporarily prohibits the professional activity of a registered investment adviser, investment adviser representative, broker-dealer, or agent.

"time and price" discretion – A limited discretionary arrangement under which a client decides which securities to buy and sell while giving their securities professional the freedom to effect transactions in those securities when they think they can get the best price.

"touting" – A form of social media and communications fraud in which a third party recommends a security in exchange for a fee but does not accurately disclose the relationship and compensation received from an issuer or broker-dealer in the advertisement.

trading authorization – when a third-party (other than the professional and his or her client) is given permission to buy or sell securities for a client.

Trust Indenture Act of 1939 – a U.S. law that requires bond indentures to be qualified by the SEC for all corporate bond issues over $5 million.

underwriter transactions – transactions between a securities issuer and the issue's underwriter(s) or transactions that take place among underwriters.

Uniform Securities Act – Model legislation that was designed for states to use (and modify) for the regulation of securities, professionals, and firms at the individual state level.

unsolicited transaction – A securities transaction that is initiated by a client.

whole mortgage–backed bond transactions – transactions involving bonds backed by payments from a group of mortgages.

withdrawal – when an adviser, broker-dealer, agent, or investment adviser representative chooses to terminate their registration at any time, using a Form ADV-W, BDW, or U5.

Index

9 781610 070935